MW01517078

Home and Homelessness

May, 2005
Beloit

for Mary –
Because you recognize
both the peril and
the fascination of
connecting the past with
your own vibrant present!
I trust that your own
"active engagement with
learning" will indeed
"change the world and
... make history."
With love, gratitude,
& great faith,
Ellen

Home and Homelessness

*in the Medieval
and Renaissance World*

edited by

Nicholas Howe

University of Notre Dame Press
Notre Dame, Indiana

Copyright © 2004 by University of Notre Dame
Notre Dame, Indiana 46556
www.undpress.nd.edu
All Rights Reserved

Manufactured in the United States of America

Library of Congress Cataloging-in-Publication Data
Home and homelessness in the medieval and Renaissance world / edited by
Nicholas Howe.
p.   cm.
Includes index.
ISBN 0-268-03069-3 (cloth : alk. paper)
ISBN 0-268-03070-7 (pbk. : alk. paper)
1. Home—History.   2. Housing—History.   3. Homelessness—History.
4. Social history—Medieval, 500–1500.   5. Social history—16th century.
I. Howe, Nicholas.
HQ513.H66   2004
304.2'3—dc22

2004011325

∞ *This book is printed on acid-free paper.*

contents

Acknowledgments   vii

Introduction   1
Nicholas Howe

Not One But Many Separate Cities: Housing Diversity   13
in Sixteenth-Century Venice
Patricia Fortini Brown, Princeton University

Space of Resistance, Site of Betrayal: Morisco Homes   57
in Sixteenth-Century Spain
Mary Elizabeth Perry, Occidental College

Social Conscience and Social Practice: 91
Poverty and Vagrancy in Spain and Early Colonial Peru
Sabine MacCormack, University of Notre Dame

Home and Homelessness in the Middle of Nowhere   125
William Ian Miller, University of Michigan

Looking for Home in Anglo-Saxon England   143
Nicholas Howe, University of California, Berkeley

Index   165

acknowledgments

It is once again a great pleasure to thank Suzanne Childs and Wendy Matlock of the Center for Medieval and Renaissance Studies at the Ohio State University. Their careful work and good cheer have been invaluable in the preparation of this volume. I must also express my gratitude to the contributors to this volume for their patience and understanding. I am happy as well to acknowledge Barbara Hanrahan and Carole Roos of the University of Notre Dame Press for their assistance during the editing of this volume.

Home and Homelessness

nicholas howe

Introduction

What traces are left behind by home? Foundation stones outlined beneath the soil, fragments of language and story passed in oral circulation, a people's memory of having come from some place across the sea or beyond the mountains. At another location: intact houses that are still inhabited, a continuous record of visual and documentary evidence that includes legal titles and surveyors' records, an identifiable place of departure in an ancestral nation.

These two evocations may seem radically different, but each proposes the same inquiry into home as both a place of habitation and a source of identity. More precisely, they ask about the literal structures people call home, as well as the legal and historical claims people lay on a place to make it home. They also suggest how the interval of time that has passed between the flourishing of the place being studied and the moment of inquiry determines the questions we can ask about home as shelter and idea. The first evocation—of foundation stones and origin tales—evokes a newly settled people, perhaps from the early Middle Ages, with an enduring oral tradition that preserved a legendary sense of the past. The other evocation belongs more likely to an early modern European people because its physical and documentary traces remain so obviously present that they cannot be read as merely historical. Neither applies to nomadic peoples who have made a range of territory into home ground by traversing it on a seasonal basis. If home need not be set immovably in one place,

as the example of nomads suggests, homelessness need not be defined as
the condition of living without a fixed domicile. Political exiles, having
found sanctuary in a welcoming nation, often identify themselves as homeless in an act of allegiance to their homeland.

Traces of homelessness are far more difficult to identify from the past
precisely because, as we know from our own time, they can be so transient.
That homelessness leaves little behind is its inherent condition and thus,
in part, its tragedy. Some traces of homelessness may survive within tales
of forced dispossession or voluntary migration, through legal statutes that
define penalties for those without a home, in archaeological discoveries of
the calamitous destruction of cities and villages. Another factor can inter-
vene in this regard: a literate, record-keeping society is more likely than
an oral culture to document (in ways that we can interpret) the existence
of homeless people. How the condition of being without a home might
differ between a literate, bureaucratic society and an oral, customary one
would be fascinating to consider, though the disparate kinds of evidence
for each would make it hard to answer.

Physical evidence, when it is available, matters a great deal to the study
of home. Details about the layout of domiciles and rooms and courtyards
and frontages on streets tell us how people made their living spaces usable
and symbolically meaningful. If these arrangements remain in place today,
even when modified beyond recognition except to the expert eye, then our
work is that much easier. Thinking about how such physical evidence survives is, of course, another way of acknowledging the importance of the
materials used by a society to build its homes. The various studies in this
volume acknowledge this element by asking how ideas of home relate to
the stones of Renaissance Venice, for example, or to the timbers of early
medieval England. One might suggest as a rule of practice that, the less
durable are the materials used to build homes, the more likely is the contemporary scholar to resort to philological and textual evidence as a means
of pursuing the topic.

Home appears most immediately in our minds as a physical structure:
the building, the material presence of walls and roof, the fact of shelter.
We are, early in the twenty-first century, a settled and domesticated people.
Our nomadic or migratory pasts seem very much behind us, for all that we
travel and wander as individuals. From our settled state, we tend to equate
home with the presence of domicile and homelessness with the absence of
domicile. The Parisian police of the 1930s, for instance, categorized the
clochards that lived under bridges along the Seine as *sans domicile fixe*, a

phrase that legally defines home as a fixed habitation.[1] Individual *clochards* would have responded that a certain section of the quai along the Seine was their home, no less fixed in their lives for lacking a street name and number. Home is, by that measure, where one makes it.

That the subject of home seems not to have been fully explored by scholars of the pre-modern world may be attributed partially to the fact that relatively few physical traces of homes survive from periods such as England before the Norman Conquest or Spain during its glorious years of Islamic rule.[2] To cite the exception—the rare Pompeii preserved in volcanic ash—is simply to underscore this larger generalization. The majority of physical structures in which people lived a thousand, or even four hundred years ago have disappeared. Faced with this absence of direct evidence, scholars must resort to more indirect ways of exploring the matter of home. Documents like wills and legal inventories offer some information about the objects and materials with which people furnished their homes; law codes provide some understanding of the legal protections afforded those who had a home and the penalties suffered by those who were homeless; visual images present some sense of the ways homes were represented as buildings and as settings for daily life. These are only a few of the approaches that appear in the five studies contained in this volume.[3]

Beyond the range of the present volume, one could easily compile an extensive list of case studies on home and homelessness: a survey of the medieval recovery of waste spaces and marginal lands to accommodate a growing population; an inquiry into how the European sense of home was altered by the rapid spread of plague in the fourteenth century; a meditation on the metaphysics of home as revealed through the dramatic narrative of *King Lear*; a kind of microhistory of London drawn from the entries in Pepys's *Diary*; a mapping of colonial naming practices by which new sites of occupation in the Americas echoed established sites in the old country. As these thumbnail sketches of yet-to-be-written studies suggest, home and homelessness matter deeply as concepts in western culture precisely because the fact of a specific domicile—a building set in a street and neighborhood and city—does not exhaust the subject but rather encourages us to think of the metaphorical and psychological resonances of home. If we treat home simply as bricks and mortar, wattle and daub, then we lose hope of understanding the deep influence that it has had on human beings, despite all of their historical and cultural variations. Each of the five studies in this volume recreates a sense of home in a specific time and place by means of its own particular set of traces and questions. And each demonstrates in compelling ways that the study of home must of necessity also be the study of homelessness, whether defined as vagrancy, outlawry, or exile.

Looking at Renaissance Venice, Patricia Fortini Brown asks how we are to translate floor plans of houses or layouts of neighborhoods into a larger understanding of that city's social and political arrangements. Working with an abundance of physical evidence, she reminds us of how necessary it is to think of home as a literal place of habitation tied to degrees of social status, financial resources, and political power. In turn, she can thus explore how the forms of urban planning practiced in Venice during this period created new classes of the dispossessed and homeless. The traditional notion of home as the site where one is rooted in place derives its metaphorical power from nature: one is like a plant and thus one has native soil. With the growth of cities, that sense of home as agrarian and rural became more a figure of speech than a literal truth. The world that Brown surveys for its ideas of home was shaped by such factors as high population density, a flourishing mercantile empire, and the presence of an important minority Jewish population in a largely Christian society. As she shows vividly, city dwellers develop notions of home that are thoroughly intertwined with representations of social prestige. Thus she designates the physical manifestations of home that were appropriate to each class, a matter determined in sixteenth-century Venice more by social origin than economic condition.

The diversity of housing in Venice makes it seem a proto-modern city. The fact that its residents, from the richest to the poorest, lived in a tightly circumscribed space corresponds to our contemporary experience of home and homelessness. The creation of the Ghetto, by decree of the Venetian Senate, to prevent Jews from circulating freely with Christians also reminds us of how much our sense of being at home in a city has its roots in premodern Europe. So too, the iconic and preserved qualities of Venice as a city in our time, as well as images of its palazzos remembered from paintings and movies, make it a more familiar and a more recognizable place than any of the others surveyed in this book.

Working from a scrupulously literal sense of home, Mary Elizabeth Perry demonstrates how essential the privacy of home can be in the survival of an outlawed religion, in this case, Islam in Spain after the Reconquista. By considering the physical spaces of Spanish houses and courtyards as protective structures that allowed Moriscos to maintain their religious faith, Perry portrays home as the place of forbidden belief; it is in the most pressing sense, the place of refuge. There is a persistent element as well of homelessness in her account of the Moriscos, both because their practices must be understood within the context of the forced deportation of Muslims from Spain and because they were a people rendered spiritually homeless when their land was conquered by the forces of another faith and their places of worship were appropriated.

In her recreation of Muslim neighborhoods in Iberia, Perry guides us through a cityscape of hidden belief in which the practice of a forbidden religion is enabled by culturally determined forms of architecture: "For centuries the people of Al-Andalus had built their houses with few windows, presenting blank whitewashed walls to the street that veiled their domestic activities from public view." In this story, the home becomes a site of resistance, a place where the forbidden may be practiced away from the surveillance of conquerors. Over time, as the Christian rulers of Iberia became more and more vigilant, the home as refuge for Moriscos turned into a site of betrayal and then, after their final deportation in the sixteenth century, it became an idea to be transported in memory to other places around the Mediterranean.

The experience of the Moriscos, as they worshipped secretly in their homes and then lost them, left deep traces on Christian Spain. Houses left behind by Moriscos often contained carvings and other decorative features that were, unbeknownst to their later Christian residents, traces of Islamic belief. Other houses contained holy writings hidden behind walls and inside of columns by the Moriscos, and then left behind when they were exiled—only to be uncovered centuries later. The house became, quite literally, the book of home. Another trace left behind, one recognized more immediately by the Spaniards themselves, was the discomfiting parallel between the subjected Moriscos and the colonized indigenous peoples of New Spain. Perry quotes a Jesuit who put the matter with epigrammatic concision: "This kingdom of Granada is a very great Indies." This parallel struck at an urgent question: what does it mean to be homeless in a land that your own people had once called home but that has since been conquered by your enemies? What does it mean to be rendered homeless without any change of physical location or circumstance?

In Sabine MacCormack's study of sixteenth-century Peru, home turns into homelessness in ways that address both the losses of dispossession and the gains of possession. She articulates the paradox that arose when the conquering Spaniards made a triumphant new home for themselves in Peru by brutally enforcing homelessness on much of the indigenous population. This same group of invaders asserted its claims to cultural superiority, and thus its moral warrant for dispossession, through its ability to keep detailed records of their seizure of Peru. MacCormack's account leads one to think as well about how much of human history has taken this double form: of possession and dispossession, of seizing another's home and then calling it one's own.

The homelessness of dispossessed peoples is very much the story of our own time and our own western hemisphere. MacCormack's account of home and homelessness in the Peruvian Andes reads in places like a document produced in the early twenty-first century by Amnesty International or Doctors without Borders. It is a report of political conquest followed by forced relocation and servitude, ending in starvation and homelessness on a massive scale. The migration of indigenous peoples after the conquest of Peru reshaped the communities of the Andes at least as much as did the original conquest. The destruction of homes as physical structures was essential to the Spanish logic of conquest and domination. A missionary friar who had lived in the Andes for ten years wrote to a co-religionist that perhaps fifty percent of the houses in what had been the empire of the Incas had been destroyed by the Spanish. Evidence such as this bears out MacCormack's conclusion that in conquered Peru there was a degree of homelessness unprecedented in Europe. Yet as she subtly demonstrates, the sources of that unprecedented poverty and homelessness must be traced not simply to Spanish conquest, as one would expect, but also to the arrival in Peru of *gente valdía* or "superfluous people" who had no reason to remain in Spain. Yet their Spanish blood gave them a degree of social status that they would never have known in Iberia. In MacCormack's vision, Peru thus becomes a site for the many different kinds of homelessness—from that of wastrel Spaniards to that of dispossessed Incans—which followed in the wake of colonization.

William Ian Miller's study of home and homelessness in Iceland is, by contrast, a test case for assessing an uncommon human phenomenon: the conquest of a land that did not entail the destruction or dispersal of a native population. When restless, seafaring Scandinavians made it their home in the tenth century, Iceland was unpopulated. The settlers built there mainly with such ephemeral materials as timber and sod but their scattered settlements were held together by a legal system of great complexity. As Njál, the crafty lawyer and hero of the greatest Icelandic saga, states: "With laws shall our land be built up but with lawlessness laid waste."[4] The conflation of home and law is especially evident in the Icelandic sagas. Njál, for instance, is killed when his enemies pursue a feud by resorting to the shameful and illegal tactic of burning down his home. To understand home and homelessness in Iceland, the modern scholar must thus rely heavily on legal and literary texts. Philology, the close reading of language in texts, holds out our best means of addressing the subject in Iceland because the words themselves are resonant with that culture's vision of home as farmstead and as legal covenant.

Writing about "the middle of nowhere," his evocative phrase for medieval Iceland, Miller forces us to consider what it meant to make a home where there had been no home before. The Scandinavian settlers made homes where before them only a scattered handful of Irish monks had improvised simple hermitages. The foundational text of early Iceland is thus the *Landnámabók*, literally 'the book of the taking of the land,' that is, the book of the settlement of Iceland. It is a meticulously detailed record of the process by which a new land is made into home. As Miller observes, this process was strongly influenced by the fact that houses and barns were constructed from materials that did not endure over the turn of generations. Thus a sense of home in early Iceland was established less by the physical presence of buildings than it was by the settlers' relation to the landscape, to stories about settlement, and to the spirits and ghosts that inhabited both landscape and stories. The narrative of Iceland, of making home in the middle of nowhere, speaks to the recurrent pattern of arrival in a new place followed by its transformation into the familiar and the domestic. It is, in the starkest way possible, about turning oneself into a native and thus not remaining a stranger in a strange land. Most compellingly, this story is possible only because the Icelanders cultivated and even, perhaps, invented a profound sense of their own past. Home, for these people, was where their past on the island began.

A significant moment in the writing of the Icelandic home was the acceptance of Christianity by the island's population in the resonant year of 1000 A.D. Religious conversion, especially in the case of Christianity, remakes the idea of home by joining it with another idea, that of heaven as the site of eternal life. That ideal of the final home stands always in Christianity as a critique of the earthly home, as a reminder that life here is transient and imperfect. The home of mortal life should thus be understood as at best a temporary abode and at worst a site of temptation and sin to be renounced willingly. The figuration of the earthly home as an imperfect version of the heavenly home informs the most haunting lyrics of Old English poetry, especially *The Wanderer* and *The Seafarer*. The animating contrast in these poems between the transience of earthly exile and the enduring home in heaven allows us to consider the ways in which home served as a cultural as well as physical construction in early medieval England. This sense that the earthly home is impermanent can be related, in tentative but nonetheless suggestive ways, to the fact that the same Anglo-Saxons who composed these poems were far more likely to build in timber than in stone.

The most immediately accessible evidence for home and homelessness in pre-Conquest England lies in the language, in its stock of words like *ham* to designate the place of habitation and *anhaga* to designate the figure of the exile who has been driven from home. That same methodology of philological and literary study employed by Miller to study Iceland offers a fruitful line of inquiry for tracing home and homelessness in Anglo-Saxon England, though attention must also be paid to the reconstructions of domestic habitations provided by archaeologists and architectural historians. If nothing else, the limited material evidence has the great benefit of making the semantic and poetic evidence read vividly and powerfully. The testimony of words and texts to Anglo-Saxon ideas of home and homelessness is all the more tantalizing when read within a culture that remembered, and even exaggerated, its history of migration from its ancestral home in northwest Europe to its arrival in the promised island of *Englalond*. Home takes on a more contingent meaning if one's current location figures not as the inevitable site of habitation from time immemorial but as a place arrived at after leaving another homeland within the span of remembered time. Put another way, the case of Anglo-Saxon England allows one to explore what it might mean to think of home through the screen of migratory memory.

As is evident from my summary, the chapters of this volume are arranged to lead the reader backward in time, from sixteenth-century Venice to tenth-century England, in a process of continuing defamiliarization. On another scale, these chapters also can be described as moving from the more materially situated studies of home as a built phenomenon to the more philological and textual studies of home as a category of the imagination. This order reflects the problems and varieties of available evidence, as suggested earlier, but it also registers the inextricable connections between home as built and as imagined, as domicile and as worldview. To speak of the movement between these two senses of home as some kind of terminological slippage or as eliding necessary distinctions is, I would suggest, to miss the necessary point that neither can exist without the other. Such connections testify in another way to the distinction framed in English by the differences between the words 'home' and 'house'. A 'house' refers only to a built structure with roof and walls, not a site of necessary familial and social obligations and rituals. Or, in Robert Frost's memorably laconic definition from "Death of the Hired Man": "Home is the place where, when you have to go there, / They have to take you in."⁵ Home is, in this vision, a place of sentiments and attachments that cannot be denied or evaded.

Our own experiences of home make it at once an utterly familiar and yet also a strangely alien subject. In daily life and language, the familiar element tends to obscure the alien. Thus we have uncountable sayings about home: "East is east, west is west, home is best," "Home is where the heart is," "Home sweet home," "A house is not a home." These are just a few of the many clichés that, we are likely to feel, tell us all we need to know about home. In our familiar idiom, they are the easy phrases thrown out in conversation to define a common setting for experience; they are the spoken versions of embroidered samplers hung on parlor walls to convey sentiments of domestic life. Like most formulaic sayings, these ones about home are likely to elicit from us a nod of agreement and also a gesture of resistance. Home is a subject about which we are likely to feel very conflicted.

In the more esoteric idiom of academic discourse, home rarely figures simply as the physical place where we sleep, do the dishes, read, make love, watch television, pass our lives. Instead, it presents itself in the guise of foreign terms as if to make exotic—or, at least, less safely domestic—this most familiar of places and categories. As we ponder the vibrating eerieness of our own experience, we speak of it as *unheimlich* from the German, meaning something like 'unhomelike'. The word necessarily carried over into English because there is no direct equivalent in the language for it. Or, struggling to identify our relation to all that we knew in the past, we speak of *nostalgia*, from the Greek for 'homesickness'. Here our use of a foreign word is more revealing because English has a perfectly usable literal translation for the Greek in 'homesickness', but that is a word English speakers usually reserve for the anxiety or sense of loss felt on first leaving home and venturing into the larger world. It denotes the response of a child or a young adult; it speaks to a predictable moment in the experience of growing into maturity. For that reason, 'homesickness' cannot adequately designate an adult's existential sense that the separation from home is not simply like an illness but in fact is an illness in its power to incapacitate. And thus 'nostalgia' finds its place in the English language along with 'homesickness'.

In the words of Ibn 'Abdun, as quoted by Mary Elizabeth Perry, "Homes are shelters in which souls, spirits, and bodies take refuge." In a counterstatement, the German writer Novalis observed: "Philosophy is essentially homesickness—the universal impulse to be home." To imagine two more different visions of home, or two more different writers, would be difficult, but both are equally necessary, for between them they establish a field by which to think about home and homelessness. These quotations stand as justification for the diverse nature of the studies in this volume. Taken together, it should be stressed, these studies establish that home as habitation and as idea belongs on a continuum that ranges from forms of domestic architecture to a communally imagined location, from a sense of individual being to a source of political self-definition.

History, like charity, begins at home. Nor is it accidental, I would add in passing, that more than a few of these studies concern themselves with issues of charity. In itself, home may not be a fully adequate way of thinking about the past, but it does bring a necessary and reassuring specificity to our understanding of that world. If home is problematic as both place and as idea, if it is at once a refuge against the world and also the site that must be fled to enter the world, homelessness arouses much less ambivalent responses in us. To be homeless seems, in most of the cultures one knows anything about, to be a condition of hardship and often unendurable suffering. To be homeless is not, in conventional usage at least, to be free of home or well rid of its tyrannies. Rather, it is to suffer a twofold deprivation of both physical and spiritual shelter. And that deprivation can strike an individual, as in the Icelandic sagas, or a tribal group, as in the Andean highlands.

Homelessness, the absence of a place in the world, has a particular relevance to our contemporary condition. As a social problem, homelessness reentered the consciousness of most Americans in the 1970s and 1980s, and now stands as a continual reminder that the most prosperous society in human history has yet to share its resources so that all of its citizens can enjoy at least the bare minimum of home as shelter. At a time when it has become increasingly common for scholars to indict the past as the source for such social ills as racism, sexism, religious intolerance, and homophobia, the persistence of homelessness in our midst stands as a judgment on our own society. Indeed, that persistence may be read as a cautionary tale of our own failure. How will the future judge us as we live in great prosperity and turn away from the homeless? Will it be any more understanding or kinder to us than we are toward those who owned slaves or persecuted gays and lesbians?

The historical study of home and homelessness cannot by itself solve our own social dilemmas. But like all good historical work, the studies in this volume remind us that the ways people in the past have thought about home and homelessness have had everything to do with the ways they defined a just and decent society for themselves.

Notes

1. For this phrase, see Brassaï, *The Secret Life of Paris*, trans. Richard Miller (New York: Pantheon, 1976).

2. For a broad and challenging survey of the subject, interested readers should consult *Home: A Place in the World*, a special issue of *Social Research* 58.1 (1991), edited by Arien Mack. This issue contains fascinating essays by, among others, Simon Schama, John Hollander, Joseph Rykwert, George Kateb, Lawrence Stone, and Mary Douglas, as well as many suggestions for further reading.

3. The contributions by Patricia Fortini Brown, Mary Elizabeth Perry, Sabine MacCormack, and William Ian Miller were originally delivered as lectures at the Center for Medieval and Renaissance Studies at the Ohio State University in 1999–2000. An additional lecture in the series by David Aers on "Home, Home-lessness, and Sanctity: Conflicting Models?" has been incorporated into his forth-coming book from the University of Notre Dame Press.

4. *Njál's Saga*, trans. Magnus Magnusson and Hermann Pálsson (New York: Penguin, 1971), 159.

5. *The Poetry of Robert Frost*, ed. Edward Connery Lathem (New York: Holt, Rinehart and Winston, 1968), 38.

patricia fortini brown

Not One But Many Separate Cities

Housing Diversity in Sixteenth-Century Venice

The notion of home is a devilishly slippery concept, as evidenced by the diversity of viewpoints in these essays. Is it a place or is it a state of mind? The philosopher can situate the home in the mind, while a pragmatist may take a more concrete approach, pointing out that body, soul, and mind are themselves situated in the home. And how do we distinguish between the notions of homeland (in the sense of a community) and of home (in the sense of a dwelling)? The two concepts, closely intertwined, are perhaps inseparable. This is particularly so for the Venetians of the late Renaissance. Like William Ian Miller's Icelanders, the early Venetians had made their homes "in the middle of nowhere" on the sand dunes of a vast lagoon in late antiquity. Even in the sixteenth century Venetians were still very much aware of the *ex novo* quality of their city. They, too, obtained their concept of home from the landscape and maintained a vivid sense of their own past. Exile was one of the worst fates to befall a Venetian. According to a popular saying, "non est vivere extra Venetiis"—to live away from Venice is not to be alive.[1]

The strongly rooted Venetians knew and defended their place in the world, and as a people were anything but homeless. Thus their experience is quite different from that of the dispossessed Peruvians and Moriscos who are also discussed in this volume: different, but not irrelevant. Venetians were famously successful in incorporating homeless peoples, such as Jews and Slavs, into their urban fabric—so successful that the French ambassador Philippe de Commynes observed with astonishment in the later fifteenth century that "most of their people are foreigners."[2] Yet this observation, while attentive to Venice's diverse population, does not capture the particularities and challenges of maintaining a remarkably stable amalgam that endured without invasion or internal revolution for over a millennium. That there was crime, misery, and incivility in this fabled city there is no doubt. But for all that, the Republic was remarkably successful in instilling a sense of civic duty and in privileging cooperation over competition within a populace characterized by a myriad of origins and conditions. It can be argued that the enduring appeal of this commonly held ideology must have been due in part to the physical environment, where virtually every island parish, each with its own church around which the houses of both rich and poor were clustered, contained a healthy mixture of that multifarious population that made up Renaissance Venice.

In 1581, the Venetian writer Francesco Sansovino spoke of "not one but many separate cities, all conjoined together." He was referring to the seventy odd islands surrounded by canals and linked by bridges that make up Venice. That is, what looked to be a single city was really an aggregation of separate islands, only apparent—as he put it—to "the subtle observer of things."[3] But if one turns Sansovino's metaphor on its side, framing it in social rather than physical terms, we can capture yet another dimension of Venice's diversity within a seeming unity. Writing as well of the ornaments, the furnishings, and the incredible richness of the houses, he claimed that each householder shared in the city's refinements and wealth, "according to their quality and condition."[4] And, indeed, this must have seemed the case to a visitor rowed along the Grand Canal, admiring the marble-clad facades and peering through velvet-draped windows at sparkling chandeliers of Murano glass. These palaces were called, Sansovino noted, *case*—houses—"out of modesty."[5]

But the "subtle observer of things" who ventured into the narrow canals and dark streets of the city would see a fuller picture that revealed, within each island city, many other cities yet. While the city of the rich was one of spacious golden chambers and richly woven tapestries, the city of the poor was often one of sparsely furnished rooms at best, or the streets at worst. What made the situation perhaps more complex than in other places was Venice's rigid hierarchy of social orders. Sansovino's reference to each householder's "quality and condition" alludes to the caste system that had prevailed in Venice since the *Serrata*—the closure of the Great Council—of 1297.[6] Since that time, the noble caste of patricians at the top held all the political power. This hereditary nobility included the doge, who was elected for life, and all the public officials—councilors, judges, senators, administrators—who rotated in and out of office for periods of a few months to several years. At the very least, all adult male patricians were entitled to sit in the Great Council.[7] In the early days patricians were usually merchants; by the later sixteenth century, they increasingly lived off their rents and other investments. But a good number of them were poor and depended upon public offices to sustain themselves and their families. During the sixteenth century, the patriciate comprised about 4.5 percent of the population.[8]

Just below the patriciate was the order of *cittadini*, an elite caste who came to be called *seconda corona* or second crown of the Republic.[9] They were for the most part merchants or bureaucrats who staffed the state offices and provided continuity in a government run by noble amateurs.[10] Like patricians, male *cittadini* dressed in long togas in public and were, from all appearances, indistinguishable from the noble caste. This group amounted to another 5–8 percent of the population. The remaining 90 percent or so of the population—the *popolani*—embraced a wide range of occupations and economic conditions, from wealthy merchants to artisans, small shopkeepers, semi- or unskilled laborers, and the truly indigent.[11]

Each of the three orders included the very rich and the very poor, for the groupings were social and political categories and not economic classes per se. There was thus no easy fit between noble rank and wealth, for not every nobleman was wealthy nor was every rich man noble. With social mobility extremely restricted and political office limited to the patrician caste, the Republic used various strategies throughout its history to deal with these disjunctions of social caste and economic class and to ensure domestic peace. These strategies included: ideological tools, as exemplified by the compelling ethos of *concordia* and *unanimitas* that prevailed within the ruling elite; political tools, such as a succession of regulations intended to discourage the formation of factions and nepotism within the patriciate; economic tools, such as the provision of grain in times of famine; and legal tools, most notably sumptuary laws, that aimed to limit ostentatious display and to ensure the rule of *mediocritas* among the affluent.[12] This essay

FIGURE 1.   Ca' Corner della Ca' Grande. Photo: O Böhm, Venice

focuses upon the Venetian home, exploring ways in which attitudes and practices pertaining to real property and housing helped to fuse together the city of the rich and the city of the poor into a well-functioning whole.

As the primary locus of family identity, the home was where the wealthy family, whether noble or not, displayed its taste, its prosperity, and its prominence. The Cornaro family, for example, proclaimed its pre-eminent position as one of the wealthiest families in the city with the construction of Ca' Corner della Ca' Grande (fig. 1). Designed in a classical style by Jacopo Sansovino in the middle decades of the sixteenth century, it was so massive as to dwarf all its neighbors and was praised as one of the four most outstanding palaces on the Grand Canal by Francesco Sansovino in 1581.[13]

But the Cornaro were at the high end of patrician affluence, and Ca' Corner was not a typical *casa da statio*—a Venetian term of dignity denoting the family palace, a residence that was one cut above an ordinary house.[14]

The *Casa da Statio*

The patrician Zuan Matteo Bembo, by contrast, lived with his family in the sestiere of Cannaregio in a *casa da statio* that might be considered more characteristic of the noble caste. Originally built in the late Trecento, the modest Gothic palace faces Campo Santa Maria Nova (figs. 2–3).[15] The Bembo coat of arms in the center of the asymmetrical facade still marks the domus, but beyond that, Zuan Matteo demonstrated an innovative approach to the age-old Venetian tradition of embedding sculpted reliefs in

FIGURE 3. Ca' Bembo and the surrounding neighborhood in Cannaregio, adapted from Giuseppe Cristinelli, *Cannaregio: un sestiere di Venezia—la forma urbana, l'assetto edilizio, le architetture* (Rome: Officina Edizioni, 1987), tavola 71

FIGURE 2. Ca' Bembo at Santa Maria Nova. Photo: author

the walls of the family home when he squeezed a classical tabernacle between the two residential floors in the wall to the left. Bembo's sculpture is really a time-spanning pastiche, the sixteenth-century aedicule containing a fourteenth-century statue of Chronos or Saturn in the form of a wild man holding a solar disc. An inscribed plaque below is supported by three male heads, carved in high relief and also datable to the fourteenth century.[16] The Latin inscription reads, in translation: "As long as this [the sun] rotates, the cities of Zara, Cattaro, Capodistria, Verona, Cyprus, and Candia [Crete] will give testimony to his actions."[17] The cities are those in which Zuan Matteo had served as *podestà* or *capitano* of the Venetian republic. In all likelihood Zuan Matteo had composed the assemblage as a personal impresa that spoke to posterity, possibly with a collateral function as totem to protect the house and its inhabitants. Among his contributions to colonial life was a fountain constructed in Candia that also survives to this day. It too was a sculptural pastiche.[18] Incorporating a headless Roman statue, it testifies to his humanist credentials and to his awareness of the evocative power of sculpture, publicly displayed.

Bembo's unusual sculpture on the facade of his home might be seen as a metaphor for the palimpsest quality of Venice itself, with the city at the center of a world defined by Venetian territories in the Terraferma, Dalmatia, and the Aegean and one in which personal identity was closely tied to civic responsibility.[19] But considering the relief in its domestic context, we find that it has another dimension: Zuan Matteo was surely proclaiming his own achievements and, in the grand tradition of the paterfamilias, the distinguished legacy that he was leaving his sons.

Zuan Matteo Bembo was well connected. A man of affairs with a long career of service to the Republic, he was married to a niece of the famous Cardinal Pietro Bembo, who treated him like a son and with whom he had a long and affectionate correspondence.[20] Indeed, Zuan Matteo was granted a copyright in 1530 to publish a number of Pietro's works in Latin and *volgare*.[21] Among Zuan Matteo's civic honors was his portrayal by Tintoretto in one of the narrative paintings in the Great Council Hall of the Ducal Palace. These canvases were, as Sansovino later reported, "all consumed by the fire of 1577, bringing great displeasure to everyone, through the loss . . . of the memories of so many excellent persons, in which the world is rarely so abundant."[22]

Despite his frequent missions abroad, Zuan Matteo had raised eight sons and two daughters with his wife, Marcella Marcello, in the house at Santa Maria Nova (fig. 4). Marcella was an accomplished woman whose

Zaccaria Bembo (1405– ~)
m. 1436 Caterina Surian

Alvise Bembo
m. 1488 Pentesilia Michiel
di Zuan Matteo (~ –1501)

Zuan Matteo Bembo
(ca. 1491–1570)
m. 1519 Marcella Marcello
di Sebastiano (1496–1555)

Liaison
with
unnamed
woman

Ettor
[natural]

Paolo
(~ –bef 1547)

Davide
(1530–1611)
m. (1) 1563
Elisabetta Donado
(2) 1577
Marina Barbarigo
di Zuan Battista

Alvise (1572– ~)
Zuan Matteo (1577–1618)

Bernardo
Andrea
(1534–
bef 1547)

Piero
(1533–1580)

Giulia
(1532–1562)
m. 1550
Girolamo
Della Torre

Lodovico
Sigismondo
Tadea
Giulio
Marcella
Giovanni
Luigi
Ginevra
Helena
Giulia (1562– ~)

Sebastiano
(1528–1564)

Marc'Antonio
(1524–1576)
m. 1557
Lucietta Bembo
di Gaspare
(~ –1612)

Zuan Matteo (1567–1629)
Gaspare (1572– ~)
Zuan Battista (1573–1610)
Piero (1575–1631)

Alvise
(1523–1570)
m. (1) 1552
Maddalena
Pasqualigo
di Zuanne
(2) ca. 1568
Cecilia Priuli
di Antonio

Augusta
(1522–
aft 1570)

Quintilio Lorenzo
(1520–1570)
m. 1546 Laura
Foscarini di Alvise
(in casa at San
Ermagora)

Zuan Battista (1544–1564)
Alvise (1547–1613)
Andrea (1548–1618)
Bernardo (1549– ~)
Marcantonio (1550–1574)
Zuan Matteo (1551–1627)
Pietro (1553–1574)
Marcella

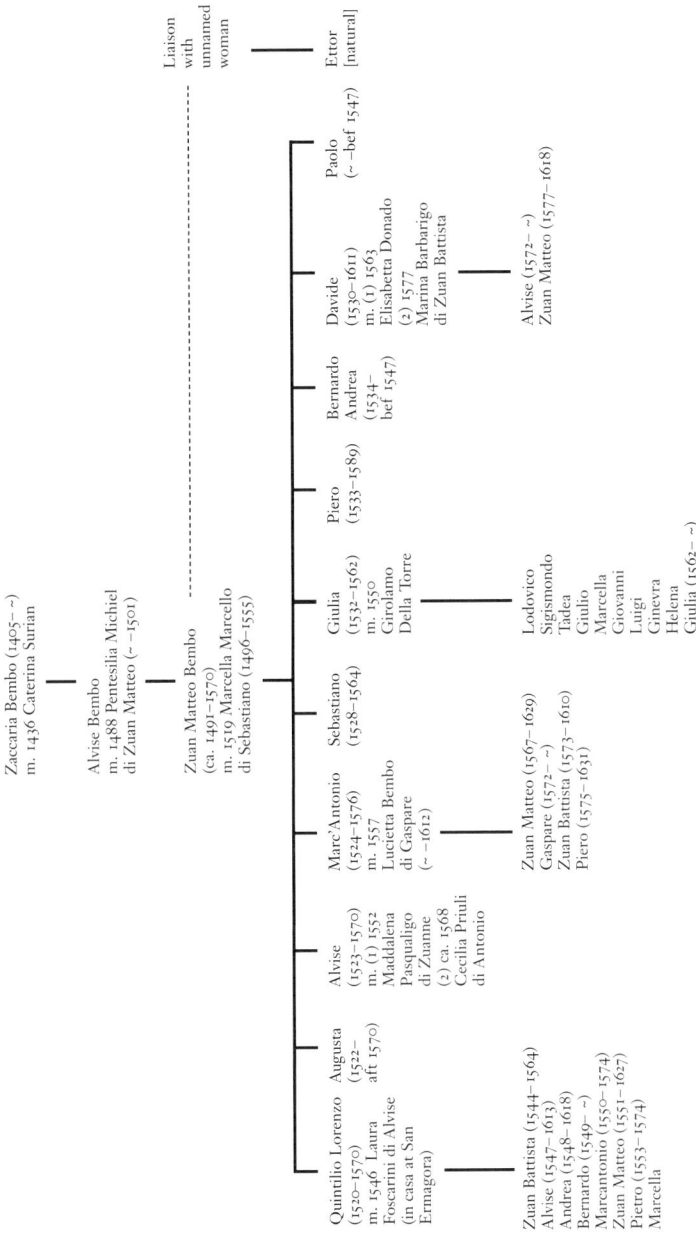

FIGURE 4. Bembo Family Tree

mother Antonia was Pietro Bembo's sister and who was herself renowned for her poetry in *volgare* and her proficiency in Greek literature.[23] By the time Zuan Matteo wrote his last will and testament in 1570, three of their sons had already died. The document offers a thumbnail sketch of Venetian attitudes about property and warrants a brief examination. In it he declares: "I wish that all my real estate, houses, and villa lands, and those few pieces of silver and furniture acquired with my money, would stay in perpetual *fedecommesso* for my four sons, Lorenzo, Alvise, Marc'Antonio and David, and their legitimate male descendants," with each share to pass on from father to sons.[24] (His fifth surviving son, not mentioned in the testament, will enter the story further on.) Each male heir was allowed to leave his portion to his daughters, but only during their lifetimes, typically as part of their dowries, after which it would revert to the male descendants. If male descendants from all of Zuan Matteo's four sons were lacking, then the estate should revert to the descendants of his brother David, again to pass from father to sons. If these direct lines should die out, then a legitimate male member of the house of Bembo should be selected by the Procurators of San Marco to inherit the estate. If the Bembo line died out entirely, then the residue of the estate should be given to the hospital of San Giovanni e Paolo "for the use and aid of the poor."[25]

And what of Zuan Matteo's daughters? Augusta, he states, "is satisfied with the legacy of 100 ducats that was left to her, and she also had twenty-five ducats more, from her mother."[26] Giulia was deceased by this time and was not mentioned. In any case, she had married into mainland nobility and would have received her share of the patrimony in her dowry. Indeed, their mother Marcella's will of 1547 had referred to both daughters and made plain that she was making the bequest of 100 ducats to Augusta "in sign of love, for a single time only, and more I do not leave her, who by grace of God is rich and is doing very well."[27] As to Giulia, her mother had declared, "that if my daughter Giulia is not married or in a convent before my death, I wish that she would have 500 ducats from all my possessions, whether from my dowry or that of my sister Madonna Giulia, and any other properties that may come to me, with this condition: that she marry one of our Venetian gentlemen or an honorable foreigner with the consent of my magnificent consort and her brothers, and if she is married before my death I do not wish her to have anything, and if she becomes a nun I do not wish her to have those 500 ducats [since] it seems to me that she could enter a very good convent with the 400 ducats that her father is leaving her." If none of Marcella's sons produce heirs, then her daughters should receive her entire estate.[28]

In accordance with Venetian custom, the testaments of both parents make plain that the bulk of the family patrimony was to pass down through the male lineage. Moreover, Marcella's stresses the importance of maintaining the purity of the bloodline: "Declaring above all that if in due course, my sons would have bastards or a bastard, they can never leave them anything of mine."[29] The rules of the game were different, however, for men. While preserving the bulk of his estate for the legitimate progeny of his legitimate sons, Zuan Matteo also provided for a natural son, Ettor, probably born after his wife's death in 1555. He was to be "governed, taught, dressed, and shod, and the masters who will instruct him, to be paid" from the proceeds of the estate. The boy was presently in the care of a tutor, but he was given leave to move in with one of his half-brothers—Zuan Matteo's legitimate sons—if he chose. The latter were, in any case, collectively obliged to support the boy until he reached the age of eighteen years.[30]

Surprisingly, Zuan Matteo does not include a fifth son, Piero, among his heirs. Namesake of Cardinal Pietro Bembo, he had entered the Church and was now bishop of Veglia. He was cited in the will only as "Monsignore, my son" in connection with a loan of 300 ducats, a favor that Zuan Matteo had also extended in various amounts to his other sons. Yet, in conformity with the Venetian legal principle of "absolute equivalence" among brothers, all surviving sons should have received the remainder in strictly equal portions.[31] So despite a legitimate will, the estate was open to question. The language of Zuan Matteo's will suggests not enmity toward Piero but rather that he was concerned, first and foremost, with posterity—so much so that he did not feel the need to endow Piero, a celibate son with a high position in the Church, with a share of his estate. But predictably, after Zuan Matteo's death, Piero contested the will, and the case went to arbitration. The dispute was between Piero and his three surviving brothers since Alvise had already died without progeny. Because the inheritance was not made "pro indiviso," the court was allowed to divide the real estate among the four parties.[32]

Zuan Matteo had written in his will that the *casa da statio* at Santa Maria Nova consisted of the principal building, "that is the upper and lower *soleri*"—the Venetian term for full-sized stories above the ground floor—along with the chamber that he had joined to it and a row of rental houses on Calle del Forno to the west. Each of the two *soleri* consisted of a long portego or sala, opening to the single large chamber that Zuan Matteo had added on the west side, and to a row of smaller chambers including a kitchen on the east.[33]

The court determined that the family home could not accommodate four households and divided it into two living units. The lower *soler*, along with the *mezzado* or mezzanine floor between it and the *piano terra*, was assigned to the heirs of Zuan Matteo's eldest son, Lorenzo, who was now also deceased.[34] Their portion also included five houses—one *casa* and four *casette*—on Calle del Forno which collectively brought in rents of 51 ducats per year. The entire upper *soler* was now given to Piero, bishop of Veglia, along with its own mezzado and the *soffitta* or attic. He also received two houses and three apartments on Calle del Forno, bringing in annual rents of 53 ducats. The courtyard with the well-head and catchment basin remained common to both properties. The two other sons, Marc'Antonio and David, divided up the remaining real estate. To David went two houses on Calle del Forno bringing in rents of 52 ducats plus an apartment not rented at the time. He was also given two houses, each described as a *casa da statio*, in the contrade of San Maurizio and San Pantalon, with rents unspecified, along with two smaller dwellings in the latter location that brought in 15 ducats of rent.[35] Marc'Antonio was given a villa and agricultural land in Ponte de Brenta, with the income that came from grain, wine, and tributes. He was also given two *case* and two *casette* on Calle del Forno yielding rents of 31 ducats and was to be paid 2 ducats per year by each of the three other parties for a total of around 33 ducats each, an arrangement that led to further litigation.[36]

Landlords and Tenants

Less than a decade later the *decima* (tax declarations) of 1582 show Lorenzo's three sons renting out the lower *soler* to another patrician, Alessandro Balbi, who paid a rent of 80 ducats per year.[37] And what of their three uncles? Piero is out of town at the time, according to his nephew Andrea, but is keeping the *soler di sopra* "as his habitation."[38] Marc'Antonio had died and his widow Lucietta is living in the same contrada with five minor children. Although she had received several small properties from her husband's estate in restitution of her dowry, she declares herself poor and sick and unable to keep all of them in good repair while supporting her children on an income of more than 90 ducats per year. The rental value of her own home, called a *casetta* in the declaration, is given as only 16 ducats.[39]

On the other hand, David, Zuan Matteo's youngest surviving son, is living in a rented *casa da statio* at San Barnaba, across the Grand Canal from

Santa Maria Nova, in the sestiere of Dorsoduro. He is paying a rather substantial rent of 100 ducats per year to another nobleman, Gabriel Zorzi, who owns the property, but is not living in it himself. David's rent is subsidized in part by his share in the rental units at Santa Maria Nova which bring in 24 ducats a year and income from a large *casa da statio* at San Boldù that was part of his wife's dowry. Like David's own family home, the latter property was divided into two living units, one on each floor, yielding a total of 160 ducats a year in rent. So although David was deprived of his ancestral home, he was ahead of the game by more than offsetting his own rent with proceeds from other properties in his possession.[40]

It should be stressed that this was not an unusual situation. The tax records show that approximately one half of the 1,230 patrician families in the city in 1582 lived in rental housing, and that the renters enjoyed the same broad spectrum of financial resources as those who lived in their own houses. Some could not afford to purchase or build a house, but others rented by choice, preferring to keep their capital liquid for investments or, as in the case of David Bembo, the balance sheet showed a distinct advantage to renting. His rent of 100 ducats was around the 80th percentile for patricians. Somewhat more than 20 percent paid 100 ducats per year or more, with the top 2.5 percent within that group paying more than 200 ducats.[41] A little more than 40 percent of patricians paid between 50 and 100 ducats and 33 percent paid less than 50. These figures suggest that there was not a *division* between rich and poor within the patriciate, but rather a continuum. Their respective resources formed a bell curve with the largest group in the center enjoying a comfortable standard of living and those at the low end living far more modestly than many a wealthy commoner.

Of those patricians who did live in their own homes, about one in eight were paying rent on part of the building to a sibling or someone else. An heir of a certain Zuan Barbarigo reported ownership in the tax rolls of 1537 of "two thirds of one half of a *casa da statio*."[42] Another patrician, Giulio Balbi, lived in the old family home at San Zulian which he owned jointly "with relatives of Ca' Balbi." These were his landlords, and he was obligated to pay rent to nine other parties.[43]

It was during this period that patrician families were encouraging only one or two sons to marry to prevent further fragmentation of the patrimony.[44] Not surprisingly, many Venetians who had large estates with several pieces of property to divide up among their heirs often insisted that the primary family home—the *casa da statio*—remain intact or at least they put limits on the subdivisions. Marco Giustinian was not atypical in ordering in his will that his *casa da statio* at San Leonardo, described as "very comfortable and honorable," was not to be divided up upon his death. Revealing that it had cost him 4,000 ducats to build, plus another 400 to 500 in expenses from a lawsuit over the property, he cautioned his sons to have "an eye to saving," a credo that had allowed him to "never fail to be able to support the house and a family of five sons and three daughters with the added burdens of wife, male and female servants, obligations, repairs, and other very great expenses," including dowries of 4,000 ducats for each daughter. He admonished his sons that "every good comes from unity" and that "fraternal love" is the key to conserving the patrimony and augmenting the esteem of the house. If his sons did not wish to live together *in fraterna*—a typical Venetian arrangement whereby the property was held in common by two or more brothers—and preferred to divide up the estate instead, so be it, but they were expressly forbidden to divide up the *casa da statio* at San Leonardo. If his sons declined to keep the house for common use, they could rent it to a third party and divide the rent in equal shares. By 1582, the three surviving sons had crafted an ingenious solution of time-sharing. Each would live with his family in the *casa da statio* for ten years at a time in rotation, and then move out into one of the other properties which they had received in the equitable division of the estate.[45] More typically adult families were dispersed. As with the Bembo family, two or more brothers or their heirs might still share a house, but married brothers just as often lived in neighborhoods that were quite distant from one another.

If the palace was a major factor in family identity, was there a loss of dignity and honor for those who rented rather than lived in homes that they owned? Not necessarily. Appearances and a noble style of living may well have been more important than a property deed. The ubiquitous coat-of-arms—inscribed on silverware and bronze objects, carved into furniture, painted on picture frames and storage chests, and woven into tapestries—created a portable family identity that could be transported from one home to another, whether rented or owned, and transmitted from one generation to the next. Indeed, the model had been set at the highest level of Venetian political life. In addition to the doge, who resided in the Ducal Palace, the Procurators of San Marco were allowed to live in state-owned signorial residences on Piazza San Marco at public expense. Since other noble homes were banned from the contrada of San Marco, this was a special privilege. A procuratorship was a lifetime appointment and the highest office in the land next to the doge. Even though paid only a token salary, the procurators were highly esteemed, with duties that involved the administration of private estates and trusts and the handling of large sums of public money. By the end of the fifteenth century, there were nine elected procurators, but over the course of the sixteenth century, additional positions would be added for those who could pay for the distinction.[46]

The apartments of the procurators were in the Procuratie Nuove, the wing on the south side of the Piazza, extending across two very high-ceilinged floors above the arcade level (fig. 5). Probably dating back to the thirteenth century, the complex was rebuilt by Scamozzi in the late sixteenth century. The wing now houses the Museo Correr, where one can get a sense of the original scale and grandeur of the interior spaces.[47] These noble tenants, although not renters per se, carried the dignity of the *casa* through the office and not through residence in the ancestral home. And yet, they were almost certainly property owners, whether they lived in their own houses or not. Patricians, consisting of less than 5 percent of the population, owned more than 70 percent of all real property in the city.[48]

Indeed, most patricians were landlords, a situation which had important ramifications. On the one hand, it helped to bridge the gap between rich and poor by encouraging direct contact between the landlord and his or her tenants; on the other, it had the potential for exacerbating class differences when properties were not kept up or tenants were evicted in hard times. Household inventories made at the time of a person's death often list account books and rental receipts attesting to the close personal involvement of the property owner in the managing of rental units, as do the *decima* tax declarations and assessments. *Decima* records survive for the sixteenth century in the form of large *buste*, each holding a mass of separate sheets, one or more for each taxpayer.[49] Declarations were either given verbally to the tax officials, who transcribed them, or written out by the property owners themselves with the name of each tenant listed meticulously, along with his or her rent.

The declaration proffered by the executors of the estate of Tomà Michiel in 1537 is typical of a landlord with large holdings.[50] Properties are listed according to parish, twelve in all, scattered throughout the city, plus a house in Burano and country properties on the Terraferma. Under San Cassan [San Cassiano] at the top of the list is *una casa*, rented to a Battista di Zuane for a very modest 4 ducats, the lowest rent on the page. Moving down the column one finds a *magazen*, or warehouse, rented to Battista dal Capello for 14 ducats, and at the bottom of the same section *una camera*—simply a room—to Bernardo Marangon for 5 ducats. The most expensive home on the page is a *casa* in the parish of San Zuanne Novo rented to Zorzi Balestrieri for 30 ducats. Such renters comprise the lower end of the

Queſte è la Procuratie, ſopra la Piazza dirimpetto al Palagio del Ser.^{mo}, Fabbrica di modello ſtimato il più ſuperbo d'Europa, inventato dal Sang.^{re} in eſa ſi conſeruano molte ſtatue famoſe laſciate per teſtamento dal Patriarca d'Aquileia l'Illmo Grimani, è la nobiliſſ.^a Libraria dell'Illmo Card.^e Beſſarioni
franco forma con priuilegio

FIGURE 5. Procuratie Nuove, from Giacomo Franco, *Habiti d'Huomeni et Donne* (Venice, 1626). By permission of the Folger Shakespeare Library

economic spectrum, but as witness the reduced circumstances of the widowed Lucietta Bembo cited earlier, there might well have been a few patricians and cittadini among the popolani. Anecdotal evidence drawn from the *decime* suggests that landlords were familiar with the tenants and their problems. The noblewoman Andriana Contarini, widow of the Magnificent Francesco, reported in her declaration that many of her rental properties "are in great ruin, so that they need many repairs. . . . And then one cannot recapture the expenses from all the rents because many of those living in them are poor people."[51] That her tenants were poor was probably accurate, but a claim that the buildings were falling apart may have been a ploy to lower the tax assessment.

Another point of contact between landlords and tenants was in their actual living arrangements. The Bembo complex at Santa Maria Nova was not unusual, with its row of little houses or apartments, sixteen in all, on Calle del Forno, next to the family palace and sharing its courtyard. At the time of the property division in 1573, these units yielded about 187 ducats per year. The rents ranged from a low 4 ducats to a moderate 30, with the mean rent about 9.5 ducats—quite similar to the *decima* declaration of Tomá Michiel's estate. In the case of the Bembo properties, the tenants included a tailor, a dyer, a spicer, a beater of gold, and six single women—Isotta, Angelica, Chiara, Medea, Lucia, and Leandra—each living in a separate unit.[52] Thus the Bembo heirs residing in the *casa da statio* lived next door to—and shared their private well with—a group of tenants, mostly women, whose rents put them at the low end of the economic spectrum of Venetian society. The complex of Bembo properties along Calle del Forno might be considered an elongated variant of the public courtyard, wherein houses were arranged around an open space with a well in the center. The *decima* of 1582 lists about 270 such courtyards, a third of which carry a noble family name signifying the double aspect of residence and investment. The status of such areas as public spaces was ambiguous, with property owners asserting their hegemony through coats of arms and other signs of family dominance. Such patterns were repeated many times over throughout the city, with poor tenants often living in close proximity to their wealthy landlords.[53]

Charitable Strategies

In a society where real estate was beginning to compete with trade as a means to generate wealth, the home also became a major factor in charitable strategies. Zuan Matteo Bembo had named a hospital as his residuary heir in case every single Bembo in Venice should die without progeny, but he also used part of a house that he owned in the contrada of San Maurizio to endow a trust to benefit the poor immediately. The building was substantial enough for him to call it a *casa grande* in his will. The *mezzado* or mezzanine below the first *soler* was rented out for 10–12 ducats per year. Zuan Matteo stipulated that these funds be used by the Procurators of San Marco to ransom prisoners at Easter and Christmas. If any of his heirs wished to recover the use of that space, they would be allowed to buy it for 200 ducats and the funds invested by the procurators for the same charitable purposes.[54] In addition to the Procurators of San Marco, the Scuole Grandi served a fiduciary function in administering such legacies.

Often such housing was built from scratch. In 1460, Tomaso Cavazza, a rich cittadino, named the officers of the Scuola Grande della Carità as

FIGURE 6.
Madonna of Mercy, emblem of the Scuola Grande di Santa Maria della Carità, relief sculpture on Rio Santa Caterina on the back of the building facing Calle dei Volti, Cannaregio. Photo: O. Böhm, Venice

executors of his will and ordered that his furniture and some property at Santa Marina be sold to build houses whose market rate rents could be used by the Scuola for charitable purposes. It took another thirty years for his wishes to be carried out. In 1491 the Scuola bought a house that was under construction with adjacent property on the Santa Caterina and built a complex of two parallel rows of houses along the Calle dei Volti. Within a decade twelve houses were in place, renting for 24 to 25 ducats each. By 1566 the complex had been reorganized and fourteen houses were bringing in a wide range of rents, from 10 to 115 ducats per annum.[55]

On the rear facade of the complex facing the Rio Santa Caterina, a large relief sculpture of the Madonna of Mercy sheltering two groups of kneeling *confratelli* under her cloak is embedded in the wall (fig. 6). On her breast is an emblem of the Scuola della Carità. A plaque below carries an inscription: "It was erected from the proceeds of the sale of the house of Tomaso Cavazza which he had left to the governors of the Scuola della Carità so that the profit would long be fruitful for the care of the poor."[56] Beneath the inscribed plaque is the Cavazza coat of arms. In contrast to most confraternity properties offered to the poor *pro amore dei*, which were marked by a simple discreet emblem, the relief at Calle dei Volti is a particularly ostentatious announcement. Why was the Cavazza plaque so elaborate? Perhaps to make clear that these homes were only to benefit the poor, and were not for the use of the poor.

Housing for the Working Poor

During the late medieval and Renaissance period a number of housing projects were also built specifically as rentals, the more modest of them intended specifically to house the working poor or those with some means to pay their own way—artisans, widows, the elderly.[57] Two architectural types predominated that distinguish them from the usual hodgepodge of random building: the diptych row house and the courtyard surrounded by apartments. The diptych model consists of a double row of attached houses with a wide alley in between, such as the Calle or Corte dei Preti located near the Arsenal (fig. 7). The project was owned by the Hospital of Saints Peter and Paul, an institution which dated back to the Middle Ages. Hospitals in that period were not just for the sick; this one was originally founded by a lay confraternity to shelter pilgrims en route to the Holy Land and the poor, as well as the infirm. In the best tradition of Venetian consensus, it was funded largely by private donations and bequests,

FIGURE 7.
View of Corte
dei Preti, Castello.
Photo: author

administered by a prior and a governing board of three nobles and two cittadini, and enjoyed the special protection of the doge. Already in place in
1500, the complex was remodeled in the early sixteenth century. In 1564,
thirty-nine units were occupied, with rents totaling 280 ducats, or around
7 ducats each.[58]

The complex has been truncated since that time, but the surviving
structures show that it was ingeniously designed, with a balance between
public and private spaces. Each row of the diptych consists of six sections,
with each section containing two living units stacked one above the other
for a total of twelve apartments. Each apartment consists of a ground floor
entrance with a staircase leading up to a whole floor above, comprising two
rooms on the *primo piano* and three on the *secondo piano*. Both units share
the same fireplace flues, one in front and the other in back (fig. 8).

FIGURE 8. Corte dei Preti, Castello. Reconstruction drawing from Giorgio Gianighian and Paola Pavanini, *Dietro I palazzi: Tre secoli di architettura minore a Venezia 1492–1803* (Venice: Arsenale Editrice, 1984), 68

FIGURE 9.
Emblem of Scuola Grande di
San Giovanni Evangelista on a
house held *pro amore dei*.
Photo: author

So, on the one hand, each unit has its own private entrance and staircase—still most desirable features in Venice—and, on the other, each has windows that look out on the calle or narrow courtyard in front, guaranteeing that no act goes unobserved. The courtyard itself with the double row of paired doorways ensures social contact among the neighbors. Beyond that, the clotheslines that stretch across the narrow calle today suggest that those who looked directly into each others' windows might be closer than those who lived one above one other in the same building. The apartments at Corte dei Preti were rented to low-paid workers at the Arsenal, so the complex should be considered affordable housing rather than an almshouse.

But there were also a number of initiatives in Venice whose sole aim was to provide housing for the poor that was either free or renting at considerably lower than market rate. This was housing offered *pro amore dei*, that is, for the love of God. In most cases it came from private individuals who left houses or funding in their wills for such purposes and named the Procurators of San Marco or a confraternity, most often a Scuola Grande, as administrators of the bequest. Houses obtained by *scuole* in this way were then assigned to poor members in good standing.[59] One still sees confraternity emblems marking such houses above the entrances of buildings throughout the city (fig. 9). Modern people might find this an unacceptable way of stigmatizing the poor, but in that period charitable gestures were supposed to be public and not hidden. Such signs fulfilled at least three functions. First, they rendered explicitly the mercy and benevolence of the Republic and its citizens. Furthermore, they testified to the symbiotic relationship between the rich and the poor and thus affirmed the social order.[60] Finally, since houses offered *pro amore dei* were presumably given only to persons of good reputation—that is, the worthy poor—

FIGURE 10.
View of Corte San
Marco, Dorsoduro.
Photo: author

possession of one of them offered testimony to the tenant's good character and virtue. Not surprisingly, reality often fell short of the ideal.

The frailties of human nature were amply demonstrated at Corte San Marco, the second type of popular housing complex cited above (figs. 10–11). Featuring a large courtyard with a well in the center and bounded by twenty-four attached houses, it was built with funds from the estate of Pietro Olivieri. Naming the officers of the Scuola Grande di San Marco as his executors, he ordered them to purchase land on which they were to build very modest homes of a quality that normally rented for 5 to 6 ducats per year. These should be given gratis, *pro amore dei,* to "poor brothers of the Scuola di San Marco who above all should have children." The fortunate

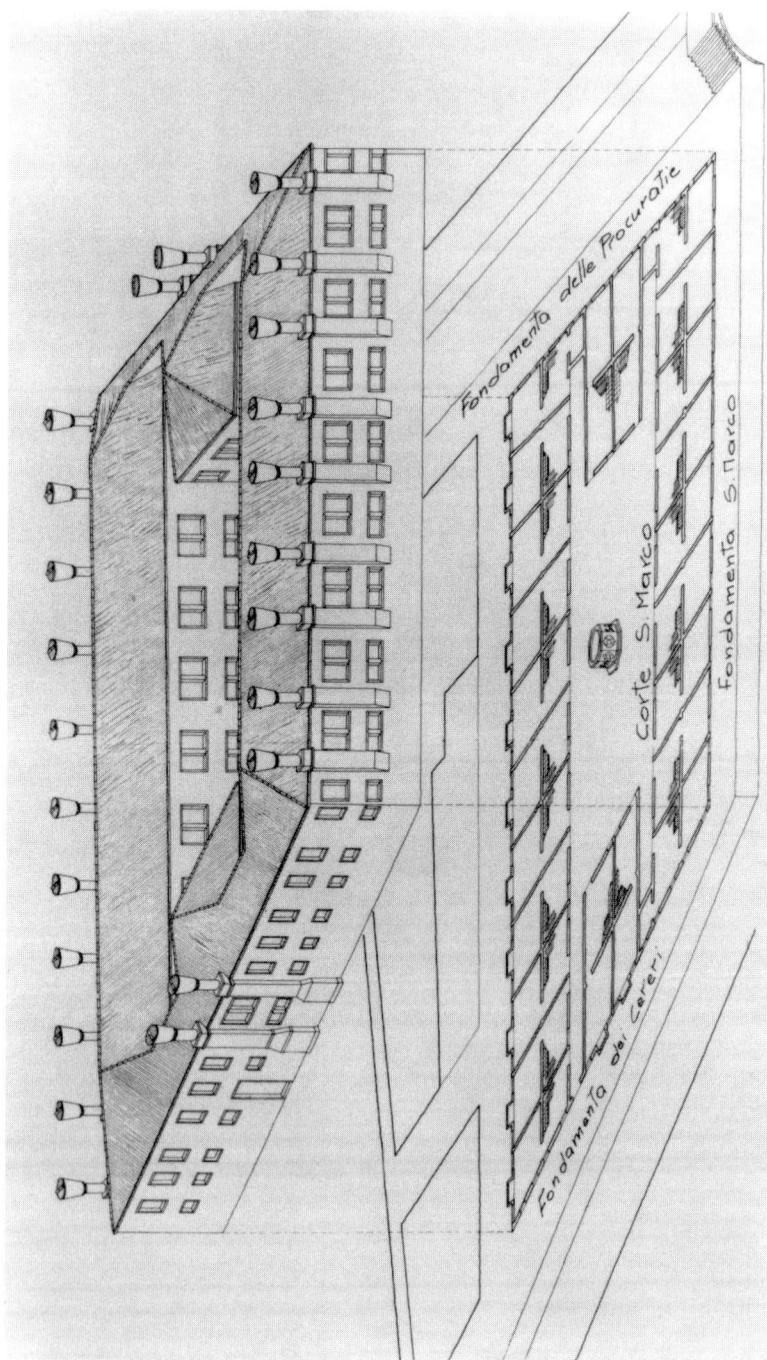

FIGURE 11. Corte San Marco. Reconstruction drawing from Giorgio Gianighian and Paola Pavanini, *Dietro I palazzi: Tre secoli di architettura minore a Venezia 1492–1803* (Venice: Arsenale Editrice, 1984), 110

tenants would be entitled to enjoy the houses during their lifetimes, and when they died the units would be reassigned to other brothers of the Scuola. Olivieri himself seems to have died in 1529. It took some time for construction to get underway, but by 1542 the houses were finally built and distributed to the confratelli.[61]

Corte San Marco was a little world unto itself. The well in the center, suitably adorned with the insignia of the Scuola, was the focal point of community life for the families who lived around it. All the homes opened only into the courtyard at that time, with access from the street outside through a single portal that could be closed off. But it was not closed off from attempts to regulate behavior, for with largesse came control. Dancing, gambling, swearing, and what were described as lascivious acts were banned by the Council of Ten in all such courtyards.[62] With little success, one suspects. And there were complaints: that there had been favoritism in the selection process, that the beneficiaries had not been sufficiently screened, and that some were not worthy and honorable men. It was also charged that many of them failed to honor the quid pro quo for receiving such benefits and did not show up to march in confraternity processions.[63]

Equally troubling was the charge that the houses were too sumptuous for the poor and that they could easily rent for 12 to 14 ducats a year.[64] Indeed, in contrast to the flats at Corte dei Preti renting for around 7 ducats apiece, the units at Corte San Marco were floor to roof townhouses with attics and *two* floors of living space above the *piano terra*. Each had four rooms in all, and those on the corners had an extra small room with windows. Aside from the all-too-human vice of envy—that others were getting more than they deserved—at play here was a notion, deeply ingrained at the time, that housing should correspond to one's social class more than one's economic circumstances.[65] For example, the family of a cobbler poor enough to live in housing offered *pro amore dei* should not be more comfortable than the families of arsenal workers of essentially the same "quality and condition" who were paying their own way.

Beyond that, people tended to think of the homes as their own property, and subletting was a common infraction. Some even joined apartments together, and cut windows and doors in walls without permission.[66] Houses were generally given at least partly furnished, and one Scuola complained that those relatives who were obliged to move out after the death of the beneficiary often stripped the houses, carrying away not only furniture such as "beds, benches, shelves and other things," but also "windowpanes, doorlocks, latches, keys, balconies, staircases and cornices."[67] Who were the tenants? Artisans, such as shoemakers, dyers, weavers, barrel-makers, and the like. Some of them may even have owned property of their own—often outside Venice—from which they received small rents that were insufficient to live on.

The competition for such houses engendered creative strategies to secure them. Knowing that large families were favored, a certain wool-worker named Hieronimo sought to tip the scales in his favor in the annual contest for free housing of the Scuola di San Rocco in 1583. He fraudulently obtained a certificate from the sacristan of his parish church and presented himself to the governors of the Scuola with his wife "and six little children, barefoot and almost naked, and he and his wife too were poorly clad and, to outward appearances, weighed down by poverty and wretchedness, the better to move you to compassion, and he said that all six children really belonged to him, although only two were his own and he had brought the others with him for the purposes just mentioned."[68] He did not receive good marks for enterprise, nor, presumably, one of the apartments.

The Non-working Poor

As to the dwellings of the truly poor, the most fortunate found homes in hospitals or hospices. Nearly a hundred such institutions can be documented by the end of the sixteenth century. These might be run by church, state, or confraternities, but the majority—about 60 percent—were private foundations. Private hospices were found in every sector of the city and were generally quite small. They were typically designated for specific categories, with the chosen groups changing over the centuries. In the thirteenth century, the majority were for pilgrims and were supported by the Church, but as lay bequests became more important in the fourteenth century, the emphasis shifted to the poor, the sick, the old, and particularly to women and orphans.[69]

While these establishments came in various sizes and configurations, the classic architectural type is exemplified by the Ospedale dei Crociferi (fig. 12).[70] It was founded as a hostel for pilgrims and the poor in the middle of the twelfth century by the Crociferi Fathers next to their monastery in Cannaregio. In 1268, Doge Ranieri Zen left it a substantial bequest of land, houses, and capital and it became known as Ospizio Zen. At this point administration of the hospice passed from the monastery to the Procurators of San Marco and the emphasis changed from the pious traveler to the sick. In the fourteenth century it was housing forty to fifty sick men and

FIGURE 12. Ospedale dei Crociferi, Cannaregio. Photo: author

women at one time, providing them with food, beds, linen, clothing, and shoes. By the early fifteenth century, the emphasis had changed again, and the hospital turned into a hospice now housing just twelve poor women.[71]

Rebuilt several times, the hospice consisted of two floors, with six bedrooms on each level—four across the front and two in back. The rooms are arranged along a common area, the equivalent of the portego in a palace, but here more of a hallway, with an oratory at the end. The ground floor was used for living space, an area that a family of means would use for storage. But many of the poor lived then, and still live, on the *piano terra*—the least desirable location in a Venetian house, given the constant problem of damp and the periodic threat of flooding. The bottom floor was raised above the pavement at some time after the late nineteenth century, precisely because of this problem, and the building is still used as a hospice for the elderly.[72]

The hospital was organized like a religious community, with the woman in charge called *priora*—prioress—and the rooms called *celle* or cells. Each woman had her own apartment and received a small stipend on Christmas, Easter, and the Feast of the Assumption of the Virgin. She was allowed to keep a cat in her room, but no other animals. There were duties both mundane and spiritual. Each woman was responsible for keeping her own rooms clean and orderly, and two were assigned to sweep and tidy up the common hallways of the hospice, "from one door to the other," on a weekly or monthly basis, as the prioress determined. In addition, the residents were asked to consent that all furnishings present in their rooms at the time of their death be passed on to the monastery. To ensure an "honorable and good example to the others," the women were not allowed to enter other parts of the adjacent church and monastery of the Crociferi. Aside from attending mass on Sundays, they were required to kneel before the altar of the Madonna in the oratory each morning to "render thanks to her, and to pray to God for the state of our most illustrious Signoria, the freedom and conservation of the monastery, and for the souls of those who have given so much good."[73]

Ospizio Priuli [also called Ospizio de' Vecchi] was a male counterpart to the Ospedale dei Crociferi, but with a significant difference: it was run by a family and not a religious order. Founded by Lodovico Priuli, son of a doge, who left money in his will and explicit instructions to build a hospice dedicated to his name saint Lodovico, it was intended to house twelve poor old men. Each would receive his own room and a stipend of 12 ducats and six cartloads of firewood per year, plus a measure of wheat each month. The hospice, built in Dorsoduro near the Church of Sant'Angelo Raffaele in 1571, follows the diptych model, with a double row of two-storied buildings flanking a blind alley. While the building has since been remodeled, the distribution of the bedrooms is essentially the same, and an oratory at the end of the right-hand wing remains intact. Lodovico left little to chance. He specified that the oldest surviving Priuli male heir must serve as prior and would participate with the executors of the estate, who included Ludovico's wife Marietta, in choosing the residents. These should be persons, he declares, "of good life, and without sons or wives, and they must be Venetians or subjects, because I do not wish in any way that the [benefits] be given to persons of a foreign country; indeed, they must have lived for thirty years or more in Venice. And if any of them should marry or gain a bad reputation, he must be replaced immediately by someone else."[74] A chaplain, "of good life and example," would live on the premises to "care for the souls of these twelve old men," and to say the mass on every feast day, but the administration of the Scuola was to remain strictly lay and secular and must not be interfered with by any priest or other ecclesiastic. Each year on the Feast of the Conception of the Virgin, a solemn mass should be sung in the oratory and dinner given to the twelve residents, which should include "malvasia wine, *bussoli* [a kind of bagel], risotto, a main course of fish because it was Advent, and other dishes to be determined by the Prior from the house of Priuli, this being his duty."[75]

The Ospizio di Sant'Agnesina on the Rio San Barnaba was intended to serve a different population. It had been founded in 1383 by Angelo Condulmer, father of Pope Eugenius IV, who left funds in his will to establish it. The hospice was run by the Scuola di Sant'Agnese and housed twelve orphaned girls of legitimate birth, noble or cittadino.[76] The number was reduced to six girls in 1526 when Sanudo visited the church. He went there on the feast day of Saint Agnes, he reported, to see "a new thing, that is six girls, eight to nine years old, who each stood on a platform, daughters of scuola members, dressed half in white and half in red with their hair down to their shoulders and wearing crowns of leaves on their heads. They live together in the house at San Barnaba with a mistress who is given 40 ducats per year to maintain them and who teaches them to read and to work [probably needlework] until they reached the right age to marry" or enter a convent. These girls, he reported, "are elected by those of the Scuola with a certain very fine order."[77] The hospice maintained its mission at least until the end of the sixteenth century. The Englishman Fynes Moryson reported in 1595: "In the cloyster of Saint Agnes, the Prioresse bringeth up six Virgins, which being of ripe yeeres, are either married or made Nunnes, and six more of good families sent thither in their place."[78]

Such foundations are typical, and the message is consistent. Charity began at home, and some poor were more deserving than others. Relatives came before friends; neighbors before strangers; confraternity members before the unaffiliated; Venetians before foreigners. And virtue was rewarded. Charity normally came with strings attached, namely that the poor recipients be morally upright and that they pray for the souls of their benefactors. San Bernardino was not far from wrong when he said, "The rich are necessary to Republics; and the poor are necessary to the rich."[79] The salvation of the rich depended on the prayers of the poor.[80]

The Shamefaced Poor

But poverty is a relative thing. Just as it was indecorous for the comfortable units of Corte San Marco to be given to humble cobblers, so too was it inappropriate for a poor noble to live in a hovel. "Poverty" could signify a loss of rank as much as a loss of financial resources, and perhaps the most troubling category of the needy were the *poveri vergognosi*—the shamefaced poor.[81] The Great Council articulated the mind-set in a decree of

1544: "It is certainly a humane and pious duty to have mercy for the poor, and especially for those, who born of honorable parents and well endowed with the goods of fortune for some time, would then by diverse accidents be reduced to a state of poverty, of which there are a great number in this city, and they are called the shamefaced poor."[82] While it was perfectly appropriate for a poor widow of a boatman to beg for alms from passersby and to lament openly about her hunger without embarrassment, it was a matter of civic shame for the widow of a nobleman or cittadino merchant who had been left destitute to do the same.

The Banca, or officers, of the Scuola Grande di San Rocco in 1591 thus listened with a sympathetic ear to an appeal from the widow of a former Guardian Grande: "If ever there was a case deserving of the Christian charity of yourselves, honorable governors of the Scuola, it is mine, that of the wretched and unhappy Filomena Stella, widow of the late honorable Missier Paulo d'Anna . . . for I am reduced to such a parlous state by the misfortunes I have suffered, in which the late Ser Paulo left me. For it is well known that nothing remains to me but the hopes I have of God and of Catholic Christians, who must consider the rank to which I was born, the parents of whom I was born, and the husband to whom I was married, for your worships know all these things, and are aware that I am brought to such destitution that I have to beg for a living from those who will pity me." Filomena requested that the Scuola give her one of its "small and lowly houses let at paltry rents of 4, 5 or at most 6 ducats a year," free of rent, or at one-half rent for as long as she lived, but the Banca did more. It voted 21–0 to offer her the first available house belonging to the Scuola that rented for 15 ducats or less, with Signor Bortolomio, a mercer at the sign of the Chalice, pledging to pay the rent on her behalf.[83] The situation was particularly poignant, given the fact that Paolo d'Anna had belonged to what was once one of the wealthiest cittadino families in the city.[84]

The Immigrant Poor

Nowhere is the principle of charity beginning at home more evident than in the laws passed in the midst of a famine in 1528 that brought droves of starving peasants into the city from the Terraferma. The high ideals of Christian charity were mixed with a desire to get beggars off the streets and out of public view. The Senate voted to select at least two or three sites where "all those poor who go through this city would be lodged, and there would be made rooms of wood with enough straw and other things to sleep on." Those who left the hostels and were found begging in public "would be arrested and put in prison and the following day flogged and sent outside the city." Those who returned "would be flogged again and taken outside, and so on each time." None of the poor who come into the city after this point were to be lodged in the places designated, "and all foreigners who are found begging must be arrested."[85]

The law of 1528 was an emergency measure, passed to deal with the crisis at hand and supported by a property tax to be paid by all those whose rents were 10 ducats per year or more. It was to end the following June, when any poor peasants who were still in the city would be loaded onto boats and sent back to the Terraferma. As harsh as the legislation may sound to us today, it marks an important shift to a collective social conscience with the State assuming responsibility for what had formerly been an individual or group—that is confraternity—initiative for the most part.[86]

Housing the Sick and Infirm

A French visitor at the end of the fifteenth century reported that there were three state hospitals in Venice with a fourth under construction. The Pietà, later famous for Vivaldi's musical orphans, was a foundling hospital that had been built on the Riva degli Schiavoni in 1346. The Lazzaretto Vecchio (later the Mendicanti) was established on an island southeast of the city near the Lido in 1423 for plague victims, who stayed there until they recovered or died; and the Lazzaretto Nuovo, a quarantine hospital, was built in 1468 on an island next to Sant'Erasmo for those who had been exposed to, or were recovering from, the plague.[87] The Ospedale di Gesù Cristo di Sant'Antonio, begun in 1474 on the eastern tip of the city proper, "for the kindly reception and charitable treatment of the poor and other wretched persons who came to that hospital from every place," was completed around 1503 with financial support from a papal indulgence.[88] Two major foundations were added in the sixteenth century: the Incurabili, on the Zattere, created in 1523 to house those suffering from syphilis; and the Derelitti (also called the Ospedaletto) at SS. Giovanni e Paolo, founded as part of the reform of 1528 to shelter vagabonds and the starving peasants.[89]

There was a general awareness that sickness and death was no respecter of persons, and of the interconnectedness of the different strata of the

FIGURE 13. Hans Heinrich Schweitzer (1618–1673), *Visiting the Sick in a Venetian Hospital*, engraving (after Titian?). Rome, Istituto Nazionale per la Grafica. Fondo Pio, Inv. 35171, F. H. 1457. By the kind permission of the Ministero per i Beni Culturale e Ambientali

well-ordered Republic. The equation is eloquently expressed in an engraving of a Venetian hospital by the Swiss artist Hans Heinrich Schweitzer (fig. 13). The room embraces the full range of humanity, from the rich man in a canopied bed to less affluent patients across the room, two to a bed, to several beggars in rags, who sit on the floor. On the wall to the upper right is a painting of Lazarus and the Rich Man, a popular pictorial theme in this period: a way of aestheticizing a social problem by elevating it to the level of art.[90]

Distributing the Poor

The law of 1528 proclaimed: "The poor people of Venice who are driven by want, and who cannot live by their own industry or manual labor on account of infirmity, shall be placed in and distributed among the hospitals or wherever it seems they can best get support. This measure shall be applied to those persons of either sex who have no fixed abode. . . . Those who are feeble [*impotenti*] and yet have a dwelling-place may on no account seek alms in the city. They must go or send to the priests in their parishes, who shall provide for their support. . . . The poor of the city must be divided and distributed among the parishes in such a way that each parish has a number of poor appropriate to its wealth and standing." Furthermore, each parish was ordered to maintain a box for support of the poor with the priest and his deputies holding the keys, and the monies collected "must be spent solely upon the assistance of the poor." But as in confraternity housing, with protection came control. The poor were not to move from one parish to another without a certificate from the parish priest.[91] Indeed, Venetian hospices for the poor can be found side by side with the great palaces of the rich, in every part of the city, except perhaps on the Grand Canal.

Inventories indicate that families of this condition had few possessions of their own: the usual chests and chairs and beds, almost always of pine rather than walnut. They are often described as old and broken, if not *triste*, or sad, in the inventory. Absent from the lists are maiolica, pewter, or silver. Very few items were decorated with carving, but chests were often painted, mostly red or green.[92] In all likelihood, they had been bought secondhand, and when money was short, they were pawned. Since the poor were often without money, these were the only things of value that could be attached, and such goods were often taken forcibly from debtors.[93] In April 1583, the house of Paolo the Pole was entered by the authorities and a ragged garment, four small pieces of green cloth, and a chest full of rags were confiscated along with candlesticks, a bed, and other items.[94] Indeed, with the secondhand trade, the lives of both rich and poor intersected with another group which had a distinctive living arrangement not of their own design—the Jews.

Rich and Poor within the Ghetto

Jews held an ambiguous status in Venetian society. Many had fled into the city during the War of Cambrai in 1509. Tolerated because of their usefulness to the city as bankers and tax-paying merchants and to the needy poor (as well as the profligate rich) as moneylenders and secondhand dealers, they settled throughout the city. But in 1516, concerned that the Jews

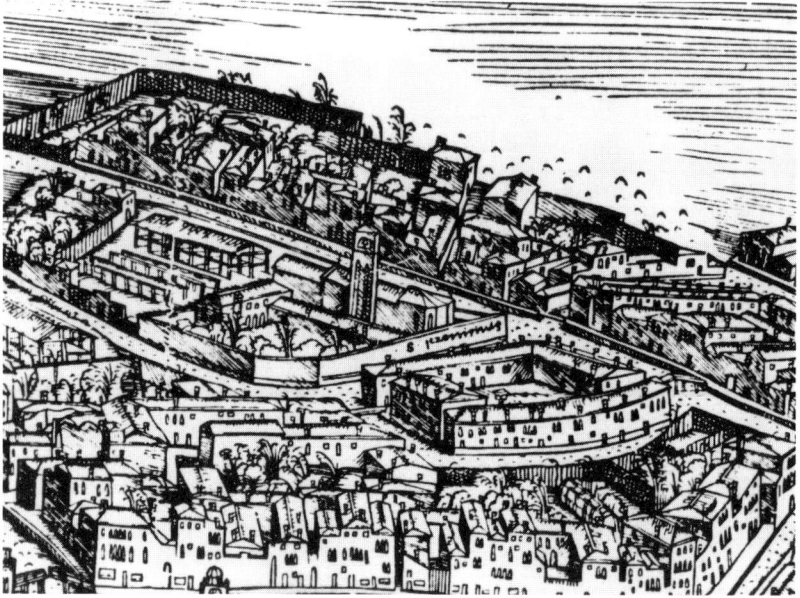

FIGURE 14. Jacopo de' Barbari, View of Venice, detail of the Ghetto area, 1500.
Photo: O Böhm, Venice

were mixing too freely with Christians, the Venetian Senate would decree: "The Jews must all reside together in the houses in the court within the Ghetto near San Girolamo, where there is plenty of room for them to live. And in order to prevent their roaming about at night, let there be built two gates . . ."[95] The site was the Ghetto Nuovo, a trapezoid-shaped island near the old public iron and brass foundries. The area, called "terren del Geto," had already been developed with rental housing around the middle of the fifteenth century by two merchant brothers, Costantino and Bartolomeo da Brolo. They constructed a cistern beneath the large campo, installed three wellheads and built a two-storey row of modest housing around the perimeter (fig. 14). It was not much different from other island parishes except that it lacked a church.[96] With the decree of 1516, the existing renters were moved out, the outside windows walled up, the Jews moved in, and rents raised by one third. The resettlement law applied to the rich as well as the poor, even to the affluent brother of Asher Meshullam, head of the Jewish community, who had rented the palatial Ca' Bernardo on the Grand Canal just the year before and was resented for flaunting his riches.[97]

The community was self-contained. Butcher shops, bakeries, banks, pawnshops, and secondhand stores were installed on the ground floors with residences above (fig. 15). To accommodate the new concentration of population, houses with as many as nine stories were constructed on the foundations of the existing buildings. The standard elsewhere in Venice was only three or four stories at most. These very plain tenements, built primarily of wood to reduce weight, did not come close to the Gothic splendor of Ca' Bernardo. Their main exterior ornaments were unadorned white Istrian stone frames on the door and window openings. But inside the walls, their interiors reflected the diversity of Venetian society at large, with inventories documenting not only the meager furnishings of the poor and dispossessed, but also the material comforts of the very rich. All such homes were rental units, since Jews were forbidden from owning real estate. To compensate, the state granted them a special privilege: the rights to one's personal rental contract that could be passed on to heirs, bestowed as dowry, given away, or sold—an early form of rent control.[98]

The Ghetto Nuovo was connected to the rest of the city by two bridges, which were locked up at night.[99] Indeed, it became a kind of open prison, with the Jews taxed to pay for boats to patrol the surrounding canals day and night and four Christian guards who imposed the curfew and controlled the access points. From the outside it looked like a fortress. Forbidden to do manual labor and to engage in professional pursuits except for medicine, Jews were allowed to lend money and engage in the highly profitable secondhand trade. The Ghetto pawnshops were frequented by the rich as much as by the poor: to facilitate liquidation of debts and the settlement of estates, to tide people over in hard times, to fill the state coffers. Clothing and home furnishings could have considerable retail value and were commonly used as collateral or pawned to raise cash. Even the rags of the poor had their market. It is not by accident that the term for a secondhand dealer—*strazzaruol*—translates as "rag merchant."[100]

The Jews had immigrated to Venice in several waves. The first group to settle the Ghetto Nuovo were the Ashkenazy or German Jews, many Italian in origin. They were followed by refugees from Spain and Portugal, known as Ponentine or Western Jews. A third group, the Levantine Jews, was recognized as a separate entity by the Republic in 1541 when an older area called the Ghetto Vecchio was built up to house them. Adjacent to the Ghetto Nuovo, it too was enclosed and guarded. The terms 'Vecchio' and 'Nuovo' thus referred not to the Jewish settlements, which were established in reverse order, but to the foundries that originally gave these

FIGURE 15. View of the Venetian Ghetto. Photo: O. Böhm, Venice

districts their characteristic names. Restricted to mercantile activity and forbidden to engage in money-lending or the secondhand trade, the Levantine Jews nonetheless became the wealthiest and most influential group of the Jewish community. The physical space of the community expanded again in 1633 when the Ghetto Nuovissimo—with the name now corresponding to the order of Jewish settlement—was rebuilt to house twenty Sephardic families.[101]

In 1528 the Council of Ten dropped a ban against synagogues and allowed the Jews to build the equivalent of the parish church. By the end of the sixteenth century there were five major congregations, reflecting the diverse origins of the population.[102] In 1581, Francesco Sansovino would write optimistically that "as a result of trade, the Jews are extremely opulent and wealthy, and they prefer to live in Venice rather than in any other part of Italy. Since they are not subject to violence or tyranny here as they are elsewhere, and they are secure in all aspects of their business . . . reposing in most singular peace, they enjoy this city almost like a true promised land."[103]

Coexisting in Venice were a number of worlds, distinct from one another economically and socially, as well as spatially. And yet they were also overlapping, interlocking, side by side. It was a tight little island, its component parts as snugly fit together as a jigsaw puzzle, with a common destiny. It should be stressed that a housing mix was characteristic of most late medieval cities,[104] but in Venice, large building blocks which housed the middling and even the poor often made it seem as if everyone was living in a palace, an illusion that helped to sustain the "myth of Venice" to foreigners and inhabitants alike. Not by chance was the city known throughout Europe as *la Serenissima*. Although the deceptively smooth surface of this most serene republic masked a society where tensions between rich and poor, landlord and tenant, native-born and immigrant, were probably as great as anywhere else, the city is notable for an absence of serious internal political upheavals throughout its thousand-year history. For all its many shortcomings, it was the strength and genius of the Venetian Republic to cement this multifaceted mosaic together into a cohesive whole. The home was a central feature in a dynamic process of inclusion that did not meld so much as it bonded and which gave the citizenry as a whole a firm sense of its place in the world.

Notes

Abbreviations:
    ASV = Archivio di Stato di Venezia
    BCV = Biblioteca di Museo Correr, Venice
    BMV = Biblioteca Nazionale Marciana, Venice

This essay, a revised version of one of the Slade Lectures in Fine Arts delivered by the author at the University of Cambridge in 2001, is included in a slightly altered form in *Private Lives in Renaissance Venice: Art, Architecture and the Family* (New Haven and London: Yale University Press, 2004).

    1. Girolamo Priuli, *I Diarii*, ed. Arturo Segre and Roberto Cessi, in *Rerum Italicarum Scriptores*, n.s. 24 (Bologna, 1924–1931), pt. iii, 331, cited in Alberto Tenenti, "The Sense of Space and Time in the Venetian World," in *Renaissance Venice*, ed. J. R. Hale (London: Faber and Faber, 1973), 33.

    2. Philippe de Commynes, *The Memories of Philippe de Commynes*, ed. Samuel Kinser (Columbia, S.C.: University of South Carolina Press, 1969–1973), II:493.

    3. Francesco Sansovino, *Venetia città nobilissima et singolare descritta in XIIII libri*, with additions by Giustiniano Martinioni, 2 vols. (Venice: Steffano Curti, 1663; reprint, Venice: Filippi Editore 1968), I:389.

    4. Ibid., I:384–385. On this issue, see Patricia Fortini Brown, "Behind the Walls: The Material Culture of Venetian Elites," in *Venice Reconsidered: The History and Civilization of an Italian City-State, 1297–1797*, ed. John Martin and Dennis Romano (Baltimore and London: The Johns Hopkins University Press, 2000), 295–338.

    5. Sansovino, *Venetia città nobilissima*, I:381.

    6. Frederic Lane, "The Enlargement of the Great Council of Venice," in *Florilegium Historiale: Essays Presented to Wallace K. Ferguson*, ed. J. G. Rose and W. H. Stockdale (Toronto: University of Toronto Press, 1971), 237–274. For two recent views, see Gerhard Rösch, "The *Serrata* of the Great Council and Venetian Society, 1286–1323," and Stanley Chojnacki, "Identity and Ideology in Renaissance Venice: The Third *Serrata*," both in Martin and Romano, *Venice Reconsidered*, 67–88 and 295–338, respectively.

    7. For the structure of the Venetian government, see Robert Finlay, *Politics in Renaissance Venice* (New Brunswick, N.J.: Rutgers University Press, 1980).

    8. For Venetian demographics, see Daniele Beltrami, *Storia del popolazione di Venezia dalla fine del secolo XVI alla caduta della Repubblica* (Padua: CEDAM, 1954), 72.

    9. BCV, cod. Gradenigo 83, "Corona seconda della veneta republica."

    10. Patricia Fortini Brown, *Venetian Narrative Painting in the Age of Carpaccio* (New Haven and London: Yale University Press, 1988), 13–16 and 23–26; and James S. Grubb, "Elite Citizens," in Martin and Romano, *Venice Reconsidered*, 339–364.

    11. See Dennis Romano, *Patricians and Popolani: The Social Foundations of the Venetian Renaissance State* (Baltimore: The Johns Hopkins University Press, 1987); idem, *Housecraft and Statecraft: Domestic Service in Renaissance Venice, 1400–1600*

(Baltimore: The Johns Hopkins University Press, 1996); and Ugo Tucci, "Carriere popolane e dinastie di mestiere a Venezia," in *Gerarchie economiche e gerarchie sociali: Secoli XII–XVIII*, ed. Annalisa Guarducci (Florence: Le Monnier, 1990), 817–851.

12. For patrician ideology in the fifteenth century, see Margaret King, *Venetian Humanism in an Age of Patrician Dominance* (Princeton, N.J.: Princeton University Press, 1986); for the sixteenth century, see Manfredo Tafuri, *Venice and the Renaissance* (Cambridge, Mass.: MIT Press, 1989).

13. Sansovino, *Venetia città nobilissima*, I:387–388. See Deborah Howard, *Jacopo Sansovino: Architecture and Patronage in Renaissance Venice* (New Haven and London: Yale University Press, 1975), 126–146; and Giandomenico Romanelli, *Ca' Corner della Ca' Granda: architettura e committenza nella Venezia del Cinquecento* (Venice: Albrizzi, 1993).

14. For the term *casa da statio* (also spelled *casa da stazio*), see Wladimiro Dorigo, "Toponomastica urbana nella formazione della città medioevale," *Rassegna* 5, no. 22 (1985): 50–51; Elisabeth Crouzet-Pavan, '*Sopra le acque salse': Espaces, pouvoir et société à Venise à la fin du moyen âge* (Rome: Ecole Française de Rome, 1992), I:509–514; and, in particular, Juergen Schulz, "The Houses of Titian, Aretino, and Sansovino," in *Titian: His World and His Legacy*, ed. David Rosand (New York: Columbia University Press, 1982), 83–84.

15. See Paolo Maretto, *La casa veneziana nella storia della città dalle origini all'Ottocento* (Venice: Marsilio Editori, 1986), 115–120.

16. Alberto Rizzi, *Scultura Esterna a Venezia: Corpus delle Sculture Erratiche all'aperto di Venezia e della sua Laguna* (Venice: Stamperia di Venezia, 1987), 321: Cat. nr. CN 431, Cannaregio, no. 5999 (S. Canzian). Cf. ibid., 470–471, cat. nr. DD 129, for a late *Gothic homo silvanus* on the facade of Casa Brass, Campo S. Trovaso 1083. See also Giulio Lorenzetti, *Venice and Its Lagoon*, trans. John Guthrie (Trieste: Edizioni Lint, 1975), 338 and 651; and Giuseppe Tassini, *Curiosità veneziane* (Venice: Fuga, 1915; reprint, Venice: Filippi, 1988), 390. The lunette-shaped plaque above the relief with three male heads is badly defaced, but the details that remain suggest the symbol of San Marco as *leone in moleca*.

17. Emmanuele Cicogna, *Delle iscrizioni veneziane*, 6 vols. (Venice: Picotti, 1824–53), III:318: DVM. VOLVITVR. ISTE IAD. ASCR. IVSTINOP. VER. / SALAMIS. CRETA. IOVIS. / TESTES. ERVNT. ACTOR. / PA. IO. SE. Mᵛ. See also Patricia Fortini Brown, *Venice and Antiquity: The Venetian Sense of the Past* (New Haven and London: Yale University Press, 1996), 285–286.

18. For the fountain, see BMV, cod. It. VII 14 (= 7418): Bernardo Bembo, *Cronica di tutte le case dell'inclitta Città di Venetia*, 68v; BCV, cod. Cicogna 3558/III: *Descritione dell'Isola di Candia*, f. 9v–10; and Giuseppe Gerola, *Monumenti Veneti dell'isola di Creta* (Venice: Istituto Veneto delle Scienze, Lettere ed Arti, 1932).

19. Brown, *Venice and Antiquity*, 285–286.

20. Pietro Bembo, *Nuove lettere famigliari . . . scritte a m. Gio. Mattheo Bembo suo nipote . . . ; nelle quali si commende particolarmente tutta la vita dell'autore, & qual fosse il suo stile nelle cose volgari in tutti i tempi* (Venice: Francesco Rampazetto, 1564). For Zuan Matteo's career, see Cicogna, *Iscrizioni veneziane*, III:318–337; and "Giovanni Matteo Bembo," q. v., *Dizionario biografico degli italiani* (Rome: Istituto della Enciclopedia Italiana, 1966), 8:124–125.

21. Marin Sanudo, *I Diarii*, ed. Rinaldo Fulin et al. (Venice, 1879–1902), 53:65 (22 March 1530): "Da poi leto le lettere, fo leto una suplication di sier Zuan Mathio Bembo qu. sier Alvise, qual vol far stampar do opere latine di suo barba reverendo missier Pietro Bembo, videlicet, de Virgilii culice et Terentii fabulis, et l'altra di Guido Ubaldo et Elisabetta Gonzaga Urbini ducibus, et un'altra volta far ristampar la Ethna monte, del ditto, et li Asolani, da lui reconzi et mutati in qualche parte, et che niun per anni 20 li possi far stampar, se non lui, sub poena etc. Et fo posto, per li Consieri et Cai di XL, di conciederli quanto el dimanda. Fu presa. Ave: 189, 6, 2."

22. Sansovino, *Venetia città nobilissima*, I:336. The paintings depicted the Story of Alexander III, a legendary event in Venetian history. See Brown, *Venetian Narrative Painting*, 272–279.

23. Pompeo Molmenti, *La storia di Venezia nella vita privata dalle origini alla caduta della repubblica* (Bergamo, 1927–29; reprint, Trieste: Edizioni Lint, 1973), II:372.

24. ASV, Notarile, Testamenti, B. 1259, n. 507 [Cesare Ziliol] (22 March 1570): "Tutti li mei beni stabeli, case, et terre, dalla villa et quelli, serrano aquistati col tratto di quelli pochi arzenti, et mobeli, con denari mei, voglio stiano sotto perpetuo fideicommisso in quattro mei figlioli mascoli, Lorenzo, Alvise, Marc'Antonio et Davit, et in loro descendenti mascoli legitimi . . ." Cf. ASV, Procuratoria di San Marco de Citra, B. 48: *Commissaria di Zuan Matteo Bembo fu Alvise of Santa Maria Nova.*

25. ASV, Notarile, Testamenti, B. 1259, n. 507: "in uso, et agiuto di quelli poveri."

26. Ibid., "Item dechiaro che Augusta fu' satisfatta del legato delli ducati cento che li fu lassato, et ha havuto anche ducati vinticinque de piui da sua madre."

27. ASV, Notarile, Testamenti, B. 1210, n. 716 (Antonio Marsilio): "Volgio anche sia dato cento ducati delli miei beni a mia fiola Augusta per segnio de de amor per una volta sola, et piu non le lasso: che per la gratia a di Dio l'è richa: e sta molto bene."

28. Ibid.: "se mia filgiola Julia non sarà maridata o monacha avanti la mia morte, volgio che l'abbia ducati cinquecento de tutti li mei beni, si della mia dota come de mia sorella madonna Julia e de qualunque altri beni mi potessi pervegnir, con questa condizion che la se marida in zentilhomo nostro venetian: overo in honorevole forestier de consentimento del Magnifico mio consorte e sui fratelli, e se la fusse maridà avanti la mia morte non volgio la habia per niente cossa alcuna, e se la andara monaca non volgio la habia dicti ducatj cinquecento, che mi par la possa andar in bonissimo monestier con li quatrocento ducatj che lassa suo Padre."

29. Ibid.: "Dechiarando sopratutto che se mei filgioli averà bastardi o bastardo non possa mai lassarle in tempo alcuno niente del mio." Cf. Chojnacki, "Identity and Ideology," 268–280.

30. ASV, Notarile, Testamenti, B. 1259, n. 507: "Lasso che Ettor, mio fiol natural, sia governato, amaestrato, vestito, et calzato, et pagato li maestri che li insegnaranno . . ."

31. Laura Megna, "Comportamenti abitativi del patriziato veneziano (1582–1740)," *Studi Veneziani*, n.s. 22 (1991): 285 and 294–296 (253–323), who

incorrectly assumed that Piero was one of the original heirs and made no mention of Alvise.

32. BCV, cod. P.D. C.2706; cf. Megna, "Comportamenti abitativi," 294–295.

33. ASV, Notarile, Testamenti, B. 1259, n. 507. For the layout, see Paolo Maretto, *L'edilizia gotica veneziana*, 2d ed. (Venice: Filippi Editore, 1978), 74–77. Cf. Ca' Bollani, rented out to Pietro Aretino, which has a plan similar to that of Bembo's before the chamber was added on the west side (Schulz, "Houses of Titian, Aretino, and Sansovino," 83–86).

34. BCV, cod. P.D. C.2706/1, f. 9: In his decima declaration of 25 June 1566, Zuan Matteo declared that he was living in the *casa da statio* at Santa Maria Nova, presumably in the *soler di sopra*, for he was renting the *soler di sotto* for 55 ducats annually until his son Lorenzo returned from Famagosta where he was presently living.

35. BCV, cod. P.D. C.2706/2 lists a total of annual rents of 109 ducats for these properties. See also Megna, "Comportamenti abitativi," 294–295, citing BCV, cod. P.D. C.2706/2 and cod. P.D. C.2706/3.

36. BCV, cod. P.D. C.2706/2, ff. 32–40; ibid., cod. P.D. C.2706/3; and ASV, Notarile, Atti, Marc'Antonio Cavanis, 1573:II, R. 3290, ff. 344–345, 376, 451, 455. Not only did Marc'Antonio engage in additional lawsuits against his brothers and nephews, but in 1605, a cousin, Dardi Bembo fu David, successfully contested the will of their great-grandfather Alvise fu Zaccaria by which Zuan Matteo fu Alvise Bembo had claimed the house in the first place. Dardi was given the *soler di sotto* while the heirs of Lorenzo fu Zuan Matteo were moved upstairs to the soler di sopra, once owned by Piero di Zuan Matteo, bishop of Veglia. The legal squabbling continued until 1686 when Girolamo and Francesco Bembo attempted, unsuccessfully, as it happens, to claim one fourth of the house from Pellegrina, the last surviving heir of Lorenzo Bembo.

37. ASV, Dieci Savi sopra le Decime, B. 164/971.

38. Ibid., B. 164/984.

39. Ibid., B. 164/1098.

40. Ibid, B. 170/794. Cf. Megna, "Comportamenti abitativi," 283.

41. Megna, "Comportamenti abitativi," 278–281.

42. Ibid., 285.

43. Ibid., 287.

44. For marriage strategies in this period, see Stanley Chojnacki, "Subaltern Patriarchs: Patrician Bachelors in Renaissance Venice," in his *Women and Men in Renaissance Venice* (Baltimore and London: The Johns Hopkins University Press, 2000), 244–256; and idem, "Identity and Ideology," 269–270.

45. Megna, "Comportamenti abitativi," 290–291, citing ASV, Notarile, Testamenti, b. 1193, prot. II, cc. 90v ff.

46. Howard, *Jacopo Sansovino*, 8–9; and Finlay, *Politics in Renaissance Venice*, 248–250.

47. Ennio Concina, *A History of Venetian Architecture*, trans. Judith Landry (Cambridge: Cambridge University Press, 1998), 220–226. On the earlier building, see Juergen Schulz, "La piazza medievale di San Marco," *Annali di architettura* 4–5 (1992–93): 139–140, who notes that procurators had lived there at least since

1319 when the Maggior Consiglio provided two additional houses near the Church of San Geminiano. See also Vincenzo Scamozzi, *Dell'idea della architettura universale* (Venice, 1615), 243, for an enthusiastic description of the apartments.

48. Megna, "Comportamenti abitativi," 271.

49. For the *decima*, see Luciano Pezzolo, *L'oro dello stato: società, finanza e fisco nella Repubblica Veneta del secondo '500* (Venice: Il Cardo, 1990), 43–45. The term *decima* comes from the 10 percent tax that was levied annually on the rental value of property, including the primary residence. Beginning in 1582, the family residence was appraised at one half its rental value, giving a tax break to those who lived in their own homes; it was later lowered to one third (see Megna, "Comportamenti abitativi," 286).

50. ASV, Dieci Savi sopra le Decime (Redecima 1537), B. 97, no. 476, f. 1.

51. ASV, Dieci Savi sopra le Decime, B. 110 [Aggiunte—1540], no. 2116: "ne sono molto ruina, tali che hanno bisogno de molti concierj. . . . E poi non si puol scuoder tutti li fittj per esser in quelle de molta povera gente."

52. Megna, "Comportamenti abitativi," 294–295.

53. Ibid., 267–270. For a magisterial study of such an enclave, see Juergen Schulz, "The Houses of the Dandolo: A Family Compound in Medieval Venice," *Journal of the Society of Architectural Historians* 52 (1993): 391–415.

54. ASV, Notarile, Testamenti, b. 125, n. 507.

55. Giorgio Gianighian and Paola Pavanini, *Dietro I palazzi: Tre secoli di architettura minore a Venezia 1492–1803* (Venice: Arsenale Editrice, 1984), 72–73.

56. Ibid.; Alberto Rizzi, *La scultura esterna a Venezia: corpus delle sculture erratiche all'aperto di Venezia e della sua laguna* (Venice, 1987), 297–298, no. 324; and Giannino Piamonte, *Venezia vista dall'acqua: Guida dei rii di Venezia e delle Isole*, 3d ed. (Venice: Stamperia di Venezia, 1992), 91 and 102.

57. See Wladimiro Dorigo, "*Exigentes, sigentes, sezentes, sergentes:* le case d'affito a Venezia nel Medioevo," *Venezia Arti* 10 (1996): 25–36; and Giorgio Bellavitis, "Il linguaggio gotico diffuso nell'edilizia minore veneziana; *domos a statio, hospicii,* e *domos a sergentibus* nella Venezia medioevale," in *L'architettura gotica veneziana*, ed. Francesco Valcanover and Wolfgang Wolters (Venice: Istituto Veneto di Scienze, Lettere ed Arti, 2000), 175–188.

58. This discussion is based upon Gianighian and Pavanini, *Dietro I palazzi*, 68–69. See also Egli Renata Trincanato, *Venezia minore* (Milan: Edizioni del Milione, 1948), 156–158.

59. See, in particular, Brian Pullan, *Rich and Poor in Renaissance Venice. The Social Institutions of a Catholic State, to 1620* (Cambridge, Mass.: Harvard University Press, 1971), 132–137; Franca Semi, *Gli "Ospizi" di Venezia* (Venice: Edizioni Helvetia, 1983); and Brian Pullan, "Abitazioni al servizio dei poveri nella repubblica di Venezia," in Gianighian and Pavanini, *Dietro I palazzi*, 39–44.

60. Dennis Romano, "L'assistenza e la beneficenza," in *Storia di Venezia* V (Rome: Istituto della Enciclopedia Italiana, 1996), 355–406.

61. Gianighian and Pavanini, *Dietro I palazzi*, 110–113. See also Trincanato, *Venezia minore*, 306–309.

62. Gianighian and Pavanini, *Dietro I palazzi*, 113.

63. Ibid., 111–113.

64. Ibid.

65. See, for example, Giacomo Lanteri, *Della economica; nel quale si dimostrano le qualità, che all'huomo & alla donna separatamente convengono pel governo della casa* (Venice: Appresso Vincenzo Valgrisi, 1560), 14; and Sebastiano Serlio, *Sebastiano Serlio on Domestic Architecture; Different Dwellings from the Meanest Hovel to the Most Ornate Palace. The Sixteenth-Century Manuscript of Book VI in the Avery Library of Columbia University*, ed. Myra Nan Rosenfeld (New York: Architectural History Foundation, 1978), 56–57. See also Brown, "Behind the Walls," 317–319.

66. Pullan, "Abitazioni al servizio dei poveri," 39–44.

67. Paola Pavanini, "Abitazioni popolari e borghesi nella Venezia cinquecentesca," *Studi Veneziani*, n.s. 5 (1981): 109–111 (63–126): "veri, serradure, chiave, cadenazzi, balconi, scale, sovaze, et ogn'altra cosa."

68. Pullan, "Abitazioni al servizio dei poveri," 41–42, citing Archivio di Scuola di San Rocco, Registro delle Terminazioni 3, ff. 71–75: "con sei creaturine picciole, scalce, et si può dire nude, et lui similmente insieme con sua moglie mal vestito, et pieno in apparenza di miseria et povertà per maggiormente concitar gli animi vostri a favorirlo, et moverli a compassione, affermando tutti sei quei figliolini esser suoi, se bene dui soli d'essi erano suoi figlioli, et gl'altri menati secco per l'intentione sopradetta."

69. See Romano, "L'assistenza e la beneficenza," 355–406; Bernard Aikema and Dulcia Meijers, *Nel regno dei poveri. Arte e storia dei grandi ospedali veneziani in età moderna, 1474–1797* (Venice: IRE, 1989); and Semi, *Gli "Ospizi" di Venezia;* and *Venice. A Documentary History, 1450–1630*, ed. David Chambers and Brian Pullan, with Jennifer Fletcher (Oxford: Blackwell, 1992), 295–322.

70. Romano, "L'assistenza e la beneficenza," 370. It is located on Campo dei Gesuiti 4905, near Santi Apostoli. See Silvia Lunardon, *Hospitale S. Mariae Cruciferorum: L'ospizio dei Crociferi a Venezia* (Venice, 1984); and Semi, *Gli "Ospizi" di Venezia*, 184–186. The present layout is similar to that of the late sixteenth century, although two bedrooms have been added.

71. Aikema and Meijers, *Nel regno dei poveri;* and Semi, *Gli "Ospizi" di Venezia,* 184–186.

72. Semi, *Gli "Ospizi" di Venezia,* 184–186. Jacopo Sansovino followed this time-honored typology for his Ca' di Dio in the mid-sixteenth century (Howard, *Jacopo Sansovino*, 112–119).

73. Romano, "L'assistenza e le beneficenza," 370–378.

74. Semi, *Gli "Ospizi" di Venezia*, 278–280, citing from Priuli's testament (3 May 1569), published in *Antichi testamenti, tratti dagli archivi della Congregazione di Carità*, ser. XI, 1883: "avvertendo di metter persone di buona vita, et senza fioi ne mugier, mache siano venetiani, over suditi, perchè in modo alcun non vogioche sieno dati (camera e ducati) a persone di paese alieno, abenchè fussero stati anni trenta et più in Venetia."

75. Ibid: "malavasia, buzolai, minestra de risi, per piatanza pesce per esser ne l'avento . . ."

76. Semi, *Gli "Ospizi" di Venezia*, 263–264, who names Pope Gregorio IV instead of Eugenius IV in error. See Tassini, *Curiosità veneziane*, 302–303.

77. Sanudo, *I Diarii*, 40:696–697; Semi, *Gli "Ospizi" di Venezia*, 263–264.

78. Fynes Moryson, *An Itinerary* (Glasgow: James McLehose and Sons, 1907), 183.

79. Cited by Romano, "L'assistenza e la beneficenza," 358.

80. Ibid., 355–406; and Pullan, "Abitazioni al servizio dei poveri," 39–44.

81. Romano, "L'assistenza e la beneficenza," 363; Pullan, *Rich and Poor in Renaissance Venice*, 372–374.

82. Romano, "L'assistenza e la beneficenza," 363: "è certo umano, et pietoso officio l'haver à poveri commiseratione, et massimamente à coloro, che nati di honesti parenti, e de' beni di fortuna per qualche tempo ben dotati, siano poi per varii et diversi accidente di quella, à povero stato ridotti, delli quali in questa città ne habbiano gran numero, et sono chiamati li poveri vergognosi."

83. Chambers and Pullan, *Venice: A Documentary History*, 319–320, citing Archivio della Scuola Grande di San Rocco, Registro delle Terminazioni 3, f. 230v (2 June 1593).

84. See Blake de Maria, "The Merchants of Venice: A Study in Sixteenth-Century *Cittadino* Patronage," doctoral dissertation, Princeton University, 2002, 56–182.

85. Sanudo, *I Diarii*, 47:81–84 (13 March 1528): "dove siano posti tutti ditti poveri che vanno per questa terra, et li siano fatte le stantie de tavola cum assai paglia et altro per dormir, nè de lì se possino partir sotto pena a chi sarà trovato fuora de ditti loci et andar per la terra mendicando et cridando la notte, da esser subito retenuto et messo in preson, et il giorno seguente fatto frustar et condutto fuora de la terra, et se'l ritornerà la seconda volta, sia iterum frustato et conduto fuora, et hoc toties quoties. . . ." Cf. Semi, *Gli "Ospizi" di Venezia*, 32–33; and Chambers and Pullan, *Venice: A Documentary History*, 303–306. The hospitals built in that period became permanent institutions. See Aikema and Meijers, *Nel regno dei poveri*.

86. Semi, *Gli "Ospizi" di Venezia*, 33; Brian Pullan, "La nuova filantropia nella Venezia Cinquecentesca," in Aikema and Meijers, *Nel regno dei poveri*, 19–34.

87. Chambers and Pullan, *Venice: A Documentary History*, 114–115, 302–303; Semi, *Gli "Ospizi" di Venezia*, 33–45. Built on the island of Santa Maria di Nazareth, the Lazzaretto Vecchio was renamed the Mendicanti and moved to the Zattere at the beginning of the seventeenth century when a new building was constructed to house orphans and beggars. For the Pietà and the Mendicanti, see Aikema and Meijers, *Nel regno dei poveri*, 197–214 and 249–271, respectively.

88. Chambers and Pullan, *Venice: A Documentary History*, 303, 307–308; Dulcia Meijers, "L'architettura della nuova filantropia," in Aikema and Meijers, *Nel regno dei poveri*, 43–69.

89. Chambers and Pullan, *Venice: A Documentary History*, 308–315; Aikema and Meijers, *Nel regno dei poveri*, 131–195.

90. Patricia Fortini Brown, *Art and Life in Renaissance Venice* (New York: Prentice Hall and Abrams, 1997), 107–109. Cf. Thomas Riis, "I poveri nell'arte italiana (secoli XV–XVII)," in *Timore e carità: i poveri nell'Italia moderna*, ed. Giorgio Politi, Mario Rosa, and Franco Della Peruta (Cremona: Annali della Biblioteca Statale e Libreria Civica di Cremona, 1982), 45–58.

91. Chambers and Pullan, *Venice: A Documentary History*, 303–306, citing ASV, Senato, Terra, Reg. for 1529, ff. 125v–127r, 3 April 1529.

92. Isabella Palumbo–Fossati, "L'interno della casa dell'artigiano e dell'artista nella Venezia del Cinquecento," *Studi Veneziani* 8, n.s. (1984): 109–153.

93. Patricia Anne Allerston, *The Market in Second-Hand Clothes and Furnishings in Venice, c. 1500–c. 1650*, doctoral dissertation (Florence: European University Institute, Department of History and Civilization, 1996), 69–71.

94. Ibid., 74, citing ASV, SNC, b. 216, Inventari d'asporti, Reg. 1, 21 April 1583.

95. Cited by Riccardo Calimani, *The Ghetto of Venice*, trans. Katherine Silberblatt Wolfthal (New York: M. Evans, 1987), 1; For the word "ghetto," see Benjamin C. I. Ravid, "From Geographical Realia to Historiographical Symbol: The Odyssey of the Word *Ghetto*," in *Essential Papers on Jewish Culture in Renaissance and Baroque Italy*, ed. David B. Ruderman (New York: New York University Press, 1992), 373–384. See also Gaetano Cozzi, ed., *Gli Ebrei e Venezia, Secoli XIV–XVIII* (Milan: Comunita, 1987).

96. See, in general, Cozzi, ed., *Gli Ebrei e Venezia*; E. Concina, U. Camerino, and D. Calabi, *La città degli ebrei. Il Ghetto di Venezia: architettura e urbanistica* (Venice: Marsilio, 1991); Donatella Calabi, "The 'City of the Jews'," in *The Jews of Early Modern Venice*, ed. Robert C. Davis and Benjamin Ravid (Baltimore and London: The Johns Hopkins University Press, 2001), 31–52; Richard Goy, *Venice. The City and Its Architecture* (London: Phaidon, 1997), 86–93; and Gianighian and Pavanini, *Dietro I palazzi*, 186–191.

97. Benjamin C. I. Ravid, "Curfew Time in the Ghetto of Venice," in *Medieval and Renaissance Venice*, ed. Ellen E. Kittel and Thomas F. Madden (Urbana and Chicago: University of Illinois Press, 1999), 237–275; Calimani, *The Ghetto of Venice*, 1–20.

98. Ibid.

99. Ravid, "Curfew Time in the Ghetto of Venice," 237–275.

100. Allerston, *The Market in Second-Hand Clothes and Furnishings*, 120–155, 197–206 and passim.

101. Calimani, *The Ghetto of Venice*, 1–20.

102. Benjamin Ravid, "Christian Travelers in the Ghetto of Venice: Some Preliminary Observations," in *Between History and Literature: Studies in Honor of Isaac Barzilay*, ed. Stanley Nash (Bnei-Brak, 1997), 115–116.

103. Sansovino, *Venetia città nobilissima*, I:368. For life in the Ghetto, see the rich collection of essays in Davis and Ravid, *The Jews of Early Modern Venice*.

104. James S. Ackerman and Myra Nan Rosenfeld, "Social Stratification in Renaissance Urban Planning," in *Urban Life in the Renaissance*, ed. Susan Zimmerman and Ronald F. E. Weissman (Newark: University of Delaware Press; London and Toronto: Associated University Presses, 1989), 21–49.

mary elizabeth perry

Space of Resistance, Site of Betrayal

Morisco Homes in Sixteenth-Century Spain

Behind the windowless whitewashed walls of their homes, domestic life was changing for Moriscos, those Hispano-Muslims and their descendants who had to convert to Christianity in sixteenth-century Spain. After 1492, when the last Muslim stronghold of Granada surrendered to Ferdinand and Isabel, Moriscos adapted their homes to growing tensions with Christian authorities. Soon required to convert to Christianity, Moriscos survived two rebellions and a forced relocation. Yet they finally had to leave their Iberian homes between 1609 and 1614, when Philip III ordered the massive expulsion of some 300,000 Moriscos from the Spanish kingdoms.

Hispano-Muslim homes developed within their own distinct historical context, but they shared significant characteristics with homes of other pre-modern peoples. In the first place, these homes were ideas as well as physical places. They provided a sense of identity not only in where one truly belonged, but also in the distinctive architecture and structural styles that developed among geographic regions, ethnic groups, and social classes. Moreover, the seeming permanence of buildings and foundations of homes outlasted generations of families and entire dynasties of rulers. In some cases, conquerors took over the homes of the conquered. These physical

57

remains evoked strong memories of one's rightful place, valued possessions of the past, and what had been lost.

Loss of homes, in fact, must be considered in any discussion of homes,
for home and homelessness are two sides of the same coin. The medieval
Arabic writer Ibn 'Abdun had cautioned his readers in the early twelfth
century to protect and watch homes.[1] The loss of them could mean the
loss of political order and economic well-being, the loss of a secure place
for faith and for civilization itself. Even more important, the memory of
losing one's home generated a powerful mythos of diaspora. More than
simply the loss of home, diaspora implied impotence, shame, and exile, a
movement to another place where it could be difficult to make new homes.

In the memory of both home and homelessness a significant source of
power developed that many people in the pre-modern world came to know
and use. This memory explained and preserved a people's sense of identity as a specific group distinct from all others. It motivated the movement
of peoples from one place to another. It justified revenge and conquest.
Filled with pathos and absurdity, hatred and devotion, this memory developed a politics of home even more basic than the politics of dynasties and
institutions in the making of the pre-modern world. While homes developed within a local political context, they also promoted the construction
and expression of power relations that extended far beyond themselves.

Like the stories of so many other people in the past, the story of
Hispano-Muslims holds remarkable relevance for our world in the twenty-
first century. Their homes tell a tale of power, for it is here that power
struggles took place as one people imposed control over another, taking
over the homes of the conquered and ordering them into exile or to live
in ghettos known as *morerías*. More than mere victims, however, the conquered people also developed power as they learned to resist and to survive, even when forced to leave their homes and look for new ones. Revealing the politics of home and homelessness, the Moriscos' story tells of the
power that oppressed people developed as well as that of those who would
not tolerate their difference. It offers lessons of urgent importance in our
own time when millions of people have been uprooted from their homes,
tens of thousands still live as refugees, and every major city of the world
faces the challenge of a growing population of people without homes.

The story of Morisco homes begins with traditions and evidence of the
Hispano-Muslim home in medieval Al-Andalus. Then, as Christians issued
decrees in 1502 and 1525 that Muslims must convert to Christianity or
leave the Spanish kingdoms, Islam retreated into the domestic space of
these homes. Here Moriscos attempted to preserve some of their Islamic

culture in resistance to increasing Christian demands of assimilation. At
the same time, Christian authorities and neighbors invaded their homes,
looking for evidence that would betray these people to the Inquisition.
Some 50,000 Moriscos from the Kingdom of Granada had to leave their
homes to be forcibly relocated when Christian forces defeated a major
Morisco rebellion in 1570. Less than four decades later, hundreds of thousands of Moriscos became homeless as they were expelled from the Spanish kingdoms between 1609 and 1614. Home for them became a symbol
of both loss and hope as they went into exile. All of these changes in the
Morisco home in early modern Spain reveal the critical role of home and
homelessness in constructing power relations so essential to our understanding the past and surviving the present.

Hispano-Muslim Homes

In his treatise on municipal government, Ibn 'Abdun recognized the
political significance of homes in medieval Al-Andalus. "Homes are shelters in which souls, spirits, and bodies take refuge," he pointed out. They
should be "protected and watched," he continued, "since goods are deposited in them and lives are guarded."[2] A refuge but also a depository, the
Muslim home provided the essential bedrock for the orderly Islamic community. Whether the mud-walled, earthen-floored hovel of poor day laborers, or the tiled and carved palaces of the wealthy (fig.1), the home derived
its strength from a fusion of spiritual, physical, and material concerns.

Within a century of the time when Ibn 'Abdun wrote his treatise about
the importance of domestic space, many Muslims had to leave their homes
as Christian forces made serious inroads into Muslim-held lands. In 1248
the Muslim ruler of Seville capitulated to the Christian army of Fernando III. About 100,000 Muslims fled their homes, seeking refuge in
nearby North Africa or in the Kingdom of Granada where Muslims would
hold out against the Christians until 1492.[3] Home for these exiles became
all the more precious, a place for preserving the family, the culture, the
true religion, and one's identity.

In Iberia, Hispano-Muslim architecture expressed the ideal of the home
as a refuge and place to preserve identity. For centuries the people of Al-
Andalus had built their houses with few windows, presenting blank whitewashed walls to the street that veiled their domestic activities from public
view. As a veil, the windowless walls concealed from public view interior
courtyards, such as that in figure 2. They hid concealed doors leading to

FIGURE 1.
The Alcázar,
Seville

FIGURE 1.
The Alcázar,
Seville

adjoining houses, and small nooks and crannies where the religious and cultural objects that were later prohibited in the sixteenth century could be hidden from view.[4] Although conjugal families usually occupied the houses, hidden doors frequently connected the houses belonging to members of a kinship group. Elders in these groups could thus maintain control over most of their kinship members, even under a change in rulers. More than merely an ideal, the architecture of these homes served as a material means to preserve the cohesion of Muslim society at its most basic level.[5]

The location of homes directly affected a sense of community that could connect them. Although Christians, Jews, and Muslims often lived side by side in the medieval towns of Iberia, they might also live in neighborhoods inhabited mostly by members of their own religions. As Christians took over areas once ruled by Muslims, they developed a pattern of requiring Jews to live in quarters called "juderías" and Muslims to live in "morerías." The Cortes of Toledo in 1480, for example, agreed to the complete separation of Muslims and Christians, and three years later Ferdinand directed

FIGURE 2.
Concealed Courtyard,
Seville

officials of the city of Seville to meet with two members of his council to determine where Muslims should be separated in that city.[6] More than simply oppression by Christian victors, religious segregation was also supported by some Muslim religious leaders. At the end of the fifteenth century the mufti al-Wansharishi warned of the dangers of living with Christians:

> One has to be aware of the pervasive effect of their [Christian] way of life, their language, their dress, their objectionable habits, and influence

on people living with them over a long period of time, as has occurred in the case of the inhabitants of Avila and other places, for they have lost their Arabic, and when the Arabic language died out, so does devotion in it, and there is consequential neglect of worship as expressed in words in all its richness and outstanding virtues.[7]

Despite official pronouncements on segregating the living quarters of religious groups, however, some Muslim families continued to live in homes in neighborhoods where Christians also lived.[8]

Yet many Muslims did make their homes in Muslim neighborhoods, where they could have their own mosques and live independently of Christians. These Muslims educated their children both at home and in the mosque or at a school attached to the mosque. Usually they taught their children "the ancient sciences" at home, and they sent their children to the mosque to learn the Qur'an and "Arab sciences." Both boys and girls could learn their "first letters" at home, but boys were much more likely to be sent to school at the mosque to learn the Arabic language.[9] This partnership between mosque and home declined as Christians took over more of the Iberian peninsula and replaced mosques with churches. Muslim parents had to take on more responsibility for educating their children in their own homes.

Muslim homes in morerías played other roles that developed their significance for the community. Often situated on slopes and narrow winding streets, the location of these houses strengthened a sense of community even as it discouraged visits from outsiders.[10] Rituals to celebrate births and marriage and mourn the dead could spill over in these neighborhoods from individual houses into the shared space of streets, plazas, and other houses. A Muslim marriage, for example, usually began with the signing of a betrothal contract in the home of the bride or groom. On the day of the wedding, women gathered at the home of the bride to bathe her, dye with henna her face, hair, hands, and feet before dressing her. Then they formed a procession to take the bride to her new home, dancing and singing through the streets.[11] Muslim homes provided the basic space for these celebrations, and they also became linked together with collective observations of life passages.

The basic issues of water and sewage further linked Muslim homes into a community. Soon after Muslims settled in Iberia, they constructed waterways that serviced their communities, probably because both their secular traditions and religious rituals placed a strong emphasis on personal cleanliness. Neighborhood fountains became a gathering place for people who came not only to fill storage vessels with water for their homes, but also to wash themselves according to the ablution ritual that Muslims tried to follow for each of the five times that they were to pray during the day.[12] Their waterways brought water to the community baths that Muslims constructed, where certain days were reserved for men and others for women. In Seville, a few private homes had their own outlets from the pipes that brought water to the city from springs at a nearby village. During the twelfth century, Muslims constructed a reservoir for Seville that stored water taken by water wheels from the Guadalquivir River. They also used underground pipes to drain streets and carry sewage away from the streets where many householders deposited their waste.[13]

In 1492, however, the fall of Granada signaled a major change for Hispano-Muslim homes and communites throughout Iberia. As this last Muslim stronghold fell to Christian forces, Ferdinand and Isabel promised their new Muslim subjects that they would be free to keep their own religion. The conditions of capitulation that they signed with the defeated Muslim king agreed that the Muslim ruler, his officers, and subjects "great or small" would be permitted "to live in their own religion," in their own system of justice and continue "the uses and customs which they observe."[14] Although some Muslims left Granada to make new homes in North Africa, many remained and expected to continue living in their homes and communities as they had for generations.

Within a decade, however, promises of peaceful coexistence collapsed. Isabel and Cardinal Archbishop Francisco Jiménez Cisneros insisted that Christians must try to convert Muslims in Granada, exasperating many with their heavy-handed attempts. Cisneros, in particular, angered the Muslims of Granada as he insisted that those Muslims of Christian descent must return to the Church.[15] When they refused, Christian authorities imprisoned them, sparking long smoldering resentments that flamed into open rebellion on Christmas Eve in 1499. Quickly spreading from the Albaicín, a Muslim quarter of the city of Granada, to the Alpujarra Mountains, Ronda, and the port of Almería, the rebellion lasted for nearly two years.

After Christian forces had finally subdued the rebels, Ferdinand and Isabel decreed that all Muslims of Granada would have to convert to Christianity or leave Castile. In the next two decades, the Crown extended this decree to Muslims in the other Spanish kingdoms. For many Muslims the decrees of compulsory conversion meant displacement. Those leaders of the rebellion in Granada who were able to elude punishment fled to the Alpujarras, a nearby mountainous region of deep ravines and tiny hamlets where few Christian authorities could intrude into Muslim lives. Other Muslims who refused baptism left Iberia where their families had lived for centuries and sought new homes in North Africa and the Eastern Mediterranean. Home for these people became less a geographical place than a refuge from punitive authorities and a space for expressing their cultural identities.

Islam's Retreat into Domestic Space

Muslims who chose to stay in their Iberian homes became Moriscos, accepting baptism either voluntarily or by force. In the early sixteenth century the Church and monarchy sought to catechize the new converts from Islam, granting them six years in which they would be expected to gradually abandon their Muslim customs and Arabic language. Christian clerics were even urged to use the Arabic language to instruct the New Christians, and Archbishop Martín de Ayala published a book of Christian doctrine in both Arabic and Castilian.[16] Royal decrees extended the protection from prosecution by the Inquisition for another twenty years, although authorities required that all Arabic books be handed in for inspection and those relating to Islam were burned in public bonfires.[17]

For the first time, many Morisco households now engaged in domestic subversion. In hollow pillars and false floors, ceilings, and walls in their homes they concealed writings in Arabic and Aljamía, a Castilian dialect written in Arabic characters. Inquisitors found some writings, and others disappeared in the ruins of these homes. But a significant number of these writings were found unexpectedly in Aragon some two and three centuries later, ranging from amulets and cabalistic notations through stories, sermons, liturgies, prophecies, and the Qur'an, itself.[18] Many of the hidden stories had belonged to an oral tradition that scholars believe were written down in Aljamía in the fifteenth century. Not all Moriscos had access to this Aljamiado literature, nor could many read it. We do not know how many actually took the risk of keeping and hiding these writings in their homes.

Although some scholars have dismissed Aljamiado writings as merely a reflection of resignation among a subject people who did not trust their strengths, I would argue that these writings so carefully hidden in their homes actually empowered Moriscos. This clandestine literature preserved Morisco stories of Old Testament heroes such as Moses and Joseph, who survived oppression and exile. It told of Rajma, the wife of Job, who carried him on her back when their villagers had banished him, building with her own hands a shelter for him and working to earn bread to feed them both.[19] "The Story of the Maiden Carcayona," another Morisco legend, tells of a handless maiden, who remained loyal to Islam despite unjust exile.[20] Aljamiado prophecies explained current suffering as just punishment for moral degradation and irreligiosity among Moriscos, but they promised that the just and merciful God would grant them ultimate political victory over their enemies.[21] Thus, Aljamiado writings played a political role in preserving legendary heroes and promoting the possibilities of keeping a forbidden culture in their own homes. Reinforcing a belief that common people could invoke supernatural powers to protect themselves, Aljamiado literature gathered together many popular beliefs and legends of a centuries-long oral tradition that helped to unify Moriscos in identifying themselves and resisting Christian domination.

As Christian authorities increasingly resolved to eliminate Muslim culture as well as Islam, Moriscos came under pressure to give up public expressions of their religion, their language, literature, music, dances, costumes, bathing, and rites of birth, death, preparation and consumption of food. Many viewed their conversions as an exercise of the Muslim tradition of *taqiyya*, or conforming externally to an oppressive regime while maintaining Islam internally. Moriscos withdrew into the privacy of their homes to carry out not only their religious rites, but also those cultural expressions of who they were as a people.[22] Even though they had to take new Christian names, Moriscos sometimes used their Muslim names privately. Ironically, the Christian belief that it was easier to control these people as family units also worked to preserve the strong Morisco traditions of family and kinship.

To many Spanish Christians and travelers from other parts of the world, Morisco homes appeared to be centers of difference. Travelers especially noted the exotic in costumes and culture that they saw in Morisco homes. In the early sixteenth century, Christoph Weiditz came from a German-speaking region to visit Granada and other parts of Spain. Particularly interested in costumes, he made many drawings and later published these in a travel book.[23] Figure 3 shows how he saw Moriscas working in their homes. In figure 4 Weiditz depicts the street dress of Moriscas, and figure 5 indicates in contrast how he saw the dress of Christian women. The drawings of Weiditz emphasized the different appearance of Moriscas, and it also depicted scenes in their everyday lives that centered around home and community.[24] Note that Weiditz's drawing of the Christian woman does not indicate that non-Muslim women also veiled themselves in this

FIGURE 3.
Morisca Sweeping Her
House, from Christoph
Weiditz, *Das Trachtenbuch
des Christoph Weiditz* (Berlin
and Leipzig: Von Walter
de Gruyter, 1927; original
1531–32). Reproduced by
permission of the Art and
Architecture Collection,
Miriam and Ira D. Wallach
Division of Art, Prints, and
Photographs, The New York
Public Library, Astor, Lenox,
and Tilden Foundations

period, although historical records imply that veiling was not limited to Muslim women. Repeatedly Christian officials prohibited all women from wearing veils.[25]

In fact, many Spanish Christians in the early modern period viewed Moriscos as non-European people whom they had conquered. Conveniently forgetting the centuries in which they had lived as neighbors and even intermarried, these Spanish Christians now adopted a policy of internal imperialism in which they could treat Moriscos as colonial subjects.[26] They subjected Moriscos to purity of blood statutes that had originated earlier as weapons against Judeo-conversos. In the sixteenth century Christians expanded these laws to prohibit people whose ancestors included either Muslims or Jews from holding certain offices and privileges.[27]

One Jesuit saw very clearly the parallel between the subject status of Moriscos and that of indigenous peoples of the New World, declaring, "This kingdom of Granada is a very great Indies."[28] Although these two regions contrasted remarkably, Granada and the Indies also shared important similarities. For example, the Christian conquest of Granada in the

FIGURE 4.
Street Dress for Moriscas,
from Christoph Weiditz,
*Das Trachtenbuch des Christoph
Weiditz* (Berlin and Leipzig:
Von Walter de Gruyter,
1927; original 1531–32).
Reproduced by permission
of the Art and Architecture
Collection, Miriam and
Ira D. Wallach Division of
Art, Prints, and Photographs,
The New York Public
Library, Astor, Lenox,
and Tilden Foundations

fifteenth century brought into the Spanish kingdom a large area of land to grant to victorious Christian warriors. It also subjected to Spanish rule thousands of new subjects who knew neither the language nor the religion of their conquerors. Conquests in both Granada and the New World opened up seemingly unlimited opportunities for converting new subject people to the God and customs of the victors.

However, Moriscos frustrated these opportunities as they continued to cling to their own beliefs and customs. Their homes became places of suspicion to Christians who did not believe that these new converts really wanted to assimilate. For a while, Moriscos agreed to pay special tributes to the Crown, which afforded them some protection from prosecution for speaking Arabic or engaging in their cultural traditions. Yet in buying time to adapt to Christian beliefs and practices, they increased suspicions that they were an obstinate people who would never assimilate.

The forcible baptism of thousands of additional Muslims during the Comunero Revolt of 1520–1521 multiplied suspicions that Moriscos were false converts. A junta of church leaders formalized these baptisms, deciding

FIGURE 5.
Dress of Christian Women
of Seville, from Christoph
Weiditz, *Das Trachtenbuch des
Christoph Weiditz* (Berlin and
Leipzig: Von Walter de
Gruyter, 1927; original
1531–32). Reproduced by
permission of the Art and
Architecture Collection,
Miriam and Ira D. Wallach
Division of Art, Prints, and
Photographs, The New York
Public Library, Astor, Lenox,
and Tilden Foundations

that these new converts must be considered Christians. The royal government now prohibited all Morisco "particularism," including songs, dances, bathing, and the slaughter of animals.[29] Any expression of Muslim culture became evidence of apostasy, or slipping back into Islam, although Moriscos were still able to buy some time from prosecution by the Inquisition. An edict of grace issued in Seville in July 1548 assured Moriscos that they would not be prosecuted for past errors nor have their goods confiscated nor taken from their heirs. Nevertheless, the edict prohibited more than one Morisco family from living together, required Moriscos to live among Old Christians and to marry their sons and daughters to Old Christians, that is, Christians with no Jewish or Muslim blood. It required Moriscos to follow burial practices of Old Christians, live faithfully as Catholics, and send their children to be instructed in the Catholic faith.[30]

As Christian authorities determined to eliminate external expressions of Morisco ethnicity, such as dress, language, ritual calendars, food, taboos, special medical and economic practices, Moriscos sought to preserve their own sense of identity.[31] They withdrew into what they hoped was safe space in their homes. Here the women maintained the fast of Ramadan in their households, healed the sick, and washed the bodies of the dead, all according to Muslim tradition. Because Muslim leaders had been exiled, these women assumed the role of teaching their children Muslim prayers in Arabic.[32] In countless everyday tasks, these women prepared food, consumed it with their families, laundered clothing and household linens, presenting it each Friday to replace soiled linen, and drew water at a fountain or well for washing the body. Such ordinary banalities became "everyday forms of resistance," in the words of anthropologist James Scott.[33] In sixteenth-century Spain, these private acts would become increasingly politicized, publicly announced in edicts of faith as grounds for denunciation of self or others to the Inquisition.[34] They provided the basis for thousands of cases in which the Inquisition prosecuted Moriscos for practicing Islam.

Although historical evidence does not prove that all Moriscos made a conscious choice to resist oppression, it does indicate that most Morisco resistance took place in the home. It suggests that some Moriscos consciously chose to resist, some unconsciously resisted, and all of them probably resisted only because of the situation imposed on them. Some of their acts must be regarded as passive resistance rather than active. And compounding all this are the interactive strategies that these people devised which combined active conscious resistance with active conscious accommodation. In my judgment, there is no question that Moriscos wanted above all to survive and to assure the survival of their families. Sometimes the imperatives of survival meant that they accommodated Christian regulations even though they might wish to resist them.[35]

Moriscas, like so many other women, became politicized as they responded to threats to their homes and families. When Christians intensified their attempts to obliterate Morisco culture, both the women and men of this community had to become more aware of the context of power in which they sought to survive and to preserve their culture. Traditional Muslim ideals for women might prescribe enclosure for them in households where men would make decisions and carry out all interactions with outsiders. In sixteenth-century Spain, however, this ideal became impossible.

Gender ideology must be considered here, for many people in early modern Spain believed that domestic space provided the only secure and "natural" place for women, regardless of their ethnicity. Fray Luis de León, who wrote *La perfecta casada* (The Perfect Wife), argued that just as the fish, which swims in peace and security in water, cannot live outside it, neither can the good woman live outside the peace and security of her home.[36]

Another writer urged parents to keep their daughters enclosed in the home where "as dragons" parents could guard their daughters' purity.[37] Biblical verses and traditional proverbs emphasized a "natural" order of the sexes that required enclosure for females, either in home, convent, or brothel. This order had to be protected in particular from women who left the security of their enclosure to wander about the dangerous spaces outside.[38]

During the sixteenth century, however, domesticity itself became dangerous, not merely to the established order, but also to those attempting to resist that order.[39] The Morisco family acted as the nucleus of a closed society that taught its young to oppose the world outside.[40] In the words of present-day cultural critic bell hooks, Morisco homes became a "site of resistance."[41] Suspecting domestic resistance, Christian authorities determined that they would penetrate Morisco homes to look for evidence of Muslim practices. They directed sheriffs to enter Morisco homes unexpectedly at meal time when they could find evidence of Muslim diet and fasting, as well as the Muslim practice of eating while seated on the floor.[42] They sent rectors and lay sheriffs to Morisco homes to find out if the children were attending the compulsory Christian schools that had been established for them.[43] Far from the refuge that the home had once been for Moriscos, their homes became the primary forum for the struggle over heresy. While inquisitors found the commonplace heretical, Moriscas made the ordinary subversive.

Despite official prohibitions of the Arabic language, Islam, and Muslim cultural practices, all of these aspects of Moriscos' lives survived. We know this because the Inquisition continued to prosecute Moriscos for apostasy. Women played prominent roles in many of these cases, such as that of Leonor de Morales, whose husband had testified against her that she had persuaded him to follow Muslim practices.[44] Moreover, other witnesses said that she danced and sang as a Muslim at weddings and that she ate while sitting on the ground, cooked meat in oil, ate meat on Fridays, changed into clean clothing on Fridays, and communicated with "other Moors." Under torture she confessed to changing into clean clothing and fasting and praying as a Muslim; but she confessed to nothing more, even though she was subjected to six turns of the cord, nor did she give names of any accomplices.[45]

In another case, witnesses accused Lucía de la Cruz along with her husband and fifteen-year-old daughter of living according to Islam.[46] Under torture she confessed to all she had been accused of and added, whether out of pain or defiance, that she washed five times each day in the Muslim manner and taught Islam to others. Inquisitors reported that she had communicated with other Moors about Inquisition proceedings against them. In both these cases, and countless others like them, inquisitors found Moriscas guilty of preserving Muslim practices in their homes, influencing others to follow Islam, and communicating with other Moors.

It should be noted here that some Moriscos, both men and women, made genuine conversions to Christianity; and some of them intermarried with Old Christians.[47] Yet all of them remained subject to suspicion. Christian authorities believed that many of them followed the Muslim tradition of *taqiyya* and merely pretended to convert. When Moriscos had called on the mufti of Oran for help in 1563, he had urged them, "Maintain prayer and give alms, even though you do it symbolically, for God is not concerned with your exterior attitude, but with the intention of your hearts." If they tell you to denounce Mohammed, he continued, "denounce him by word and love him at the same time in your heart."[48]

For years Moriscas carried on this subversive but covert—and sometimes unconscious—resistance to Christianization in the privacy of their homes where they determined cooking and eating practices and set the schedule for changing into clean clothing. They taught the Arabic language and Muslim prayers to their children, perhaps unconsciously falling back on traditional practices. But a conscious choice to resist seems clear in those cases of women who hid their children so they would not have to attend schools established to Christianize them. According to one official report, the women were the most "obstinate" in resisting attempts to Christianize Moriscos.[49]

Homes and Betrayal

After the middle of the sixteenth century, Christians determined to break Morisco resistance through increased pressure on their homes. In 1565 clerics in Granada deliberately broke with their previous policy of persuasion and adopted a new policy of repression that opposed every aspect of Morisco culture. These prelates asked the Crown to send away from the homes of the "most principal Moriscos" their sons who would have to live in Old Castile "at the cost of their parents" so that they would better assimilate and learn Christianity.[50] Sharing the prelates' impatience with Moriscos' slowness in assimilating, the Crown adopted most of their recommendations in the next year, adding a prohibition of all Arabic speech and books within three years.[51]

At the same time, economic developments undercut the stability of many Morisco homes. From mid-century, heavy new taxes on raw silk production threatened the only livelihood that many Moriscos had, and they could no longer freely export their silk.[52] In addition, authorities revised the boundaries of their farms and fined Moriscos who did not have written title to the land that they had farmed for generations. They refused to accept titles written in Arabic. Moriscos who could not pay the fines simply lost their land.[53]

Unable to support their families, some Morisco men left their homes. They fled from the areas of most effective Christian oppression and abandoned all pretense of assimilation. From shelters on the coast of North Africa many of them sailed to attack and enslave Christians who lived along the Spanish coast. Others remained in remote interior areas of Andalusia, such as the Alpujarra Mountains, where they formed bandit gangs as *monfíes* and attacked Old Christians, aiming especially at clerics, merchants, and innkeepers. Regarded as a criminal by Christians, the monfí was hailed as a "hero of liberty" by Moriscos.[54]

Monfíes quickly joined the Morisco rebellion that erupted in the Alpujarras on Christmas Eve in 1568. As the rebellion spread, atrocities escalated on both sides, and homes became targets rather than refuges. When Moriscos of a particular place decided to rebel, they would attack the local church and Old Christian residents. Then, in an effort to protect them from vengeful Christians, the Moriscos would take their wives and children and livestock to nearby mountains where many of them made homes in natural caves.[55] Food became scarce, and the extreme cold penetrated their caves. As Moriscos began to surrender, the marqués of Mondéjar promised to try to get pardons for them, but he could not protect them from his own Christian soldiers.[56] Moriscos trying to escape these soldiers moved further into the mountains, fleeing from cave to cave. At one place Christian soldiers found two large caves sheltering some 800 Moriscos.[57]

Women and children took active part in the conflict on both sides. Armed only with "stones and roasting spits," Morisco women joined the men in the battles, fighting and dying beside them.[58] According to a Christian who participated in the January 1570 battle of Galera, the women fought "with such bravery, that it was marvelous to see." He noted in particular their "valiant captain," a woman named Zarçamodonia, "large in body, with strong limbs," who led troops in combat and killed eighteen men by her own hand in this one battle.[59] Despite her valor and that of the other women and children who hurled stones to defend their stronghold, Christians captured Galera and killed hundreds of their captives, including

400 of these women and children.[60] They spared the lives of another 4,500 women and children, most of whom they sold as slaves.

For the defeated Moriscos, the rebellion ended in the fall of 1570 with death, enslavement, and lost homes. Morisco boys younger than ten and one-half years and girls younger than nine and one-half years were not to be enslaved, but distributed among Old Christians to be raised as Christians. However, a royal pragmatic of 1572 noted that "from ignorance or malice" some Christians had sold Morisco children even younger after branding them on the face as a slave.[61] Families fortunate to remain intact had to gather in relocation centers for further instructions. They came by the tens of thousands, unwilling to leave their homes but too frightened to disobey the royal decree of forced relocation, well aware that the armies of Philip II had finally—after struggling for nearly two humiliating years—defeated the Morisco rebellion.

Determined to punish the rebels and prevent further armed eruptions against his authority, Philip II ordered the dispersion and relocation of some 50,000 Moriscos from the Kingdom of Granada.[62] Individual Moriscos of Granada petitioned the king for exemption from the order of dispersion because they and their families had been Christians for generations. The petition of Ysabel de Padilla, for example, described her as "a New Christian of Granada from long ago," and many other Moriscos described themselves as "Moriscos of peace" who had not participated in the armed rebellion.[63] Philip II, however, maintained firmness in the face of poignant pleas. Whole families now had to leave their homes in suddenly depopulated villages. Monasteries and landlords that had depended on Moriscos' labor to cultivate their fields and bring in the harvest protested in countless letters and petitions to the Crown.[64] In response, royal authorities promised to help them resettle Old Christians in the vacant homes of these Moriscos, a project not entirely successful.[65]

Christian authorities rounded up the Moriscos of Granada, sending some to Almería to board ships that would take them to other Spanish ports. Others they gathered in Albacete, forming them into units under armed guards to march north and west to towns and cities of Castile where few Moriscos lived. A report from Albacete on 3 November 1570 assured the king of compliance with his order, explaining that Moriscos were being formed into groups of 500, each to be moved under the direction of a captain and two officials. Moriscos were arriving in Albacete so quickly, the report added, that on one day 4,000 entered the town, and on the following 6,000.[66] These Moriscos would suffer great hardship, hunger, and cold during their relocation journeys. One group of 1,700 Moriscos had to travel three months, continuing northward to León because other cities along the way were already filled with relocated refugees. With little food, clothing, or shelter, they crossed high plateaus and mountain passes, burying their dead along the way.[67] Another group of 300 Moriscos lost more than half their number as they made their way to Mérida in Extremadura.[68] At least one-fourth of the Moriscos, it has been estimated, died during the journeys of relocation.[69]

Most Old Christians in the cities and towns that were ordered to receive the displaced Granadan Moriscos regarded them with great suspicion.[70] Some 4,300 Moriscos were sent to Seville, for example, where the archbishop imposed a close ecclesiastical scrutiny. Now not only required to attend instruction by a cleric on Sundays and feast days, Moriscos were also to pay each time for the instruction and to pay a fine if they missed it. Priests of parishes in which Moriscos had settled were made responsible "to know how they live, and not to consent to their speaking Arabic, nor that they teach it to their children; and they must see that they do not live too many together, nor that they meet together, because in this way they hide their language and customs."[71] Clearly, the new homes of these relocated Moriscos would not afford them the refuge and space of cultural identity and resistance that they had found in their former homes.

In fact, these new homes seemed to harbor treachery more than refuge for these Moriscos. The great majority of acts for which the Inquisition prosecuted them were domestic acts, carried out within their homes. Not surprisingly, a large number of Moriscos were betrayed not only by outsiders, but by their own family members. Note that Leonor de Morales, whom we discussed above, was denounced by her husband. The parents of María Jérez, a fifteen-year-old Morisca, testified against her that she had participated with them in Muslim rites and traditions.[72] Inquisitors prosecuted Leonor Hernández when her son told them that she kept the Muslim faith and had taught it to him and his brother.[73] In thousands of cases, inquisitors questioned prisoners to get them to implicate other family members.

Despite this dangerous and hostile world in which the very stones seemed to be watching them, Moriscas continued their resistance. Even after inquisitors caught and condemned them, some found ways to communicate with other Moriscos in prison, refused to name accomplices, and resisted inquisitorial authority. One outraged cleric reported that a Morisca sentenced to wear the *sanbenito*, a penitential sack-like garment meant to humiliate her, asked inquisitors for another *sanbenito* for her young son "because he was cold."[74] Another Morisca requested a new *sanbenito* because her old one was wearing out.[75] Historical records do not tell us whether these women made their inquiries sincerely or in a conscious attempt to ridicule the power of the Inquisition.

Morisco resistance spilled out beyond their homes, and in 1580 authorities in Seville uncovered a network in which many Moriscos had planned to begin another rebellion. On 20 June 1580, the head of the city council of Seville announced that Moriscos who had been relocated in Seville from Granada had been holding meetings to prepare for an armed uprising that would begin in just eight days.[76] Under the leadership of Fernando Muley Enríquez, the official reported, these Moriscos expected victory with the aid of Turks and North Africans. Mobilized by this news, the city council issued special instructions for city residents. Christians could go to the Plaza de Armas to get weapons and instructions when an alarm was sounded, and they were also subject to stand watch in the city. In contrast, Moriscos were now to become prisoners in their own homes, forbidden to leave their houses by night or day. Only Morisco women could go out during daylight and then only to get provisions for their homes.[77] Despite these precautions, the rebellion did take place, but on a very small scale; its leader and his son were soon captured.

Partly in response to the uprising of 1580, Christian authorities took measures to maintain better control over Moriscos. The Crown directed local officials to remove and relocate any Moriscos still remaining in Granada, adding that guards must accompany these people to protect Moriscos' wives and daughters and property from attack.[78] One official who reported on carrying out this task noted that some of these people were widows with children, and all were poor and had been raised from childhood in Christian homes where they had never learned Arabic. He asked the Crown for money to provide warm clothing and food for their journey.[79] Church leaders in towns and cities that received the relocated Moriscos directed their parish priests to send in reports of where these Granadan Moriscos had been relocated and how they were living, from 1581 to 1589.

The 1589 census of Moriscos in Seville shows that many of them lived in homes far different from those idealized by either Ibn ʿAbdun or Christian officials. Slaves, who often lived separately from their masters in Iberia, congregated together in the same household without any blood or marital relatives, and so did widows in post-dispersion Seville. Although nuclear families appear in the census, female adults outnumber male adults by 35 to 31. This population imbalance can be explained by the numbers of adult men who went into captivity, galley service, slavery, or voluntary emigration to mountain hideouts or North Africa.[80] Many widows and women without husbands lived together in *corrales*, those buildings around a common courtyard where inhabitants shared water from a fountain, the company of a common bench, a play area for children, and neighbors to keep watch.[81]

Although Christian officials declared that Moriscos should live scattered among Old Christian neighbors, they must have found it difficult to enforce such regulations. In practice, Moriscos tended to congregate in three or four parishes in Seville, with one third of them living in Triana, a section of the city across the river from the rest of the parishes.[82] Availability of affordable housing probably played a major role in decisions of where to live, and the cost of living undoubtedly kept many Moriscos living together in a single structure even when they shared no blood or marital ties. To Christian authorities, these households sheltered potential conspirators of rebellion and spies for the Turks.[83] Officials transformed Morisco homes into snares by arresting one person who, under interrogation and torture, would betray others of the household.

Yet some people, both Christians and Moriscos, held out hope for peaceful coexistence through assimilation or acculturation.[84] Although ecclesiastical authorities doubted that most Moriscos had sincerely converted, some clerics asked how these people could possibly understand Christianity when they had not received instruction and did not understand the language in which priests spoke and preached to them.[85] Moriscos' hopes for a reconciliation between Islam and Christianity had peaked in 1588 with the discovery in Granada of writings that became known as the *Libros Plúmbeos*, or leaden books. Written in Arabic and crude Latin, these writings were believed to be ancient testaments of the common ground between Islam and Christianity, presenting an Islamic version of the Trinity: "There is no God but God and Jesus, the Spirit of God."[86] Despite the firm belief of many (including the archbishop of Granada) that the writings were genuine, Innocent XI later declared them to be forgeries in 1682 and condemned the Arabic passages as attempts to defile the Catholic faith.

Expulsion and the Morisco Home

Proposals for how to solve the "Morisco question" seemed to doom the Morisco home and family in the late sixteenth century. Some clerics called for stricter punishments of Moriscos who refused to assimilate. "It is very strange," observed Pedro de Valencia, "that Spain which encircles the sea and the land, from the ends of the East and those of the West, to Chile, to China, to Japan" looks to convert the infidels in these places, "and does not take care nor diligence to convert and confirm the faith of these people within its own houses who are baptized and should be taught and confirmed."[87] Alternative solutions proposed enslaving all Moriscos or sending them in groups to live in colonies in places such as Naples, Sicily, Lombardy, Flanders, the Indies, or interior Spain far from the coastline.[88] Alonso Gutiérrez proposed branding Moriscos and assigning them to live in groups of 200 families under the control of a chief who had the power to forbid marriage as a way to limit their "very great multiplication."[89] In addition, he discussed the possibility of limiting Morisco propagation through castration, which the bishop of Segorbe had proposed in 1587.[90]

Increasingly, Christian authorities considered expulsion as a solution to the problems with Moriscos, but they had to consider many complicating factors, such as economic issues. On the one hand, Christian nobles in Aragon, Valencia, and Granada opposed the expulsion of Moriscos as economically detrimental—not simply for landowners dependent on Morisco vassals for producing income from their land, but also for all people of the empire. In the words of the count of Castellar, to expel the Moriscos would be "the universal ruin and desolation of this kingdom."[91] In contrast, commoners resented the economic success of Moriscos whom they saw as retailers eager to make money that they hid or took out of Spain.[92]

Political issues added further complexity to the expulsion debate. Nobles in particular wanted to limit powers of a nascent central state that infringed on their own regional powers, but most ecclesiastical leaders sided with the central monarchy in its decision to expel the Moriscos. The resistance of these people, after all, seemed to reveal the failure of attempts to impose the Church over them. Political imperatives of the infant central state tipped the balance against the Moriscos, who served as a common enemy or "counter-identity" that could unite all the different regions in this polyglot empire.[93]

After years of debate, Philip III issued decrees to expel the Moriscos from the Spanish kingdoms between 1609 and 1614. In Andalusia, Moriscos were given only thirty days to leave Iberia, forbidden to pass through the kingdoms of Aragon and Valencia.[94] They had to try to sell their houses, furnishings, and other property, converting any money into clothing that they could wear in layers, or into gold and silver that they could attempt to sew into their clothing to smuggle out of Iberia. Some Moriscos, believing that expulsion was imminent, evidently began to try to sell their property even before the expulsion decree was issued in Seville in 1609. Here the expulsion decree caustically observed that Moriscos showed they wanted to live away from Spain, "for they have begun to dispose of their estates, selling them for much less than they are worth."[95] Countless Old Christians benefited from the urgency with which Moriscos had to liquidate their homes and property.

As they moved to leave Iberia, Moriscos had to transform their homes from a physical place that would have to be abandoned into a transportable ideal of refuge which they could take with them. Some 300,000 Morisco men, women, and children would leave Spain, a few to return, but most to seek to make their homes elsewhere.[96] Defending his decision as one based on consultation with theologians and "learned persons," Philip III declared that all Moriscos well enough to travel should be expelled because "such are the most obstinate of their bad sect, and that with their bad doctrine and example, they are enough to inflict them on the children."[97]

The question of what to do with children of the Moriscos provoked some of the most emotional debate. They were baptized, after all, and might be raised as good Christians. As one courtier advised Philip III, children under a certain age should be kept in Spain and separated from their parents "so they do not fall into the same errors."[98] Yet others argued that to take Morisco children away from their parents would make the expulsion all the more difficult, and it would create the problem of how to care for the children. Assured that Old Christians could be found who would raise the children and that their parents could be consoled by telling them that these children would be nothing but a burden to them on their journey—perhaps even dying on the way—Philip III ended the argument.[99] He decided that Moriscos going to Christian lands could keep their children of any age, but those embarking for "infidel lands" must leave behind their children under the age of seven years.[100]

Morisco families preparing to leave their homes now had to prepare to leave their youngest children as well. Some made desperate appeals that their families be exempted from the expulsion, and others asked trusted Christian friends to take in their children as they left. In Seville authorities took some 300 children from Morisco parents preparing to embark during the expulsion. These children were held under armed guard in warehouses near the port until they could be moved to the homes of Old Christians who agreed to raise them, usually in exchange for their future labor.[101] After the expulsion some Moriscos attempted to return to Spain, hoping to find the children they had left behind or to see again the houses that had once been their homes. Some came back to claim money and precious metals that they had hidden because they could not take them out of Spain.

Moriscos gathered at the points of embarkation "voluntarily" and "quickly," according to one Christian account.[102] They went as happily as Christians go to their churches, this cleric wrote, and the women wore their best clothing. One woman gave birth at the port of embarkation, then said she was ready to leave and walked on board the boat. Another Christian writer declared that the Moriscos took much gold and silver as they left, although it was forbidden; women wore most of it sewn into their clothing.[103] Some believed that Moriscos left full of hope for returning later to their homes in Spain, but it is also possible that they left with hopes for making new homes elsewhere or that they chose to act with bravado simply out of defiance.

Not surprisingly, Morisco accounts of the expulsion tell a different story. Licenciado Molina, a Morisco from Granada, sent a letter dated 25 July 1611 from Argel to a Christian friend in Trujillo.[104] His group of 1,000 exiles had gone to Marseilles from Spain, but within a few days of their arrival the French turned against them as spies of the king of Spain. Within fifteen days, he wrote, most of their money had been taken and their lives were in danger. They decided to try to find a better place to make their home, but in Italy the people wanted them only to work as servants, workers in the fields, or "other low offices." Moving on, they arrived in Argel to live among other Moriscos who had come from Extremadura, La Mancha, and Aragon. Here Molina was able to realize that the expulsion was divinely inspired, for he had seen signs that from a thousand years ago had foretold what had happened to the Moriscos. But God would send a king who, "with only the word of God," would conquer the world.

Although Moriscos spread throughout the world in their diaspora, those from the same towns in Spain often settled together. Some made their way to the Western Hemisphere, despite laws that prohibited Judeo-conversos and Moriscos from this part of the Spanish Empire.[105] About 30,000 Moriscos went to France, one of the few Christian countries where they could go and take their youngest children; but fewer than 1,000 remained there as prejudice grew against them. Other Moriscos settled in Venice and Rome, in Salonica and Agde. For many, however, these places were merely stopovers during their long trip to Turkey, where the Ottoman bureaucracy carried out a policy of assisting the Moriscos wherever they settled.[106] The great majority settled in North Africa and made new homes in which they could keep their faith and attempt to preserve the traditions of their Hispanic-Muslim past.

Moriscos who made their way to Tunisia found important support from the Ottoman governor for Tunisia, Utman Dey, and a pious Tunisian who convinced other Tunisian families to take in and shelter Morisco families.[107] They opened mosques and prayer sites as refuges for the exiles and defended them against local xenophobia. Utman Dey undoubtedly saw an opportunity to create a community of immigrants dependent on him who would help to counterbalance Tunisians who opposed their Turkish rulers. Many of these Morisco immigrants created agricultural colonies in the north of Tunisia where political instability had resulted in nomadism and agricultural instability. Those Moriscos who did not engage in farming carried out artisanal work in ceramics, soap, and silk production. They made new homes, formed guilds, and even monopolies.[108] These exiles lived openly as Muslims, and yet they also preserved some of their Hispanic-Muslim culture and a love for their previous homeland. The eloquent *Cántico* of Ybrahin Taybili, a Morisco who came to Tunisia from Toledo, celebrated a strong belief in Islam while also expressing the Moriscos' love for the land and language in which they had been raised.[109]

The expulsion of the Moriscos left tens of thousands of formerly Morisco homes empty in the Spanish kingdoms. In November 1609 the marqués of Carazena reported that 1,000 houses had been left unoccupied in Valencia and noted an advertisement that invited people to come from the Azores to repopulate them.[110] A month later the marqués of los Velez wrote to Philip III to remind him about the urgency to repopulate his estate with workers to replace the Moriscos who had been expelled.[111] Some Moriscos would even attempt to return to Spain after they had been expelled, and the king commissioned the count of Salazar to find and punish them. According to one courtier, Salazar had found more than 800 fugitive Moriscos in one location and had sent them to galley service.[112] Moriscos risked a great deal in attempts to return to reclaim young children they had left behind or treasure they had hidden when they left. Most could hide their Morisco identity only by avoiding their former homes and neighbors who might recognize them.

Official expulsion orders declared that Morisco children left behind were not to be enslaved, but to be raised as good Christians by Old Christians in Spain.[113] Some of these children made their homes with friends of their families or in seminaries already established for Morisco children. In 1615 the Casa de Niñas, which had been founded in Valencia in 1606, housed forty-four Morisco girls between the ages of five and seventeen years. It was directed to place these girls in private homes where they would "serve," but also continue in the instruction that they had received in the school.[114] Other Morisco children were given letters of commission which placed them under the protection of a Christian family that would put them to work. Usually, boys were taken by rural families that wanted them to work in the fields, while girls often remained with families in towns where they worked as domestic servants.[115] Families who provided homes for these children were told not to treat them as Moriscos, but as if they were their own children "so that with this and with good doctrine and teaching, they will completely forget their birth and become as Old Christians."[116]

The gap between actual and ideal homes continued, however, even in Christian homes where a Morisco presence continued long after their expulsion. For years Morisco women and men had constructed and crafted these homes with brick work and stucco, tiled fountains, interior court-yards, and carved ceilings. They left their mark in homes both lowly and splendid. During the sixteenth century, for example, many Morisco artisans had labored in Seville to build and decorate the palatial Casa de Pilatos of the Enríquez de Ribera family. Some years later the elaborate carvings on one gallery arch of this noble home would catch the eye of a visitor who could read Arabic. To his great amazement, the visitor saw that the carvings duplicated the arabesques and lines of Arabic letters to spell out a bold message of defiance: "Eternal happiness for Allah."[117]

Notes

I wish to thank Nicholas Howe and members of Dialogica and of the Occidental Writing Network for helpful comments and suggestions on earlier drafts of this essay.

1. *El tratado de Ibn 'Abdun*, published about 1100 C.E., quoted in Jacinto Bosch Vilá, *La Sevilla islámica, 712–1248*, no. 92 of *Historia de Sevilla*, ed. Francisco Morales Padrón (Seville: Universidad de Sevilla, 1984), 242.

2. Ibid., 242.

3. Alonso Morgado, *Historia de Sevilla* (Sevilla: Andrea Pescioni y Juan de León, 1587), 102.

4. Julio Caro Baroja, *Los moriscos del Reino de Granada (Ensayo de historia social)* (Madrid: Artes Gráficas, 1957), 264–265. This architectural "veiling" could be compared with the cultural veiling of women when they left the home. See my book, *The Handless Maiden: Moriscos and the Politics of Religion in Early Modern Spain*

(Princeton, N.J.: Princeton University Press, 2004), 6–9; and also my essay, "Behind the Veil: Moriscas and the Politics of Resistance and Survival," in *Spanish Women in the Golden Age: Images and Realities*, ed. Magdalena S. Sánchez and Alain Saint-Saëns (Westport, Conn., and London: Greenwood Press, 1996), 37–53.

5. Bernard Vincent, *Minorías y marginados en la España del siglo XVI* (Granada: Diputación Provincial de Granada, 1987), 8–15; and Andrew C. Hess, *The Forgotten Frontier: A History of the Sixteenth-Century Ibero-African Frontier* (Chicago and London: University of Chicago Press, 1978), 144.

6. Pascual Boronat y Barrachina, *Los moriscos españoles y su expulsión: Estudio histórico-crítico*, 2 vols. (Valencia: Francisco Vives y Mora, 1901), note at I:96–97; and Celestino López Martínez, *Mudéjares y moriscos sevillanos* (Sevilla: Rodríguez, Giménez, 1935), 32.

7. Quoted in L. P. Harvey, *Islamic Spain 1250 to 1500* (Chicago: University of Chicago Press, 1990), 58. Al-Wansharishi, who died in 1508, was a mufti from Fez whose legal opinions (*fatwas*) were collected into *Kitab al-Mi'yar*, the source of this quotation.

8. López Martínez, *Mudéjares*, 34–35, for Seville; for a recent study of Muslims and Christians living together in three villages of southern Aragon, see Mary Halavais, *Like Wheat to the Miller: Community, Convivencia, and the Construction of Morisco Identity in Sixteenth-Century Aragon* (New York: Columbia University Press, 2002), esp. chapter 1.

9. Julián Ribera y Tarragó, *La enseñanza entre los musulmanes españoles: Bibliófilos y bibliotecas en la España musulmana* (Córdoba: Real Academia de Córdoba, 1925), 34–35, 72, and 84–85.

10. Caro Baroja, *Los moriscos del Reino de Granada*, 264–265.

11. Bernard Vincent, "Las mujeres moriscas," in *Historia de las mujeres en occidente*, ed. Georges Duby and Michelle Perrot, trans. Marco Aurelio Galmari (Madrid: Taurus, 1992), 3:592; Julián Ribera, *Historia de la música árabe medieval y su influencia en la española* (Madrid: Editorial Voluntad, 1927), 236–237; and Ana Labarta, "Contratos matrimoniales entre moriscos valencianos," *Al-Qantara* 4 (1983): 57–87.

12. Juan Aranda Doncel, "Las prácticas musulmanas de los moriscos andaluces a través de las relaciones de causas del tribunal de la inquisición de Córdoba," in *Las prácticas musulmanas de los moriscos andaluces (1492–1609)*, ed. Abdejelil Temini (Zaghouan: Centre d'Etudes et de Recherches Ottomanes, Morisques, de Documentation et d'Information, 1989), 11–26, esp. 17.

13. Information on the water and sewage systems of Seville is in Bosch Vilá, *La Sevilla islámica*, 228–233; and Antonio Collantes de Terán, *Sevilla en la baja edad media. La ciudad y sus hombres* (Sevilla: Ayuntamiento, 1977), esp. 84. Described as "caños," the pipes ran both above and below ground; and they were often said to be made of lead. For an important local study of baths in medieval Valladolid, see Magdalena Santo Tomás Pérez, *Los baños públicos en Valladolid. Agua, higiene y salud en el Valladolid medieval* (Valladolid: Ayuntamiento de Valladolid, 2002).

14. For the capitulations of 1492, see Luis Marmol Carvajal, *Historia del rebelión y castigo de los moriscos del reino de Granada*, vol. 21 of *Biblioteca de Autores Españoles* (Madrid: Atlas, 1946), 146–150. These capitulations are also quoted in

Florencio Janer, *Condición social de los moriscos de España, Causas de su expulsión, y consecuencias que ésta produció en el órden económico y político* (Madrid: Real Academia de la Historia, 1857), 18–19.

15. Cisneros, according to one historian, especially disliked "elches," as Christians who had converted to Islam under Muslim rule were known; see Ciezar Nicholás Cabrillana, *Almería morisca* (Granada: Universidad de Granada, 1982), 16. Harvey, *Islamic Spain*, also discusses the elches, 330–331.

16. Martín de Ayala, *Doctrina Christiana en lengua araviga, y castellana* (Valencia: Joan Mey, 1566), Biblioteca Nacional (hereafter BN) ms R–8782.

17. The burning of writings in Arabic and Aljamía is discussed in Antonio Domínguez Ortiz and Bernard Vincent, *Historia de los moriscos. Vida y tragedia de una minoría* (Madrid: Revista de Occidente, 1978), 19–21; and in A. R. Nykel, *A Compendium of Aljamiado Literature* (New York and Paris: Macon, Protat Freres, 1929), 27–28.

18. For more on these concealed writings and their discovery, see Nykel, *A Compendium*, 29–30; F. Guillén Robles, *Leyendas moriscas*, 3 vols. (Madrid: M. Tello, 1885); Luce López-Baralt, *Islam in Spanish Literature, From the Middle Ages to the Present*, trans. Andrew Hurley (Leiden: E. J. Brill, 1992), 171–174; Julián Ribera and Miguel Asín, *Manuscritos árabes y aljamiados de la biblioteca de la Junta* (Madrid: Junta para Amplicación de Estudios é Investigaciones Científicas, 1912), v–xviii, 138, 156–157; and Gerard Wiegers, *Islamic Literature in Spanish and Aljamiado* (Leiden and New York: E. J. Brill, 1994). Additional kinds of writings included treatises on magic and popular beliefs, legends, laws, prescriptive literature, medicine, Arabic grammars and vocabularies, and polemics against Christians.

19. Many of these Morisco versions of biblical stories appear in the Qur'an, and they are also published in Antonio Vespertino Rodríguez, *Leyendas aljamiadas y moriscas sobre personajes bíblicos* (Madrid: Editorial Gredos, 1963). For Rajma and Job, see Vespertino Rodríguez, *Leyendas aljamiadas*, 272–299; and Guillén Robles, *Leyendas moriscas*, I:225–263. For an anaysis of Rajma and the Morisco story of Job, see my essay, "Patience and Pluck: Job's Wife, Conflict, and Resistance in Morisco Manuscripts Hidden in the Sixteenth Century," in *Women and Texts and Authority in Early Modern Spain*, ed. Marta Vicente (Burlington, Vt. and Aldershot, Hampshire: Ashgate, 2004).

20. Guillén Robles, *Leyendas moriscas*, I:42–53 for the Castilian version, and 181–221 for the Aljamiado version. This story provides the central metaphor for my book, *The Handless Maiden*, and is discussed especially in chapter 1, 25–52. A few sources refer to "Arcayona," but the Aljamiado version specifies "Carcayona," and it presents a different conclusion than the Castilian version.

21. Prophecies are reprinted in Mercedes García Arenal, *Los moriscos* (Madrid: Editora Nacional, 1975), 55–62; three of these legends were translated for the Inquisition in Granada and are included in Marmol Carvajal, *Historia del rebelión*, 169–174. The Mancebo de Arévalo's *Breve Compendio* and chapter 58 of Iça de Segovia's *Breviario Sunni* contain strong apocalyptic messages that Weigers discusses in *Islamic Literature*, esp. 168, 240–242.

22. Most scholars believe that *taqiyya* originated with Muslim Shi'as living under Sunni domination, particularly those dissenters who joined the secret societies of

Isma'ilis, Nusayris, and Druses. See, for example, H. Lammens, *Islam, Beliefs and Institutions*, trans. Sir E. Denison Ross (London: Methuen, 1968), 168; *The Shorter Encyclopaedia of Islam*, ed. H. A. R. Gibb and J. H. Kramers (Ithaca, N.Y.: Cornell University Press, 1961), 561–562; and see surah 16:106 of *The Holy Qur'an: Text, Translation and Commentary*, trans. and comm. by Abdullah Yusuf Ali, 2 vols. (Cambridge, Mass.: Hafner, 1946), I:685.

23. Christoph Weiditz, *Das Trachtenbuch des Christoph Weiditz* (Berlin and Leipzig: Von Walter de Gruyter, 1927, orig. from the Netherlands, 1531–32). I want to thank Ida Altman, who first told me of this source, and the Office of Special Collections of the New York City Public Library, which has given permission to reproduce these illustrations. Weiditz's drawings are also reprinted in Christoph Weiditz, *Authentic Everyday Dress of the Renaissance: All 154 Plates from the "Trachtenbuch"* (New York: Dover, 1994).

24. Weiditz's emphasis on Morisca difference could be interpreted as an early form of orientalism, which Edward W. Said discussed for a later period in his book, *Orientalism* (New York: Pantheon, 1978).

25. For example, in 1639 the city council of Seville approved for the fourth time the prohibition against women covering their faces; see Archivo Municipal de Sevilla (hereafter AMS), Sección 4, siglo XVII, Escribanías de Cabildo, tomo 29, número 18. For more on cultural veiling of women, see Leila Ahmed, *Women and Gender in Islam: Historical Roots of a Modern Debate* (New Haven, Conn.: Yale University Press, 1992); and Lila Abu-Lughod, *Veiled Sentiments: Honor and Poetry in a Bedouin Society* (Berkeley: University of California Press, 1986).

26. I discuss internal imperialism more fully as a "political imperative" of the growing Spanish state in my essay, "The Politics of Race, Ethnicity, and Gender in the Making of the Spanish State," in *Culture and the State in Spain 1550–1850*, ed. Tom Lewis and Francisco J. Sánchez (New York and London: Garland, 1999), 34–54.

27. Henry Kamen, *Inquisition and Society in Spain in the Sixteenth and Seventeenth Centuries* (Bloomington: Indiana University Press, 1985), discusses these statutes esp. 115–133; but note that he also shows opposition to the statutes and that they were especially aimed at *conversos*, or baptized Jews. An excellent historical study of purity of blood statutes is Albert A. Sicroff, *Los estatutos de limpieza de sangre: Controversias entre los siglos XV y XVII* (Madrid: Taurus, 1985). For a theory of social boundaries believed necessary to separate purity and profanity, see Mary Douglas, *Purity and Danger: An Analysis of Concepts of Pollution and Taboo* (New York and Washington: Frederick A. Praeger, 1966). See Fredrik Barth, ed., *Ethnic Groups and Boundaries* (Boston: Little, Brown, 1969), esp. 31, for boundaries of exclusion that prevent pariah groups from assimilating.

28. Padre Román, quoted in Vincent, *Minorías y marginados*, 108.

29. Domínguez Ortiz and Vincent, *Historia de los moriscos*, 22.

30. Archivo Histórico Nacional (hereafter AHN), Inquisición, libro 1254.

31. For important insights into the political significance of ordinary events and rituals in the home, see William H. Beezley and Linda A. Curcio-Nagy, "Introduction," in *Latin American Popular Culture: An Introduction*, ed. William H. Beezley and Linda A. Curcio-Nagy (Wilmington, Del.: Scholarly Resources Books, 2000),

xi–xxiii. Anthropologist Hank Johnston explores the "microsociological" field of "the private, the primary, the mundane and quotidian," in his *Tales of Nationalism, Catalonia, 1939–1979* (New Brunswick, N.J.: Rutgers University Press, 1991), esp. xiii.

32. Inquisition records are full of information about women's roles in this resistance; further discussion is in Ricardo García Cárcel, *Herejía y sociedad en el siglo XVI. La inquisición en Valencia 1530–1609* (Barcelona: Ediciones Penínsulas, 1980), esp. 299; E. W. Monter, *Frontiers of Heresy: The Spanish Inquisition from the Basque Lands to Sicily* (Cambridge and New York: Cambridge University Press, 1990), esp. 226–227; and Vincent, *Minorías y marginados,* esp. 139. A similar incursion into domestic space took place earlier as the Inquisition prosecuted Judeo-conversos; see Deborah S. Ellis, "Domesticating the Spanish Inquisition," in *Violence against Women in Medieval Texts,* ed. Anna Roberts (Gainsville, Fla.: University Press of Florida, 1998), 195–209; and Renée Levine Melammed, *Heretics or Daughters of Israel? The Crypto-Jewish Women of Castile* (New York and Oxford: Oxford University Press, 1999).

33. James C. Scott, *Weapons of the Weak: Everyday Forms of Peasant Resistance* (New Haven and London: Yale University Press, 1985), xvi.

34. For example, see the Edict of Faith in AHN, Inquisición, libro 1244, folios 105–109.

35. Scott, *Weapons of the Weak,* 27, points out that the powerless engage in deferential or "onstage" behavior even as "backstage" they engage in resistance.

36. Fray Luis de León, *La perfecta casada* (1583), in *Biblioteca de Autores Españoles* (Madrid: M. Rivadeneyra, 1855), 37:211–246.

37. Juan de la Cerda, *Vida política de todos los estados de mugeres; en el qual se dan muy provechosos y Christianos documentos y avisos, para criarse y conservarse devidamente las mugeres en sus estados* (Alcalá de Henares: Juan Gracian, 1599), 242r.

38. See, for example, Juan de Espinosa, *Diálogo en laude de las mujeres* (1580), ed. Angela González Simón (Madrid: Consejo Superior de Investigaciones Científicas, 1946), 258. For more on gender ideology in early modern Spain, see Mary Elizabeth Perry, *Gender and Disorder in Early Modern Seville* (Princeton, N.J.: Princeton University Press, 1990).

39. This, of course, was true for Judeo-conversos as well. For recent work on Judeo-conversas, see Melammed, *Heretics or Daughters of Israel;* and three essays by the same author: "Sephardi Women in the Medieval and Early Modern Periods," in *Jewish Women in Historical Perspective,* ed. Judith R. Baskin (Detroit: Wayne State University Press, 1991), 115–134; "Sixteenth-Century Justice in Action: The Case of Isabel López," *Revue des études juives* 145, 1–2 (1986): 51–73; and "Women in (Post-1492) Spanish Crypto-Jewish Society," *Judaism* 41, 2 (Spring 1992): 156–168. Also, see Ellis, "Domesticating," 195–209.

40. Johnston, *Tales of Nationalism,* 49, points out a similar role for Catalan families during the Spanish Civil War.

41. bell hooks, *Yearning: Race, Gender, and Cultural Politics* (Boston: South End Press, 1990), 45.

42. See the "Instrucción" and "Informe" reprinted in García Arenal, *Los moriscos,* 106–125.

43. Francisco de Borja de Medina, S.M., "La Compañía de Jesús y la minoría morisca (1545–1614)," *Archivum Historicum Societatis Jesu* 57 (1988): 69–73, for reports on schools established by Jesuits especially in Granada.

44. AHN, Inquisición, legajo 2075, número 11, dated 1601.

45. As in much of medieval and early modern Europe, the Inquisition used torture not for punishment, but to ascertain the "truth." In this case, it examined Leonor de Morales using the *potro*, a rack to which the body and limbs were bound, with the examiner tightening the cords by turning them. Six turns would have been very severe. For more on the Inquisition and torture, see Kamen, *Inquisition and Society*, 174–177.

46. AHN, Inquisición, legajo 2075, número 11, dated 1601.

47. The 1589 census reports very few cases of intermarriage, but for a very interesting case of intermarriage raising issues of assimilation, see AHN, Inquisición, legajo 2075, número 31, "Relación de causas de fe," discussed in Mary Elizabeth Perry, "Contested Identities: The Morisca Visionary, Beatriz de Robles," in *Women and the Inquisition*, ed. Mary E. Giles (Baltimore: The Johns Hopkins University Press, 1998), 171–188. For Moriscos who became Christian prelates and attempted to Christianize other Moriscos, see Borja de Medina, "La Compañía de Jesús," esp. 77. More recent work on assimilating Moriscos of Aragon is by Halavais, *Like Wheat to the Miller*; and see James Tueller, "The Assimilating Morisco: Four Families in Valladolid Prior to the Expulsion of 1610," *Mediterranean Studies* 7 (1997): 167–177; as well as the same author's *Good and Faithful Christians: Moriscos and Catholicism in Early Modern Seville* (New Orleans: University Press of the South, 2002).

48. "Respuesta que hizo el mufti de Oran a ciertas preguntas que le hicieron desde la Andalucía," dated 3 May 1563, reprinted in García Arenal, *Los moriscos*, 44–45.

49. "Informe de Madrid a Valencia sobre instrucción de los moriscos," included in García Arenal, *Los moriscos*, 116–125, esp. 122.

50. Domínguez Ortiz and Vincent, *Historia de los moriscos*, 32.

51. Jaime Bleda, *Coronica de los moros de España* (Valencia: Felipe May, 1618), 657–659.

52. Hess, *The Forgotten Frontier*, 131.

53. Domínguez Ortiz and Vincent, *Historia de los moriscos*, 31–32.

54. Vincent, *Minorías y marginados*, 173–176.

55. Marmol Carvajal, *Historia del rebelión*, describes this pattern in many places, such as at 219.

56. Ibid., 248.

57. Ibid., 360.

58. The phrase is in *Relación muy verdadera sacada de vna carta que vino al Illustre Cabildo y regimiento desta ciudad* (Seville: Alonso de la Bar, 1569), n.p. For more on Moriscas participating in the rebellion, see Bleda, *Coronica de los moros*, esp. 695; Ginés Pérez de Hita, *Guerras civiles de Granada* (Granada: University of Granada Press, 1913, orig. 1595), Part II, chapter 20; and Marmol Carvajal, *Historia del rebelión*, esp. 312–314.

59. Pérez de Hita, *Guerras civiles*, Part II, chapter 20. I want to thank Mark Groundland for pointing out this and several other accounts of Morisca participation in the rebellions.

60. This was the January 1570 battle of Galera, reported by Marmol Carvajal, *Historia del rebelión*, 312–314.

61. *Pragmática y declaración sobre los moriscos del Reyno de Granada* (Madrid: Alonso Gómez, 1572), n.p.

62. For a 4 February 1571 memorial containing this decree, see Archivo General de Simancas (hereafter AGS), Cámara de Castilla, legajo 2161, part 1; another addressed to all his subjects and dated 24 February 1571 is in AGS, Cámara de Castilla, legajo 2166. Some historians believe that the relocation affected 80,000 Moriscos; see Domínguez Ortiz and Vincent, *Historia de los moriscos*, 55–56.

63. The plea of Ysabel de Padilla is in AGS, Cámara de Castilla, legajo 2169, which describes her as "cristiana nueva de viejo"; this same legajo contains many petitions from "moriscos de paz."

64. For example, see the petition of the city of Almería in AGS, Cámara de Castilla, legajo 2172; that of the dean and council of the church of Almería, in AGS, Cámara de Castilla, legajo 2180; and that of the abbess and convent of La Concepción in Almería, in AGS, Cámara de Castilla, legajo 2170.

65. Memorial of Philip II, 4 February 1571, in AGS, Cámara de Castilla, legajo 2161, pt. 1; reports of Rodrigo de Monsalve, who was commissioned by Philip II to find new settlers to live in depopulated areas of Granada, are in AGS, Cámara de Castilla, legajo 2164, ff 30–88. For more on the repopulation of Granada, see Margarita María Birriel Salcedo, "Las instituciones de la repoblación del Reino de Granada (1570–1592)," in *Hombre y territorio en el Reino de Granada (1570–1630). Estudios sobre repoblación*, ed. Manuel Barrios Aguilera and Francisco Andújar Castillo (Almería: Instituto de Estudios Almerienses, Universidad de Granada, 1995), 89–132.

66. AGS, Cámara de Castilla, legajo 2157.

67. See the 9 December 1570 report of Cristóbal de la Aguila who accompanied this group, in AGS, Cámara de Castilla, legajo 2157.

68. The 4 January 1571 report of the governnor of Mérida in AGS, Cámara de Castilla, legajo 2160.

69. Domínguez Ortiz and Vincent, *Historia de los moriscos*, 52.

70. Old Christians of La Mancha, however, welcomed the Granadan Moriscos for their artisanal and agricultural skills; see Carla Rahn Phillips, "The Moriscos of La Mancha, 1570–1614," *The Journal of Modern History*, On-Demand Supplement (1978): D1067–D1095.

71. *Constituciones del Arçobispado de Sevilla* (Seville: Alonso Rodríguez Gamarra, 1609), 19–20; see also Antonio Domínguez Ortiz, *Orto y ocaso de Sevilla. Estudio sobre la prosperidad y decadencia de la ciudad durante los siglos XVI y XVII* (Seville: Diputación Provincial de Sevilla, 1946), 57.

72. AHN, Inquisición, legajo 2075, número 11.

73. AHN, Inquisición, legajo 2075, número 8.

74. Damian Fonseca, *Justa expulsión de los moriscos de España: con la instrvccion, apostasia, y traycion dellos: y respuesta á las dudas que se ofrecieron acerca desta materia* (Rome: Iacomo Mascardo, 1612), 126.

75. Memorial of Fr. Nicolás del Río to Philip III from Valencia, 13 June 1606, quoted in García Arenal, *Los moriscos,* 127; also, see Bleda, *Coronica,* 883.

76. López Martínez, *Mudéjares y moriscos,* 57.

77. Ibid., 58–62.

78. Philip II's order to Francisco de Molina, dated 17 December 1583, is in AGS, Cámara de Castilla, legajo 2186.

79. Report of Don Esteban Nuñez, dated 26 January 1584, in AGS, Cámara de Castilla, legajo 2187.

80. Vincent, *Minorías y marginados,* 140, refers to voluntary emigration as "a masculine phenomenon." Cf. Carla Rahn Phillips, "Morisco Household and Family Structure in the Late Sixteenth Century," *Estudios en Homenaje a Don Claudio Sánchez-Albornoz en sus 90 Años,* 5 (Avila-Buenos Aires: Fundación "Claudio Sánchez Albornoz" and Instituto de Historia de España, 1990), 373–388, who found that in 1571 Morisco households in Ciudad Real were more likely to have male heads of households than Old Christian households, primarily because Old Christian men had been called to military service.

81. The 1589 census is in AGS, Cámara de Castilla, legajo 2196.

82. The regulation against Moriscos living together is in AGS, Cámara de Castilla, legajo 2196, and is also repeated in *Constituciones del Arçobispado.* See the population figures reported in AGS, Cámara de Castilla, legajo 2196; and also the discussion in Francisco Morales Padrón, *Sevilla: La ciudad de los cinco nombres* (Madrid: Turner, 1987), 92.

83. Two contemporary examples are Bleda, *Coronica de los moros,* 891; and Pedro de Valencia, "Tratado acerca de los moriscos de España," *Obras varias* (Zafra, 1606), BN ms 8888, passim.

84. For acculturation, see Thomas Glick and Oriol Pi-sunyer, "Acculturation as an Explanatory Concept in Spanish History," *Comparative Studies in Society and History* 11, 2 (1969): 136–154; I discuss assimilation and Moriscos in "Moriscas and the Limits of Assimilation," in *Christians, Muslims, and Jews in Medieval and Early Modern Spain: Interaction and Cultural Change,* ed. Mark D. Meyerson and Edward D. English (Notre Dame, Ind.: University of Notre Dame Press, 1999), 274–289.

85. The Jesuit Ignacio de las Casas argued that Moriscos were "baptized and not converted" because they had received no instruction in Christianity; quoted in Borja de Medina, "La Compañía de Jesús," 14.

86. López-Baralt, *Islam in Spanish Literature,* 200. An interesting description of the Libros Plúmbeos and their discovery is by a contemporary, Adam Centurion, *Información para la historia del Sacromonte, llamado de Valparaiso y antiguamente Illipulitano junto a Granada,* Part I, 1632, which is in the Biblioteca Capitular de Sevilla 56–3, detras 13. A more recent analysis is A. K. Harris, "Forging History: The Plomos of the Sacromonte of Granada in Francisco Bermúdez de Pedraza's *Historia eclesiástica,*" *Sixteenth-Century Journal* 30, 4 (1999): 945–966.

87. Pedro de Valencia, "Tratado acerca de los moriscos de España," *Obras varias* (Zafra, 1606), BN ms 8888, 103r–104.

88. Ibid., 72r-74, 83–83r.

89. See his "Informe" of 1588 reprinted in Boronat y Barrachina, *Los moriscos españoles*, I:634–638. His phrase is "grandísima multiplicación," 635.

90. Domínguez Ortiz and Vincent, *Historia de los moriscos*, 70–71.

91. His report is included in the memorial of P. Sobrino of September 1609, which is reprinted in García Arenal, *Los moriscos*, 247–250. Domínguez Ortiz and Vincent, *Historia de los moriscos*, 146–147, discuss the nobles of Aragon, Valencia, and Granada as defenders of Moriscos. The 1589 census of Moriscos in AGS, Cámara de Castilla, legajo 2196, noted the livelihoods for many of the people, both women and men. Prohibited by guild restrictions and purity of blood statutes from many offices, occupations, and professions, Moriscos worked primarily as retailers, nonskilled artisans, and day laborers. Women specialized in preparing and selling food, and some made hats and kept shops.

92. For example, see Bleda, *Coronica de los moros*, 905–906.

93. For more on this argument, see my essay, "The Politics of Race, Ethnicity, and Gender," 34–54; and Anne Norton, *Reflections on Political Identity* (Baltimore: The Johns Hopkins Univerity Press, 1988).

94. *Traslado de la Cedula Real que se publicó en la ciudad de Córdova a diez y siee dias del mes de Enero. En que manda el Rey nuestro Señor que salgan de todos sus Reynos y Señoríos, los Christianos nuevos del Reyno de Granada, Murcia, Andaluzia, y Villa de Hornachos* (Córdova, 1610).

95. *Cédula real sobre los moriscos*, dated 28 December 1608, Biblioteca Nacional (hereafter BN) ms VE 195–19. Note that the expulsion decree for Moriscos in Valencia had already been issued.

96. For numbers involved in the expulsion, see Domínguez Ortiz and Vincent, *Historia de los moriscos*, 200; and the discussion of different estimates in Miguel Angel de Bunes Ibarra, *La imagen de los musulmanes y del norte de Africa en la España de los siglos XVI y XVII. Los characteres de una hostilidad* (Madrid: Consejo Superior de Investigaciones Científicas, 1989), 81–94.

97. *Declaración del Bando que se a publicado de la expulsión de los moriscos* (Sevilla: Alonso Rodríguez Gamarra, 1610), n.p. BN VE 44–68.

98. Informe of 27 August 1609, from Juan de Ribera, reprinted in Boronat y Barrachina, *Los moriscos españoles*, II:523.

99. Suggestions for consoling Morisco parents are in the consulta from Segovia dated 1 September 1609, quoted in Boronat y Barrachina, *Los moriscos españoles*, 524–526. A report from the Royal Council dated 15 September 1609 suggests how Morisco children left by their parents can be raised, quoted in ibid., 549–550.

100. *Declaración del Bando*, n.p.

101. AGS, Contaduria Mayor de Cuentas, legajo 415, 2a, número 60, gives accounts for the cost of the embarkation and some of the costs of the care of the children. See also Domínguez Ortiz and Vincent, *Historia de los Moriscos*, 186–190, for the embarkation and leaving of children in Seville. For a discussion of how Morisco children should work to repay guardians, see J. Ripol, *Diálogo de consuelo*

por la expulsion de los moriscos de España (Pamplona: Nicholas de Assiayn, 1613), BN R–14165. An important essay on the children left behind is by François Martínez, "Les enfants morisques de l'expulsion (1610–1621)," in *Mélanges Louis Cardaillac*, ed. Abdeljelil Temini (Zaghouan: Fondation Temini pour la Recherche Scientifique et l'Information, 1995), 499–539.

102. Bleda, *Coronica de los moros*, 1001.

103. Fonseca, *Justa expulsión de los moriscos de España*, 273.

104. This letter is reprinted in appendix CXXXII in Janer, *Condición social*, 350–351; it is also included in Ripol, *Diálogo de consuelo*, 75–77r.

105. Information on the destinations of the Morisco exiles comes from Domínguez Ortiz and Vincent, *Historia de los moriscos*, 226–231. For Moriscos in the Western Hemisphere, see the interesting article by Peter Dressendörfer, "Crypto-musulmanes en la Inquisición de la Nueva España," in *Actas del Coloquio Internacional Sobre Literatura Aljamiada y Morisca*, ed. Alvaro Galmés de Fuentes (Madrid: Editorial Gredos, 1972), 475–494.

106. Hess, *The Forgotten Frontier*, 121.

107. Miguel de Epalza, "Trabajos actuales sobre la comunidad de moriscos refugiados en Túnez, desde el siglo XVII a nuestros días," in *Actas del Coloquio Internacional Sobre Literatura Aljamiada y Morisca*, ed. Alvaro Galmés de Fuentes (Madrid: Editorial Gredos, 1972), 430–431.

108. Ibid., 431–433.

109. Luis F. Bernabé Pons, *El Cántico islámico del morisco hispano tenecino Taybili* (Zaragoza: Institución Fernando el Católico, 1988); note also the important Introduction by Miguel de Epalza, 5–26.

110. AGS, Estado, legajo 218, notice to king, 3 November 1609.

111. AGS, Estado, legajo 213, letter of 7 December 1609 to the king.

112. Luis Cabrera de Córdoba, *Relaciones de las cosas sucedidas en la corte de España, desde 1599 hasta 1614* (Madrid: J. Martin Alegria, 1857, orig. 1623), 522.

113. Don Juan de Mendoza, *Declaración del Bando que se a publicado de la expulsión de los moriscos* (Sevilla: Alonso Rodríguez Gamarra, 1610), n.p.

114. François Martínez, "Les enfants morisques," 524.

115. The phrase used is "cartas de encomienda." See Domínguez Ortiz and Vincent, *Historia de los moriscos*, 251; and Martínez, "Les enfants morisques," 527.

116. Consulta from Segovia, 1 September 1609, quoted in Boronat y Barachina, *Los moriscos españoles*, II:525.

117. Joaquín González Moreno, *Aportación a la historia de Sevilla* (Seville: Editorial Castillejo, 1991), 197.

sabine maccormack

Social Conscience and Social Practice

Poverty and Vagrancy in Spain and Early Colonial Peru

In 1526, the Spanish humanist Juan Luis Vives, a man respected throughout the learned world of Europe and a friend of Erasmus, addressed a treatise on *How to Help the Poor* to the city fathers of Bruges, where he had been living for the last fourteen years. The work mingles reflections on the causes of poverty with practical advice about how to lead folk surviving in idleness on the fringes of society to join the community and to live productive lives. Why this mattered is clear from what Vives wrote. On the roads leading to Bruges, able-bodied vagrants and thieves who refused to work made travel unsafe and lived by laws of their own or none at all.[1] If vagrants on the roads and in the countryside were a problem because they formed a quasi-independent society remote from their more respectable neighbors, the poor within the city walls were only too close at hand: they smelt bad, they were an offense to the eyes and brought moral and physical contagion to the city.[2] They disturbed the course of worship with their begging, and many of them were rapacious and arrogant, which was why respectable citizens did not like giving them alms. For, as Vives asked, alluding to a sermon about helping the poor by Augustine, "what is more insupportable than an arrogant beggar?"[3]

91

Yet, that was not the whole story, for, as Vives viewed matters, human beings are inherently creatures of need, and everyone is in need of something: "some are in need of money, others in need of health, or of a sense of enterprise." In effect, "whoever is in need of help by another is poor, and requires compassion." Hence, almsgiving was not merely a matter of giving money, but of "performing any kind of action whereby human need is relieved."[4] It was therefore wrong to blame only vagrants and the poor for the troubles and inconveniences that befell the good citizens of Bruges.[5] The powerful and affluent were also responsible and it behooved them to employ their resources to help the rest. "For unless we are prepared to go and live elsewhere, we are not at liberty to disregard or disobey the precepts of our magistrates . . . and likewise we must not withhold our material resources when the city calls on them or avoid contributing to its welfare," the point being that people acquired their possessions not in isolation but thanks to living with others as members of a society.[6] As regarded practical remedies, Vives recommended that the city fathers should pay a salary to some "trustworthy men," who would see to it that those who could work were taught a trade, that the children of the poor went to school and learned useful habits, and that the sick and disabled who really could not work were housed and cared for.[7] In short, the task confronting the city was to help vagrants and the poor to join the larger community, to share in its values and contribute to its resources.

During subsequent decades, views and solutions similar to those recommended by Vives were reiterated by Spanish jurists and theologians,[8] one of whom, Domingo de Soto, addressed a treatise to the Infante Don Felipe, the future Philip II, in which he reviewed existing Spanish legislation on the subject of poverty and vagrancy and suggested additions and modifications that were actually being turned into law during those same years.[9] Just as Vives, Soto, and others recommended, these Castilian laws mandated that idle persons and vagabonds, *holganzanes y vagamundos*, should practice a trade, thereby leaving the many small charitable institutions and hospitals that were to be found in Castilian cities to care for those who really needed help.[10] Those who could not avoid begging were to obtain a permit and to renew it every year, and had to stay within six leagues of the place of their birth.[11] *Pobres vergonzantes*, people who were too shy to beg, were to be discreetly assisted in their homes,[12] and the entire operation was to be supervised by *hombres buenos*, good and trustworthy men of the locality, just as Vives and Soto recommended. The only people who, on paper at least, were allowed to wander freely and without a permit were the blind.

Consider the story of Lazarillo, "little Lazarus," de Tormes, hero of a Spanish picaresque novel published in 1554. The anonymous author of this engaging small work was a person of learning, and appears to have known some of the theoretical literature on poverty and vagrancy. At any rate, the life of Lazarillo suggests that the recommendations offered in this literature could be implemented successfully. Little Lazarus began his life as beggar, vagrant, and thief when his mother apprenticed him, still a small boy, to a blind man. Cut loose from the fragile economy of his mother's household, Lazarillo spent years on the road by begging, stealing, and deceiving people in the service of various masters, and he learnt skills of survival in this wandering life that were quite distinct from those needed to survive by his work, just as Vives had observed was the case among the vagrants living in the countryside surrounding Bruges. At last Lazarillo was reintegrated into society by being made to practice a trade, that of town crier of Toledo.[13] Along with his trade, he acquired as wife the maid of his patron, the archpriest of San Salvador, who from time to time presented Lazarillo with a load of grain, some meat, and his discarded shoes. Also, the archpriest ordered Lazarillo to rent "a little house,"[14] thereby completing the young man's transformation from vagrant, deceiver, and thief to resident of the imperial city of Toledo.

The life of little Lazarus was, on the surface at least, a success story,[15] and that in more than one respect. After his troubles and trials, he came to enjoy the benefits of a sedentary existence and could, as he expressed it himself, "lay something by for old age." In the larger scheme of things, his experiences on the road exemplify precisely the ills that Spanish social reformers and legislators of the day had in mind when they wrote about vagrants, the poor, and homeless. Finally, Lazarillo's story suggests ways in which these ills could be remedied. Poverty was endemic in early modern Spain,[16] but those who thought about it in the mid-sixteenth century did so in fundamentally upbeat terms: even though poverty would never disappear altogether, it could, if handled correctly, be managed and contained.

In Peru, during these same years, the small minority of Spaniards who paid attention to the poor, to vagrants and beggars, had no such hopes, because poverty was of a different nature, and on a different scale. Like Vives and Soto, the men who drafted legislation in Castile believed that in the last resort, the relief and control of poverty and vagrancy were tasks pertaining to the state, whether this was the city of Bruges or Habsburg Spain. In Peru, by contrast, there was, for the time being, no real state. The Inca empire had functioned as a system of redistributing resources among the many polities that the Incas controlled. In redistributing resources, the Inca ruler did on an imperial scale what regional lords had traditionally done, and were continuing to do among their own people, thereby preventing the problem of poverty from arising in the first place, because everyone, even the "weak," *huaccha*, were included in this age-old Andean system of exchange.[17] But when in 1532, the Spanish invaded Peru and murdered the Inca emperor Atahuallpa, they also dismantled imperial redistribution, without putting any equivalent in its place. That was only one aspect of the upheaval generated by the invasion. In 1550, the missionary friar Domingo de Santo Tomás, having worked in the Andes for ten years, wrote to the Infante Don Felipe, that in the course of the long wars of conquest and internecine rivalry among Spaniards, about half of all the houses in the former empire of the Incas had been destroyed, and the people who used to live in them had died or fled.[18] In Cuzco, the former Inca capital, the palaces and houses in the city center were taken over by the invaders, without a thought for the original inhabitants.[19] Fields lay abandoned, and entire regions were left desolate. Among survivors, Fray Domingo thought, the poor by far outnumbered the rich. A certain Juan Griego, who wrote a despairing letter about the condition of the country to Philip II in 1567, estimated that there were 15,000 poor persons for every 1,000 rich ones.[20]

Not only was poverty in the Andes on a different scale from the peninsular variety, it also raised a host of ethical questions that were quite new, or, if not new, were thought about for the first time in these recently conquered lands. In 1557, Domingo de Santo Tomás and some other friars made a deposition in Lima on behalf of two surviving sons of the Inca Atahuallpa. Fray Domingo traveled there in the company of one of these sons, Don Diego Ylaquita. Like his brother Don Francisco Ninancuro, Don Diego was poor and homeless. "This Don Diego," Fray Domingo stated in his testimony,

> came with me to Lima in order to be refreshed by my company. I said to him that he ought not to come because he would die [from the sudden change of climate] but he said that he only wanted to come and die speaking out before the Viceroy and not to die of hunger and shame, seeing so regularly how the servants of the Christians, and the African slaves of the Spanish possess the fields and the houses . . . and so at present he is living in the house and convent of the holy lord Saint Dominic awaiting the coming of the Viceroy.[21]

Consensus was building up among a number of influential Spaniards that the Incas had been rightful rulers of Peru, and that the judicial murder of Atahuallpa, which at the time had been justified by a host of specious arguments, was by any account a grave wrong. The matter was made worse by memories of the event that were during these very years surfacing among some of the *conquistadores* who had been present. These men were now saying that Atahuallpa, once he realized that his death was inevitable, had commended his young sons to the care of Francisco Pizarro, the leader of the Spanish invasion, who had promised not to betray this sacred trust: all the more sacred since Atahuallpa had died a baptized Christian.[22] But Pizarro did betray the trust. How else could one explain that Atahuallpa's sons, now grown men, were homeless vagrants in their own land? What was true on the grand scale of the sons of Atahuallpa, and other impoverished members of the Inca royal lineages, was true to a lesser but still very serious degree of thousands of Andean people who had lost their homes and livelihood as a result of the invasion and conquest of their land. For poverty of this kind, and involving so many people for whom Christ had also shed his blood, there was, as Fray Domingo and others after him were accustomed to observe, no real remedy.[23] At any rate, the "shadow of a hospital" that was erected in Lima to shelter sick and homeless Indians, and the "house of recollection" for the abandoned daughters of Spaniards and Indian women that were being founded in several other cities, along with the hospital and the convent of Santa Clara for mestizo girls in Cuzco,[24] and other similar institutions elsewhere, could not begin to address the problem of poverty, homelessness, and vagrancy in Peru.

Even so, life continued, and over the years, gave rise to forms of social consciousness which, for all their Spanish origins, were specific to the Andes. In 1545, the silver mines of Potosí were discovered, and within a few years, thousands of Indians were working there. In Inca times, Andean people had taken turns, *mita*, at performing certain tasks away from home both for the Inca state, and also for their own communities. The Lupaqa from Lake Titcaca, for example, regularly sent masons to erect buildings for the Inca in Cuzco, while others among them tilled fields at lower altitudes to provide the community with crops that did not grow in the highlands. Such workers were known as *mittayoc*, men who worked in turn.[25] This method of organizing labor was adapted by the Spanish to exploit the mines of Potosí. Like a number of other men of the church, Domingo de Santo Tomás was appalled, since, as he wrote to the Council of the Indies, sending *mittayoc* to Potosí, uprooting them from their communities, amounted to depriving them of their freedom and condemning them to poverty and deprivation, even death.[26] Also, the climate of Potosí was cold and inhospitable, and the fact that nothing grew there, so that even fodder for animals had to be brought from far away by llamas or "on the shoulders of Indians," along with the resulting high prices all added up to make of Potosí a "mouth of hell into which every year many people descend whom Spanish greed sacrifices to its god."[27] In Spain, Fray Domingo's letters were studied and annotated with some care, and led to several royal decrees prohibiting forced labor and the displacement of Indians from their homes.[28]

But were the Indians really being forced? In the mind of the lawyer Polo de Ondegardo, an expert on many Andean matters, the question was far from clear, and therefore, being governor, *corregidor*, of Potosí, he assembled the Andean lords whose people were working in the mines to "declare and state what was their intention, because neither their Spanish master nor any other person could compel them [to work in Potosí]."[29] Almost unanimously, the lords declared that their people came to work in the mines of their own free will. Being native to the high Andes, they liked the climate, and the sterility of the place was not a problem because

> when they come for their turn, they bring from home some food and their llamas and when they return they bring from Potosí shawls and coca and other things, and their mothers and brothers look after their fields and plantings at home and so they find their sustenance ready when they return. And those who are strong men and who work well bring back jewels[30] and silver bracelets and silver, and with this they buy what they need.[31]

With all the advantages of Potosí, there was, however, a darker side. Asked whether the tribute that the Indians were required to pay to the Spanish was excessive, the lords provided only indirect answers. For example, some of them said that

> they come from a village of Collao called Guaqui through which the armies of Gonzalo Pizarro and of Carvajal . . . and of the captain Diego Centeno passed many times, and they stole the livestock and their clothes and everything they owned and that in their country, because it is cold, they do not harvest maize, and the potatoes do not grow well because in some years they shrivel with the frost.

In Siquisica, marauding Spaniards had stolen 5,000 llamas, and elsewhere, no llamas at all were left. Working in Potosí, therefore, supplied the where-withal to pay tribute and provided opportunities to remedy the impover-ishment that had been brought on by a long decade of warfare and destruc-tion.[32] In addition, the mines yielded revenue for the ever depleted treasury of His Majesty the King. It thus seemed that the pragmatic Polo de Onde-gardo was right, and Domingo de Santo Tomás, for all his passionate dedi-cation to improving the lot of Andean people in Spanish Peru, allowed his ideals to run away with him.[33]

That, at any rate, was a possible conclusion in the early days of min-ing in Potosí. But after 1565, yields dropped drastically, to recover only when the process of amalgamation was developed on a large scale, in the early 1570s, with mercury imported from Spain and from Huancavelica in Peru.[34] Meanwhile, the work at Potosí, carried out in ever deepening mine shafts, became grimmer and more dangerous, and the *mita*, whatever it may have been at the start, turned into a system of highly organized com-pulsory labor[35] without which, so many people feared, Peru would face economic ruin. As the mining engineer Luis Capoche explained to the Viceroy Conde de Villar in 1585, without the silver from Potosí,

> merchandize would lose the value it has, the fleets would not sail, and customs dues would not be paid, for without the silver circulating in the kingdom, it would not be possible to communicate and conduct ex-change and commerce with Castile.

However, all this trading and exchanging had a terrible cost since, in Ca-poche's graphic phrase, "the poor Indian is the currency with which every-thing anyone wants is being obtained."[36]

"Poor Indian" was not just a manner of speaking. The mortality rate of miners in Potosí was high, and those villagers who were able to find and pay for substitutes who would serve in the *mita* in their stead did so. Oth-ers left their homes and resettled elsewhere in order to avoid going, and every time a *mita* train left a community, those who stayed behind bade farewell to those who had to go with tears and lamentation, as though they were departing never to return: with good reason, for many of the *mit-tayocs* never did return. Potosí itself was changing. In the center, religious orders were building churches with elegantly carved stone facades, and the ample houses of Spaniards and creoles lined the streets, while *mittayoc* lived in tiny adobe huts on the other side of the river that separated the

Spanish side of town from the *cerro*, the mountain where the silver was being mined.[37] According to a description of the early seventeenth century, the Indians

> sleep on the hard and damp floor, and stretching out on some straw is comfort and luxury. The houses are low, so that usually one has to enter bending down on all fours, and in only a few of them is it possible to stand up. In these small humble dwellings they keep their bedding and habitation, a hearth to prepare food, and their kitchen ware, which normally is only some pitchers and old pans. They never light a candle except when someone is seriously ill.[38]

In the early days of Potosí, Indians working the mines were tilling nearby fields, but subsequently, increased competition for land led to litigation in which many of those fields and the dwellings on them were acquired by Spaniards.[39] By this time, Domingo de Santo Tomás and the others, who amidst the horrors of conquest had hoped and worked for a society in which Indians would be the king's free vassals, just like Spaniards, were no longer alive. With their passing, different ideas about poverty, vagrancy, and homelessness came into play, most of which were based on the assumption that not just the mining *mittayoc* but Indians in general were in the technical sense *miserables*, "wretched ones," people without resources.[40]

This notion, as understood in Peru in the 1580s and subsequently, was composed of several components. Europe also had its *miserables:* the sick, prisoners, widows and orphans, all of them people who could not work, for whose sake good Christians gave alms and performed the works of mercy that were mandated by the Church: these were the people whom Vives regarded as entitled to society's support. Obviously, many Indians in Peru were *miserables* in this sense, although no equivalent to the multifarious network of charitable institutions that abounded in Spain was ever developed for their sakes.[41] Indians were and remained a conquered population, whom Spaniards endowed with characteristics that were designed to explain and ratify their lowly position in society. In this sense, Andean *miserables* were quite different from the European kind.

Andean people obeyed their lords, and most of all the Inca, with an awe and respect that had surprised the first Spaniards to reach the Andes as much as did the affluence and good order of the Inca empire, for which Europe offered no parallels, except perhaps in Roman times. Yet, these same Spaniards, many of them proud and overbearing men, found Andean folk to be fearful, submissive, and devoid of initiative. As the adventurer Don Alonso Enríquez de Guzman observed: "These Indians are feeble of body and spirit, and in general, by their nature, they lack ability and resourcefulness."[42] Later on, Spaniards would complain that the Indians obeyed their lords blindly and labored without any sense of enterprise or "desire for riches."[43] Official inquiries conducted during the 1570s confirmed these impressions. Andean witnesses who were interviewed in these inquiries seemed to be saying that the success of Inca government was to be attributed to coercion: the Incas had forced people to work,[44] and also, all over their empire, they had "reduced" small communities living scattered in remote places to ordered villages with streets and houses,[45] and in some instances, they had moved entire populations.[46] These were precisely the tasks that during the later sixteenth century Spanish authorities believed they themselves must perform once more, if Peru were ever to become something other than a land of "poor Indians" who were dominated by their rapacious and overbearing lords.[47]

But that, in the opinion of many Spaniards, was only part of the problem. Seeing just how timid Andean people were or had become in Spanish times, vagrancy presented an entirely new challenge to the task of maintaining the fabric of society. From the beginning, those who ruled Peru complained about *gente valdía*, "superfluous people," who arrived from Spain with no intention to work. Legislation for the Indies that closely echoed peninsular equivalents and the precepts of Juan Luis Vives and Domingo de Soto repeatedly mandated that these rootless individuals should be helped to settle in a fixed place and to cultivate the land or practice a trade.[48] But to little purpose. Another recourse was to send the vagabonds back to Spain.[49] This also proved inefficacious, since there were always more idlers arriving. Efforts to keep vagrants out of Peru continued, however. In 1581, for example, the king's instructions for the Viceroy Martín Enríquez included this clause, which itself echoed several earlier laws and instructions from the Crown:

> We have been informed that Spanish vagabonds who are not married live among Indians and in their villages, and inflict much insult and injury on them, taking away their women, their children and their possessions by force, and committing other insupportable outrages. To put a stop to such offenses, you shall see to it that none of these persons live among Indians or in their villages, by punishing them severely . . . [and] you shall arrange for idlers to settle with masters whom they can serve, or learn a trade to make a living for their sustenance. And if this is

insufficient, or they will not obey, you shall at your discretion exile some of them from the land, so that the remainder, in fear of the penalty, live off their work.[50]

Six years later, as the Viceroy Torres y Portugal wrote to Philip II in 1586, not much had changed:

Those among the vagabonds and persons of unsound lifestyle whom it has been possible to discover are being removed from the land, especially those who have been living in Indian villages, because they habitually steal from and maltreat the Indians, and commit other excesses to the Indians' detriment.[51]

Where thus in Europe, vagrants were at worst a nuisance, thieves and deceivers who made travel unsafe, and might end up as rowers in His Majesty's galleys, as almost happened to Guzmán de Alfarache, hero of another picaresque novel that was first published to much acclaim in 1599,[52] in the Andes, the matter was much more serious. Here, by virtue of being Spanish, vagrants enjoyed a privileged status that would not have been theirs in the Peninsula. Not only was it next to impossible for Andean lords and village authorities to rid themselves of unwelcome Spaniards, they were also obliged to house them free of charge in the way stations, *tambos*, that Indians were still maintaining along major roads and many lesser ones, just as they had done in the time of the Inca.[53] As a result, in the Andes, the task of controlling vagrants, however unsuccessfully performed, acquired an urgency it did not possess in the Peninsula.

Yet, here also, opinions as to what should or could be done, and especially as to whether or why it should be done, varied. Some Spaniards believed that the Indians had brought their sufferings on themselves by committing "sins against nature," and by diverging from other ethical norms that Europeans considered god-given. This argument, framed initially to justify the invasion of the Inca empire, was repeated subsequently by way of easing the consciences of the conquerors and their successors, and was taken up once more in the volume of model sermons for use in Indian parishes that was published in 1584 at the behest of the Third Council of Lima. One sermon inculcated Christian family relations. Taking for granted, quite wrongly, that "poor Indians" were living in houses with several rooms, and not in single-room cottages, preachers were to insist that sisters and brothers must not sleep "all together, as often happens."[54] In the same vein, young men and women should not walk about together before being married. "This is a great sin of yours," preachers were to say:

> It is for this sin and others which you commit that God has permitted that you are persecuted and are enslaved as though you were animals, because you choose not to live like human beings, but like horses and llamas of the field, without order or cleanliness of either soul or body.[55]

Another sermon was about charity and almsgiving, about loving one's neighbor as oneself, a practice that was, so the fathers of the Council thought, sadly lacking in Andean communities:

> You should love one another well and do good to one another, acting not as you did in times past and as many of you, or almost all of you do nowadays, for you take no care of the sick, the old and the poor, but ignore and disregard them, because you only respect and serve the rich and those who wield power over you, and provide you with a living. This is what your forefathers did, and it is not the law of Jesus Christ.[56]

Not that the Spanish were blameless: *inter alia*, they forced villagers to work without pay, took their women as servants and mistresses, and stole their property, just as the king's instructions to the Viceroy Martín Enríquez described. But as matters stood, in the view of the Council, there was not much to be done in the here and now. "You are little poor ones, and powerless," and the Spanish take "your poor possessions,"[57] preachers were instructed to say to their Indian charges. Yet ultimately, Christianity offered a consolation: "when you see yourselves persecuted by such evil men, you should raise your eyes to heaven, for he who will avenge you abides in heaven."[58]

This teaching had long established European roots. In Europe, the works of mercy were designed to relieve the suffering of *miserables*, but were not intended to transform society. The naked beggar on whom in El Greco's painting Saint Martin is dropping half his cloak would most likely remain cold and homeless. Likewise, the beggars whom Zurbaran depicted receiving small loaves of bread from one of the friars of Guadalupe in Extremadura would return to the monastery, hungry once again, the next day. In short, these paintings, like many others of their kind, depict human need and the Christian virtue of giving, without any suggestion that the shape of society in itself could require change. Reformers and legislators projected that the able-bodied poor were capable of helping themselves by working and of thus becoming self-supporting. This did not mean, however, that they ought to move beyond their station[59] up the social hierarchy and be exposed to the numerous temptations of wealth and power.[60] Lazarillo de Tormes acquired a trade, but of all trades, that of town crier was the most humble. In a similar vein, the sermons that the Third Council envisioned should be preached in Andean parishes accepted as given a state of affairs in which the Indians owned no more than their "poor possessions."[61] The Council's position was in some ways not so different from that of Juan Luis Vives, who likewise thought that poverty was an upshot of sin: some people's greed resulted in the neediness of others. At the same time, so Vives believed, the poor themselves also were at fault: for often, their bad habits were directly to blame for their deprivations.[62] However, the Council differed from Vives in polarizing the results of sinfulness. Where Vives recommended ways of modifying the results of sins committed by all and sundry, the Council did not: in the here and now, Andean people would suffer for their sins, while the conquerors would enjoy the fruits of their rapaciousness in peace and quiet.

With all that, the discourse of poverty was one thing, and the reality quite another. Specifically, in Peru, "the little poor ones" did much more than raise their eyes to heaven in the way that preachers who had been schooled in European ways of confronting the poor recommended. The mines of Potosí generated much misery, but they were also a source of wealth never heard of, and not all of it stayed in the hands of Spaniards. The supplies of food and clothing that were traded in Potosí's market by the Andean nobleman Don Diego Caqui of Tacna generated a fortune that competed with those accumulated by Spanish mine-owners.[63] Other Andean lords, among them Don Joan Ayavire Cusara, whose ancestors had been great men in the time of the Inca, still ruled over thousands of Andean families and made themselves indispensable to the Spanish by helping to organize the *mita* of Potosí. This was another source of prestige and wealth,[64] on the basis of which some of these lords petitioned the king for coats of arms with which to adorn the portals of their mansions.[65]

The market of Potosí that made Don Diego Caqui rich also offered opportunities to more humble folk. Among them were the family members of miners who traded goods from their villages, and the miners themselves who received part or all of their wages in unrefined ore which they were accustomed to sell in that market. In 1579, four years before the Third Council met in Lima, some Spaniards in Potosí were busy asserting that some of the ore that the Indians were selling had been stolen from mine-owners and that to prevent such thefts, the sale of ore by Indians should be prohibited altogether. After much inconclusive discussion and official inquiry into the functioning of the market in Potosí, the Viceroy Toledo consulted a group of theologians residing in Lima who all agreed that as free persons, the Indians had the right to buy and sell: and if some of the ore was stolen, so one of the theologians declared, "Let everyone watch what he buys."[66] But many Spanish Potosinos were not satisfied, so that Martín Enríquez, the next viceroy, obtained a further expert opinion, that of the Jesuit José de Acosta, a prominent participant in the Third Council, who almost certainly contributed to the model sermons that the Council published. However, Acosta had no sympathy for the arguments of the mine-owners. Reiterating the earlier opinions, Acosta added that "the Indians ought to be supported whenever possible, because we live in their land and are getting rich by their labor."[67] To make the position quite clear, the Jesuit added some explanations to his opinion, pointing out that all theological authorities were agreed that stealing for survival was not a mortal sin.[68]

How much more are these Indians justified in stealing, since they cannot survive by their work, because their wage is low. Such a person, according to natural law, may take what is his due from the one who oppresses him, because not only must he feed and clothe himself, which is what we owe even to a slave, but also, the Indians are supposed to get rich and to thrive, just as we do in their land.[69]

This bold idea, that *miserables* living in huts on the outskirts of Potosí were entitled to steal and ought to get rich, broke with a host of established European conventions. At this very time, when the Council was meeting, and when the mines of Potosí were producing their highest yields, other long cherished social theories began to shift, first in Peru, and then in Spain. From the very beginning, Spanish officials in Peru had accepted it as one of their primary obligations to augment the royal revenue: initially, this was accomplished by surrendering a fifth of the gold and silver that was plundered from Inca shrines and burials to the royal treasury, and later, it was done by organizing Indian tribute payments, some of which were passed on to the Crown. Another important part of royal revenue was the Crown's share of the silver from Potosí. But how secure was all this income?

Repeatedly, government inspections revealed that population figures had declined drastically since the time of the Inca, and staffing the *mita* became ever more difficult, this being one of the reasons why an increasing proportion of work associated with the mines came to be performed by more highly paid voluntary workers.[70] At century's end, warfare was no longer a significant cause of death among Indians, but epidemics of European diseases like measles continued taking a toll.[71] So did the burden of taxation and oppression by Spaniards, which, as the Viceroy Velasco informed Philip III in 1597, was transforming the face of Andean landscapes and societies:

> The labor and vexation that the Indians endure in mining, farming, raising stock, and hauling goods in this kingdom are unbearable and grow with each day. They are becoming fewer because everything weighs on those who are helpless, *miserables.* The Spanish are not coming here to work but to exploit them and their small possessions. Indians travel thirty, fifty, a hundred, and two hundred leagues from their villages to the mines of Potosí and other mines, where they are kept for two, four, six months, or a year. With being absent from their homes, the insupportable work and the evil treatment they receive, many die, or flee . . . leaving behind their houses, lands, wife and little children.[72]

Two years later, the viceroy returned to the same topic with more urgency:

> The Indians, to escape from the labors and vexations they suffer in their villages, absent themselves and flee, and they hide in fields, mountains, and ravines. The outcome is the desolation of their settlements to such an extent that from Cuzco and higher up . . . the [villages] are all empty and abandoned. And hence, there is no one to pay the taxes pertaining to his Majesty, . . . or to perform the *mitas* of Potosí.[73]

The voluntary exile that many Indians were choosing transformed society because throughout the Andes, villagers who stayed put and were therefore enrolled in the tax registers were joined by strangers, *forasteros,* who often were not.[74] Migration, whether it was for the *mita* and therefore forced, or for flight and voluntary, reshaped Andean communities as profoundly as did the invasion itself. In light of these upheavals, the king's wealth came at times to be perceived not merely in financial but also in human terms: the most crucial part of that wealth were the Indians who paid the tribute and worked in the mines.[75] In legislating against vagrancy in the Andes, therefore, and in urging the Crown to curtail tribute payments, the king's ministers were indeed pursuing an old established program of maintaining the social fabric by keeping everyone in their proper and accustomed place. But at the same time, they were seeking to protect, however ineffectively, the Indians on whose labor rested the fabric not just of society, but of empire.

What made the matter more pressing at century's end was the enduring financial crisis that dogged the Spanish Crown.[76] This crisis led the king's advisors in Spain to rethink established policies in terms reminiscent of what had already been suggested in Peru. In the Peninsula also, peasants were leaving their homes, just as Indians were doing in the Andes, so as to escape from heavy taxation and other burdens. In an opinion, *consulta*, of 1619, the Council of Castile took the innovative step of advising the king to reduce taxation by way of increasing his subjects' wealth, and hence, in due course, his own wealth. "Depopulation and the shortage of people," the Council wrote,

> are now more serious than has ever been seen or heard since your Majesty's ancestors began governing these realms, because, without any possible doubt, this Crown is in the course of being utterly annihilated and ruined if Our Lord, through the instrumentality of your Majesty's piety and greatness, does not send the remedy that we hope for. The cause arises from the excessive burdens and tributes that have been imposed on your Majesty's vassals, who, aware that they cannot withstand them, must without fail abandon their children, wives, and houses if they are not to die of hunger.[77]

In seven tersely reasoned points, the Council suggested remedies for this state of affairs: apart from lowering taxes and freeing peasants from dues and services to the nobility, the king must avoid needless expenditure by reducing the number and size of his favors to nobles and churchmen, and he must prevent resources being siphoned from the provinces to the capital, where they were merely being wasted on luxuries that brought no advantage to the country. In short, the *consulta* stated, as the king's ancestor Alfonso X had understood back in the thirteenth century, the king of poor subjects would himself be poor, which was why it behooved Philip III to see to it that his subjects prospered.[78] In Peru, viceroys and others had been arguing in support of such policies for decades,[79] but without success. In Castile likewise, the *consulta* of 1619 was discussed at length but was not implemented.

However, even though these projects did not at the time become policies, they mark a shift in social awareness. In Italy, opinions resembling

those of the *consulta* of 1619 had already been aired in an influential treatise by Giovanni Botero, who also realized that the wealth and power of a
ruler could indeed be calculated on the basis of the revenue at his disposal,
but that a ruler's true wealth resided in the number and prosperity of his
subjects.[80] Neither Botero nor the Council of Castile in their *consulta* recommended stealing as a remedy for desperate poverty. Nonetheless, their
opinions share ground with that of Acosta who thought that the Indian
miners of Potosí ought to get rich, even if it were at the cost of stealing a
little ore from Spanish mining entrepreneurs. The positive view that Acosta
took of the desire to get rich was in itself a novelty of sorts, and went hand
in hand with the idea, expressed in Peru by some of Acosta's contempo-
raries, that it might be possible to inculcate in Andean people a desire to
become rich, and to develop their sense of well-being and acquisitiveness,
codicia.[81] Such an evolution would be a corrective to the Indians' proverbial
and often criticized submissiveness and timidity. Yet, *codicia* was not normally viewed as a laudable quality. Rather, in catechisms and manuals for
confession of the period, it was featured regularly as a sin to be repented
of and corrected.[82]

However, the extremes of human suffering and of appalling human
conduct that were the order of the day in sixteenth-century Peru played
havoc among long established European ways of confronting poverty,
homelessness, vagrancy, and the host of ills that accompanied them. Traditional procedures of providing help paled into insignificance in the face
of the poverty and desperation of Don Diego Ylaquita who walked from
Cuzco to Lima with Domingo de Santo Tomás in 1557, and of countless
other Andean people whose lives were engulfed in the whirlwind of invasion and conquest, not to mention the many who died. During subsequent decades, the economic and political forces that produced inhuman
working conditions in Potosí and also in the *obrajes* that Spaniards organized throughout the Andes defied comprehension and analysis. The Indians were accused of lacking charity; but then, as Domingo de Santo Tomás,
Acosta, and many others were only too aware, traditional Christian almsgiving did not and could not begin to address the suffering that had come
about. Remedies that might have worked in Europe merely looked paltry
in the Andes. In the interstices of these dilemmas, a handful of notions
raised their heads that undermined the entire system of values and precepts that was being deployed to keep the Andean situation under control.
Perhaps the most surprising of these notions is Acosta's suggestion that
miserables might steal a little and get rich.

At any rate, the reality that the system of values that the Spanish had willy-nilly imposed on Andean people was imploding itself did not escape the notice of one of the most incisive and indeed brilliant social critics of his time. This is the Andean historian Felipe Guaman Poma de Ayala. Guaman Poma devoted one section of his long illustrated work to a portrayal of the activities of men of the church in Peru, where the failure of these Spaniards to live by their own precepts is a recurring theme. A subsection is about almsgiving. Except for a Franciscan friar who is depicted giving a small loaf to a young Andean man, the other givers of Christian alms are Andean people helping Spaniards.[83] In his description of the activities of the age groups of people as organized by the Incas, and still operative to a certain extent in his own time, Guaman Poma shows how it happened that for the most part, Indians needed no alms, because they had among themselves no *gente valdía*, idle or superfluous people. This was not a matter of finding work for displaced persons in the way that Vives and Soto had described, and Spanish legislation mandated. Rather, it was a matter of not having any displaced persons in the first place, because roles were distributed within Andean communities in such a way that everyone could be useful. The old supervised young children. Little boys when older watched llamas and caught birds. Little girls picked flowers and helped their mothers. Members of the community worked the fields of mothers with very young children, because "it is very just that the mother should be exempt from work to raise the child." "For all that they were barbarians and gentiles," Guaman Poma added in an ironic aside to his Spanish readers, "the Inca kings ordered that this law of the Indians of old be observed."[84] Even the sick, the blind, and the lame had something to offer:

> They provided entertainment, talking and telling jokes, for example dwarves and hunchbacks. . . . Among those who were able to work and assist, those who had eyes helped by looking, those who had feet walked, those who had hands wove and worked at looking after stores and as keepers of records and stewards. . . . Those Indians, men and women, followed a very fine order of serving God and of multiplying, of filling the land with people, for the greatness, increase, and service of the majesty of the Inca, and of the princes, dukes, counts, and marquesses of this realm.[85]

That Guaman Poma was not inventing this social system merely to criticize the Spanish is clear from plentiful colonial documentation that shows the system still functioning: as for example when the *mittayoc* of Potosí whom Polo de Ondegardo interviewed stated that their fields were being tilled, ready for their return, by those who had stayed at home. Nonetheless, Guaman Poma did address concerns of his time. People had multiplied in the time of the Inca, just what was not happening in Spanish times. Also, Guaman Poma understood better than anyone else how Andean and Spanish social conscience and social practice intersected. For example, according to the constant refrain, Indians had no charity. As though it were to prove that this was not simply an empty prejudice, Spanish officials on occasion observed that the Indians hated hospitals and did what was in their power to avoid paying for them.[86] What Guaman Poma explained was that in effect it was perfectly true that the Indians had no "charity," the reason being that in a society ordered by Andean traditions, there was no need for it. Regarding the sick, the blind, the lame, the mute, dwarves, and hunchbacks:

> They had their fields, houses, and property, and support in return for their contribution, and so there was no need for a hospital or for alms, with this holy social and public order of the realm, which was unlike that of any other kingdom whether of Christians or of unbelievers.[87]

The realization, which pervades Guaman Poma's work, that Spaniards, so far from teaching Indians Christian charity, came to the Andes requiring support, lives on today. There is a profound truth in the perception by contemporary Indians that creoles and *mestizos* need food from them, food that they are unable to grow themselves in the harsh Andean climate, and for which they have nothing to offer that is of equivalent value.[88]

We began with vagrants and the poor in Castile during the second quarter of the sixteenth century. They lived in a society that felt confident that it could find room for the less fortunate and to a certain extent did so. In Peru, during these and subsequent decades, homeless Indians who were displaced during the Spanish invasion and the civil wars that followed, along with vagrants from the Peninsula, men who expected to survive by virtue of being Spanish in a conquered land, made for homelessness, poverty, and vagrancy on a scale unprecedented in Europe. The Peruvian civil wars were not yet quite over when the mines of Potosí were discovered, and added to the existing crowd of displaced people thousands of migrant workers who were expected, and in due course forced, to commute over long distances between their home villages and Potosí. Elsewhere in Peru also, forced labor away from home uprooted Indians from their villages and created a new sector in the population: *forasteros*, foreigners, people who settled away from their homes in order to be exempt from *mita* work and other exactions of the Spanish. In Peru, the recourses of Spanish societal providence and of Christian charity, much reduced as these were when exercised on behalf of the conquered, were unequal to assisting all those who in the Peninsula would have received, here and there, help of some kind.

In the face of this Andean crisis, two things happened. Andean communities, drawing on institutional structures rooted in their own past, took care of their people in ways that were not particularly discernible to the Spanish, who accused Indians of lacking "charity." Simultaneously, the Spanish concept of the role of Christian charity in society was changing. Self-help, long appreciated as useful in remedying poverty and vagrancy, became more important: here, the old doctrine that stealing to improve one's desperate lot was not a mortal sin acquired a very new significance. Meanwhile the afflictions that most visibly beset Peru in the 1580s, overtaxation, and the resulting flight of country folk from their homes, were at this very time also observed in Castile and occasioned urgent comment:[89] in effect, the reports that Peruvian viceroys were sending to the Crown described conditions in the Peninsula as much as they described those in the Andes.

In this context, another ancient doctrine, that the wealth of the king's subjects was tantamount to the king's own wealth, resurfaced. For all that these ideas were old, they described situations that were quite new, which was why the ideas themselves now acquired an entirely different import. Theorists and legislators of the earlier sixteenth century envisioned that charity and self-help, locally orchestrated under the distant auspices of the state, would provide assistance so as to maintain the established order of society. Such suggestions were still made at century's end and beyond, but the envisioned outcome had shifted from maintaining order to augmenting and preserving the king's wealth and that of his subjects.[90] Along with thinking about wealth, whether it was that of the king, or that of his subjects, in terms that were in effect new, economists and political theorists were conceptualizing the persons of the king's subjects differently than had been the case earlier, because the society being described had changed. During the earlier sixteenth century, vagabonds and the poor were felt to be a problem, more often than not, because they were idle and superfluous, *holganzanes y gente valdía*. Such people were still mentioned in the early seventeenth century, but in a new context. The primary difficulty in Spain and Peru now was, not so much that there were superfluous people, but that there were not enough people to go around.[91] Concurrently, when

Juan Luis Vives, Domingo de Soto, and the author of the *Lazarillo* were writing, Spain was an expanding empire. Some eighty years later, at the time of the *consulta* of 1619, expansion had given way to preservation as the primary aim of diplomacy and military strategy. In such a world, historical demography made its first infant steps. In a work advocating the advantages of honest work and inveighing against the dangers of idleness—for had not the Roman poet Catullus said, "idleness has destroyed kings / and flourishing cities" (Otium reges prius et beatas / Perdidit urbes)[92]—the Jesuit Pedro de Guzman in the footsteps of Giovanni Botero compared the population of Spain to that of France, Germany, and Italy. The figures were sobering: France, with less territory than Spain, had 14,000,000 people, Germany and Italy had 10,000,000 each, and Spain had only 4,000,000, while at the same time maintaining an empire twenty times the size of that of Rome.[93] As Guaman Poma so rightly observed at this very time, in such a world, the principal contribution of Peru was not so much its silver, for all that it filled the king's coffers, but the growing number, and above all the well-being, of its people.[94]

Notes

I thank Javier Barrios, Osvaldo Pardo, and Geoffrey Parker for their comments on an earlier version of this essay. Javier Barrios also most generously gave me a copy of his transcription of the document cited in note 38.

1. Johannes Ludovicus Vives, *De subventione pauperum*, in his *Opera omnia*, ed. Gregorio Mayans (Majansius), vol. IV (Valencia, 1783), Book II, chapter 1, pp. 466–467.

2. Ibid., Book I, chapter 5, p. 435; Book II, chapter 1, p. 466.

3. Ibid., Book I, chapter 6, p. 437: "Quid intolerabilius superbo paupere?" Augustine, *Sermo XIV* (in *Sancti Aurelii Augustini sermones de Vetere Testamento*, ed. C. Lambot, *Corpus Christianorum*, vol. 41 [Turnholt, 1961]), 2: "Quis autem ferat et inopem et superbum?" See also *Sermo XXXVI*, 7: "Si enim vix toleratur dives superbus, pauperem superbum quis ferat?"

4. Vives, *De subventione*, Book I, chapter 2, p. 426: "inops factus homo: tota eius vita et salus in aliorum auxiliis sita est . . . ut aliis desit pecunia, aliis sanitas, vel ingenium, . . . ; aliis inopia haec instrumentum est magnarum virtutum . . . quisquis ergo aliena ope indiget pauper est, et ei misericordiae est opus quae Graece elemosina dicitur, non in sola percuniae erogatione sita, . . . sed in omni opere, quo humana indigentia sublevatur."

5. Ibid., Book I, chapter 2.

6. Ibid., Book II, chapter 2, p. 469: "Neque enim libertas est communibus magistratibus non subjici et parere, . . . nec aliquis potest eximere bona sua curae

et imperio civitatis nisi simul civitatem exeat" since he acquired his possessions "beneficio civitatis."

7. Ibid., Book II, chapters 3–4.

8. See also Gabriel de Toro, *Thesoro de misericordia divina y humana, docta y curiosamente compuesto por fray . . .* (Salamanca: Juan de Junta, 1548); C. Pérez de Herrera, *Amparo de pobres*, ed. M. Cavillac (Madrid, 1975).

9. *Ad maximum atque adeo clarissimum Hispaniarum principem. D. Philippum invictissimi Caesaris Caroli V. primogenitum Fratris Dominici Soto Segobiensis theologi ordinis praedicatorum Salmanticae professoris ac prioris conventus S. Stephani In causa pauperum deliberatio.* Colophon: Salmanticae In officina Ioannis Giuntae trigessima Ianuarii Anno domini 1545. Bound with this text is the Spanish translation by the author, *Al muy alto y muy poderoso señor el Principe de España don Philippe primo-genito . . . Deliberacion en la causa de los pobres del maestro fray Domingo de Soto cathe-dratico de theologia en Salamanca . . .* Colophon: Salamanca . . . A treynta de Henero . . . 1545 (Biblioteca Nacional, Madrid University 10380).

10. See Linda Martz, *Poverty and Welfare in Habsburg Spain. The Example of Toledo* (Cambridge, 1983); Maureen Flynn, *Sacred Charity. Confraternities and Social Welfare in Spain, 1400–1700* (Ithaca, N.Y., 1989) concentrates on Zamora.

11. *Recopilación de las leyes destos reynos hecha por mandado de . . . Don Felipe Segundo . . .* (Madrid, 1640), Book I, title 12, law 6: holganzanes and vagamundos must return home; law 7, beggars need a license. See also Linda Martz, *Poverty and Welfare*, chapter 1 on Vives and Spanish legislation. On vagabonds who are not being considered under the rubric of poverty, see *Recopilación* VIII.11.1–3, 6, 11; also VIII, title 24, where, frequently, corporal punishment for vagrancy and theft is being commuted into service in the galleys.

12. On *pobres vergonzantes*, see the often repeated law (first issued in 1525, repeated 1528, 1534, 1540, 1558) *Recopilación* I.12.18; see also law 26 (p. 56b). The conceptualization of this kind of poverty is ancient: it was already mentioned in the fourth century by Ambrose of Milan in his treatise *De officiis* II.15.69: "plurima autem genera liberalitatis sunt, non solum quotidiano sumptu egentibus, quo vitam sustinere suam possint, disponere et dispensare alimoniam; verum etiam his qui publice egere verecundantur, consulere ac subvenire" (in J. P. Migne, *Patrologia Latina*, vol. 16 [Paris, 1845], cols. 120–121). Discussion of the social and economic problems posited by the poor continued throughout the century and beyond, and, as circumstances worsened towards the end of the sixteenth century, with increasing urgency; see Miguel de Giginta, *Tratado de remedio de pobres* (edited with introduction by Félix Santolaria Sierra [Barcelona, 2000]). The work was first published in 1579, and recommends that the poor be gathered in poor houses, where their lives and work could be supervised. See further below, notes 89–93.

13. The beauty of this profession was that all that Lazarillo needed was a loud voice, which he had already: he therefore did not have to undergo any further training for his trade such as Vives suggested should be offered, see *De subventione pauperum*, Book II, chapter 3, pp. 472–473; see also Book I, chapter 6, p. 438.

14. *La vida de Lazarillo de Tormes, y de sus fortunas y adversidades*, ed. Alberto Blecua (Madrid, 1984), Tratado 7.

15. For other aspects of *Lazarillo* which I cannot explore here, see the admirable essay by Antonio Rey Hazas, "El 'caso' de Lázaro de Tormes, todo problemas," in *Carlos V y la quiebra del humanismo político en Europa (1530–1558)*, vol. 3, ed. Jesús Bravo Lozano and Félix Labrador Arroyo (Madrid, 2001), 277–300; see also Paula Jojima, "La pobreza en *El Lazarillo de Tormes* como metonimia de una crisis de valores," in the same volume, 311–339. See also George A. Shipley, "Lazarillo Was Not a Hard-working Clean-living Water Carrier," in *Hispanic Studies in Honour of Alan D. Deyermond. A North American Tribute*, ed. John S. Miletich (Madison, Wisc., 1986), 247–255. But the fact remains, Lazarillo did settle down.

16. J. N. Hillgarth, *Mirror of Spain* (Ann Arbor, 2000), 79, mentioning the impressions of Flemish nobles accompanying Charles V to Spain in 1517; see also pp. 87, 92, 268. See further José Antonio Maravall, *La literatura picaresca desde la historia social (Siglos XVI y XVII)* (Madrid, 1986), 21–85, discussing changing attitudes toward poverty, ranging from acceptance during the late Middle Ages, to criticism of the poor in the course of the sixteenth century, to concern with poverty as a profound social problem in the early seventeenth century.

17. For a now classic account of the system, see J. V. Murra, *The Economic Organization of the Inca State* (Greenwich, Conn., 1980), chapter 6. For *huaccha* see Diego González Holguin, *Vocabulario de la lenga general de todo el Peru llamada lengua Qquichua o del Inca* (Lima, 1608; 1989), 167–168.

18. Archivo General de Indias, Seville (hereafter AGI), Lima 313, letter by Domingo de Santo Tomás to Prince Philip dated Lima, 1 July 1550: the poor outnumber the rich, and "tan gran parte de Republica pobre," fol. 6r; "lobos hambrientos," fol. 2v.; "de la gente, ganados, pueblos, edificios, heredades y de todo lo demas . . . no ay al presente la mitad," fol. 1r. In 1539, Vicente de Valverde, then bishop of Cuzco, wrote to the same effect to Charles V: "Vine atravesando por mucha parte desta tierra, y ví tanta perdicion en ella, que habiéndola visto antes, no pude dexar de sentir gran pena, porque, ansi como por la nobleza de la gente natural della y la habilidad que para las cosas de nuestra santa Fee tiene, como por la riqueza y grosedad de la tierra se debe tener mucho cuidado della. Ansi viendo la perdicion, comueve á quien queria á gran compasion . . . certifico a V.M. qui si no me acordara del sitio desta ciudad [i.e., Cuzco] yo no la conosciera, á lo menos por los edificios y pueblos della, porque cuando el gobernador Don Francisco Pizarro entró aqui, y entré yo con él, estaba este valle tan hermoso en edificios y poblacion, que en torno tenia, que era cosa de admiracion vello" (in *Colección de documentos inéditos relativos al descubrimiento, conquista y colonización de las posesiones españolas en América y Oceanía*, vol. III [Madrid, 1865], 92–137 at pp. 95–95).

19. See *Fundación española del Cusco y Ordenanzas para su Gobierno*, ed. Horacio H. Urteaga and Carlos A. Romero (Lima, 1926), 36–45.

20. AGI, Lima 121, *A su magd. De juan griego de 16 de deziembre de 1567. A la C.R. mt. Del rrey Don Phelipe nro senor en su mano:* "Si ay mill hombres rricos ay quince mill pobres."

21. AGI, Patronato 188, Ramo 6, fol. 13: "el dho don Diego se vino con este testigo a esta ciudad para sustentarse con su compania y que diziendole este to no vayas que te moriras dixo que no queria sino venir y morir una vez dando bozes delante del sisorrey y no morir de hambre y de verguença tantas vezes viendo que

los yanaconas de los cristianos e negros de los españoles tienen las chacaras e casas . . . y asi al presente esta en esta cassa y convento del señor santo domingo esperando la venida del visorrey." The poverty of the sons of Atahuallpa was not merely a figure of speech, nor was it relative. See, for further testimony, "Informaciones Coloniales sobre libertad y tratamiento de los Indios," in *Revista del Archivo Histórico del Cusco*, vol. 2 (Cusco, Archivo histórico del Cusco, 1951), 225–244, "Informacion sobre la libertad de los indios hecha a peticion del Sr. Gregorio Lopez, del Conzejo de Indias, y visitador de la Casa de Contratacion de Sevilla sobre la libertad de los Indios fha en sevilla a 23 de junio (1543)," pp. 243–244 (p. 15 of the original document in AGI, Patronato 231 R.4): "Hijos de atabalipa . . . andan muriendo de ambre . . . uno de estos o dos an tomado los frayles de santo domingo para adminystrallos y otros muchos hijos de señoras y disen e se andan con mucha necesidad muriendo de ambre que no tienen casas ny tierras que se las an tomado todas y de gente comun de yndios anda gran cantidad necesitados e pobres demandando limosna con una cruz en la mano."

22. AGI, Patronato 188, Ramo 6, fols. 5, 12, answers to question 9.

23. AGI, Lima 313, letter of 1 July 1550, fol. 2r: "pues tambien por ellos derramo su sangre." "No hay remedio" is a refrain in Guaman Poma de Ayala, *Nueva Crónica y buen Gobierno*, ed. J. V. Murra, R. Adorno, and J. Urioste (Madrid, 1987) (hereafter Guaman Poma, *Crónica*), e.g., p. 873, on removing Indians from their villages to work elsewhere: "Ves aqui, cristiano, como no se an de ausentarse lo pobres yndios y salir de su rreduciones con tanta molestia de todo este rreyno. Y no ay rremedio." Domingo de Santo Tomás, letter of 1 July 1550, f.1r: "Acerca de la deshorden pasada dende que esta tierra en tan mal pie se descobrio y de la barbareria crueldades que en ella a avido y espanoles an usado asi en el descubrimiento della como en lo demas hasta muy poco a que a empecado a aver alguna sombra de horden no ay que hablar. Pues ya no tiene otro Remedio." Stephen Porter, *Destruction in the English Civil Wars* (Dover, N.H.: Alan Sutton, 1994) is a carefully documented study of its topic. Although warfare in the conquest of Peru was of a different nature from that during the English Civil Wars (in particular, there was much less siege warfare in Peru than in England), the book nonetheless helps to get a picture of the destruction and displacement of people that warfare in Peru brought about. Several if not all of the letters of Domingo de Santo Tomás in AGI, Lima 313 and AGI, Charcas 135 were published in Emilio Lisson y Chaves, *La iglesia de España en el Perú* (Seville, 1943–1948), which I have not been able to consult.

24. Kathryn Burns, *Colonial Habits. Convents and the Spiritual Economy of Cuzco, Peru* (Durham, N.C., 1999), chapter 1, on Santa Clara in Cuzco; for "una sombra de hospital para los naturales" in Lima, see Domingo de Santo Tomás, letter of 1 July 1550, fol. 6v. For a casa de recogimiento for mestizas in Lima, founded by the marques de Cañete, see Robert Levillier, *Gobernantes del Perú. Cartas y Papeles*, vol. I (Madrid, 1921), 270–291: "Carta del Marques de Cañete . . . a S.M. . . . Los Reyes 15 Sept. 1556," at p. 287; see also p. 380, for the same institution in 1561, now used by Spanish women, much as Burns describes for Santa Clara in Cuzco.

25. Diego González Holguin, *Vocabulario de la lengua general de todo el Peru llamada lengua Qquichua o del Inca* (Lima, 1608; 1989), 243. The recent and important work by Ignacio González Casasnovas, *Las dudas de la corona. La política de*

repartimientos para la minería de Potosí (1680–1732) (Madrid, 2000), in its introductory first part (pp. 3–86) describes the period here surveyed in terms of the establishment of a mercantile economy in Upper Peru, shedding much light on political and economic processes that are here only touched upon. One of the book's strengths lies in its analysis of the transformation of Andean social structures that was brought about by the *mita*.

26. AGI, Lima 313, letter of 1 July 1550, fols. 3v–4r. Cf. Jeffrey Cole, *The Potosí Mita 1573–1700. Compulsory Indian Labor in the Andes* (Stanford, 1985).

27. AGI, Lima 313, letter of 1 July 1550, fol. 3v: "se descubrio una boca de ynfierno por la qual entran cada ano . . . grand cantidad de gente que la cobdicia de los espanoles sacrifica a su dios y es unas minas de plata que llaman de potosi." This same letter by Fray Domingo has also attracted the attention of a noted theologian of liberation, see Enrique Dussel, *A History of the Church in Latin America. Colonialism to Liberation* (Grand Rapids, 1981), 169 at n. 138, where the same passage about the mouth of hell is quoted. Here and elsewhere, theologians of liberation have deliberately connected their own thought with that of some sixteenth-century men of the church (e.g., Dussel, pp. 51 ff.) in order to highlight the unique experience of Latin American Christians, and their unique contribution to theological understanding.

28. Legislation of this kind began with the 'New Laws,' promulgated in 1542, thanks to the efforts of Fray Domingo's fellow Dominican Bartolomé de las Casas. In Peru, the Laws provoked years of civil war, thanks to which only some of them remained in force, and were reiterated, among them the decrees prohibiting forced labor. See Isacio Pérez Fernández, *Bartolomé de las Casas en el Perú* (Cuzco: Centro de studios rurales andinos Bartolomé de las Casas, 1988), 133–138, 160–166, 227–230, 243–245.

29. AGI, Justicia 667, N.1 fols. 238–272: "Cumplimiento e diligencias que la Justicia de la villa de la plata hizo cerca de la libertad que los yndios queestan en las minas de potosi tienen de yrse a sus tierras sinque nadie selo impoda." Potosí año de 1550, at fol. 242: "que declarasen e dixesen su voluntad porque ni su amo ni otra persona alguna no los podia compeler a ello."

30. Chipana, cf. González Holguin, *Lexicon*, pp. 111–112.

31. AGI, Justicia 667, N.1, fol. 243: "quando vienen con la myta traen de sus tierras alguna comida con su ganado y quando tornan a su tierra llevan de este asyento mantas e coca e otras cossas y que sus madres y hermanos les hazen sus chacaras y sementeras en sus tierras y hallan su comida para quando buelben. y que los que son buenos yndios y trabajan bien llevan chipanas y braceletes de plata y plata a sus tierras con que compran lo que an menester."

32. AGI, Justicia 667, N.1 fol. 246: "que ellos son de un pueblo del collao que se llama guaqui por el qual han passado los exercitos de goncalo pizarro y de caravajal . . . y del capitan diego centeno muchas vezes y que les han robado el ganado y la ropa y todo lo que tenian y que en su tierra por ser fria no se coxe maiz y las papas se da mal porque se queman de las heladas algunos anos." This kind of response recurs throughout the document. See further on this inquiry, Peter Bakewell, *Miners of the Red Mountain. Indian Labor in Potosí, 1545–1650* (Albuquerque, 1984), 40–46.

33. See also Luis Capoche, *Relación general de la villa imperial de Potosí*, ed. Lewis Hanke in *Biblioteca de autores españoles* (hereafter *BAE*) 122 (Madrid, 1958), 159–160, about the *cedula real* of 1552, prohibiting forced labor. When the Viceroy Cañete tried to implement it, the Indians thought he was "hombre loco" for thinking they had a choice about working in Potosí. As regards the opinion of Polo de Ondegardo that the Indians worked at Potosí voluntarily and by choice, it is shared, for the colonial period, by C. Sempat Assadourian, Heraclio Bonilla, Antonio Mitre, and Tristan Platt, *Minería y espacio económico en los Andes siglos XVI–XX* (Lima, 1980), 43; the authors distinguish between the 'complex work' of professional miners whom they consider to have been voluntary workers, and the 'simple work' of the *mita* laborers. There is no easy way of reconciling this conflict between current research results of this kind and the very widespread opinion held by conscientious persons at the time, that the vast majority of workers in Potosí (and also Hunacavelica, see below) would have preferred to be otherwise employed (cf. below n. 70). For a collection of opinions of the colonial period about mining, see Nadia Carnero Albarran, *Minas e Indios del Perú, Siglos XVI–XVIII* (Lima: Seminario de Historia Rural Andina Centro de Investigaciones Historico-Tecnologicas San Marcos/Ingenieria, 1981).

34. For the mining of mercury at Hunacavelica, where also *mita* labor was used, see Guillermo Lohmann Villena, *Las minas de Huancavelica en los siglos XVI y XVII* (Lima, 1999, a reprint of the book's first edition Seville, 1948).

35. For statistics of yields, see Peter Bakewell, "Registered Silver Production in the Potosí District 1550–1735," *Jahrbuch für Geschichte von Staat, Wirtschaft und Gesellschaft Lateinamerikas* 12 (1975): 67–103; this article is the source of the much reproduced graph of silver production from 1550 to 1735. Cf. Josep Barnadas, *Charcas. 1535–1565* (La Paz, 1973), 353–377, with a table of yields from 1550–1600 facing p. 360 that gives a more detailed picture showing that the sources are not as clearcut as might be thought. See also David Brading and Harry Cross, "Colonial Silver Mining: Mexico and Peru," *Hispanic American Historical Review* 62 (1972): 545–579. On labor, see Cole, *The Potosi Mita;* regarding royal qualms of conscience about forced labor, Bakewell, *Miners,* 54 ff., and Cole, *Labor,* 19–20 and chapter 4 passim. For the later period, see also Luis Miguel Glave, *Trajinantes. Caminos indígenas en la sociedad colonial siglos XVI/XVII* (Lima, 1989), chapter 4, "El virreinato peruano y la llamada 'crisis general' del siglo XVII."

36. Capoche, *Relación general de la villa imperial de Potosí,* 115: "todas las mercaderías perderían el precio que tenían y cesaría el venir de las armadas e intereses de almojarifazgos, porque no habiendo plata en el reino no era posible comunicarse ni tener trato ni comercio en Castilla"; and p. 168: "el pobre del indio es una moneda con la cual se halla todo lo que es menester."

37. On the Andean miners leaving home amid rituals of mourning, see Thomas A. Abercrombie, *Pathways of Memory and Power. Ethnography and History among an Andean People* (Madison, Wisc., 1998), 233–234. Bartolomé Arzáns de Orsúa y Vela, *Historia de la Villa Imperial de Potosí,* ed. Lewis Hanke and Gunnar Mendoza (Providence, 1965) was more interested in describing festivals than the buildings, the foundation of which those festivals celebrated, but nonetheless gives some details; see book 3.3 for the Franciscan church; book 5.14 for that

of the Augustinians; book 5.20 for that of the Jesuits; also book 4.1 for Potosí's patron saints.

38. Biblioteca del Palacio de Santa Cruz, Universidad de Valladolid, Manuscrito 511: "Tocante a las cosas del Reyno del Pirú. Relación del estado y cosas del Pirú hecha por d. Luys de Quiñones Ossorio, Tesorero de Potosí, sacada de la larga esperiençia q. tiene de aquel Reyno y de la comunicaçion con personas muy graves y experimentadas dél, especialmente de una relaçion de los obispos del Cuzco, Quito y Popayan, y del Protector General del Pirú, y de los Padres de la Compañía de Jesús: Sus camas es el suelo duro y humedo, y quando tienen mucho regalo y comodidad es echandose sobre un poco de paja. Las casas son baxas, de manera q.muy de ordinario es menester entrar en ellas como a gatas, muy inclinado el cuerpo, y en pocas puede una persona estar en pie. Y siendo las casas tan pequeñas como baxas, en ellas tienen su camas y habitaçion, y fuego en q.adereçan de comer, y su ajuar q.lo ordinario es algunos cantaros y ollas viejas. Y jamas ençienden candela para alumbrarse, si no es algun enfermo estando muy malo."

39. On Potosí in the late sixteenth and first half of the seventeenth centuries, see Peter Bakewell, *Silver and Entrepreneurship in Seventeenth-Century Potosí. The Life and Times of Antonio López de Quiroga* (Albuquerque, 1988), 22 ff., 28–35.

40. Cf. Alonso Ramos Gavilán, *Historia del Santuario de Nuestra Señora de Copacabana* (Lima, 1621; ed. Ignacio Prado Pastor, Lima, 1988), Book II, ch. 32, pp. 373 f., about Potosí: "conocida . . . entre todas las naciones del mundo por aquel admirable cerro que a dado a la cudicia Española mucha mas plata que el tiene de tamano. . . . No dejaré de condenar toda mi vida la crueldad con que tratan a estos miserables Indios casi a una mano todos los ministros." Ramos Gavilán goes on to compare the labors of the Indians to the labors of Israel in Egypt. Like the Egyptians doubled the labors of the Israelites, so the Spanish double trials of Indians: "haziendoles trabajar de dia y de noche, doblandoles molestissimas tareas, que quando la cudicia haze oficio de obrero no hay peon tan alentado que no parezca lerdo."

41. For Spain, cf. above n. 10; on care for orphans in Cuzco, see Burns, *Colonial Habits*, 113–116; see also below n. 86. Recent research has greatly improved our understanding of what was at issue in the theological and cultural indoctrination of Andean people by the Church (see, for example, Kenneth Mills, *Idolatry and Its Enemies: Colonial Andean Religion and Extirpation, 1640–1750* [Princeton, 1997]), whereas ecclesiastical, and indeed secular, efforts to help the poor, the sick, and the outcast have been studied much less. Some material is presented and analyzed in the second volume of Jean-Pierre Tardieu, *L'église et les noirs au Pérou. XVIe et XVIIe siècles*, 2 vols. (Paris, 1993). I have not been able to consult Pedro Revoredo, *Fundaciones, capellanías y dotes. Breve historia de su origen, evolución y estado actual* (published by Sociedad de Beneficencia Pública de Lima, 1937).

42. Alonso Enríquez de Guzman, *Libro de la vida y costumbres de Don Alonso Enríquez de Guzman*, ed. Hayward Kenniston, *BAE* 126 (Madrid, 1960), p. 143b: "estos yndios son fiebles de fuerças y d'esfuerços de juyzio, y naturalmente en general emenguados de todo género y manera de maña."

43. Capoche, *Relación*, p. 158a: "ni viven con codicia de riquezas." See also Capoche, *Relación*, p. 158b, commenting on a mining accident that happened because the mineowner failed to maintain the mine shafts in good repair. But the

Indians who died had done nothing to object to the state of the mine: "por esto se puede inferir cuan humildes son los indios y simples, pues teniendo causa para no oir ni ver la mina, se quisieron ofrecer a la muerte antes que hacer falta a su amo."

44. For an early example of this opinion, see Levillier, *Gobernantes*, vol. I: "carta informacion a S.M. del conde de Nieva . . . y Comisarios del Peru, acerca de la conveniencia de perpetuar las encomiendas"; Lima, 4 May 1562, pp. 395–471, at pp. 439–440: "Ninguna cosa los yngas señores de ellos tuvieron mas delante de los ojos conociendo la condicion de los yndios que heran poco amigos de trabajar quedar orden como la dieron y proveyeron para que no toviesen ociosidad ni fuesen holganzanes y continuamente travajasen como se entienede que les compelian a traer 440 piedra a cuesta desde quito al cuzco . . . y de chile al cuzco."

45. Ibid., at p. 428, stating that the Incas created large populations in the Collao, because there the climate required that some community members produce harvests at lower altitudes.

46. Murra, *The Economic Organization of the Inca State*, which is the published version of his dissertation of 1955, remains fundamental; for state settlers and related categories of people, see chapter 8; María Rostworowski, "Dos manuscritos inéditos con datos sobre Manco II, tierras personales de los Incas y mitimaes," in her *Ensayos de historia andina. Elites, etnias, recursos* (Lima, 1993), 147–167.

47. This perception of a certain unchangeability in the character of different groups and nations operated also in Europe, and was ultimately derived from Ptolemy, who attributed differences between cultures and nations to climate, and hence, to diet. Among the earliest applications of this theory to the Americas is that by Bartolomé de las Casas, for whom the many positive features he perceived in Native Americans was in part the result of the climate of the New World, see his *Apologética Historia Sumaria*, ed. Edmundo O'Gorman, 2 vols. (Mexico City, 1967), Book II, chapters 33–39 (vol. 1, pp. 169–207). In accord with this widespread theory, Alonso Enríquez de Guzman explained the submissive character of Andeans by reference to their diet, see *Libro de la vida*, p. 143b: "les mengua las fuerças por falta de mantenimientos porque no comen sino leves viandas de calavaças y una manera de melones y vatatas y otras yervas cozidas con una manera d'espeçia que se llama ají, y esto con todas las cosas . . . alguna vez, aunque pocas, comen ovejas." On "reducing" Andean populations into villages, see Juan de Matienzo, *Gobierno del Perú*, ed. G. Lohmann Villena (Lima, 1967), part I, chapter 14, providing a basic plan for such villages, which was often implemented, including in Potosí: compare Matienzo's plan (p. 50) with the plan of Potosí in Bakewell, *Silver and Entrepreneurship*, 33.

48. *Recopilacion de leyes de los reynos de las Indias mandadas imprimir . . . por . . . Don Carlos II* (Madrid, 1681; Madrid, 1973): the title Vagabundos y gitanos includes the following measure of 1533, reissued in 1555, 1558, and 1569. VII.4.4: *inter alia*, Spaniards, mestizos, and Indians living as *vagabundos y holgazanes sin assiento, oficio ni otra buena ocupacion* should be settled in pueblos, away from Indians. The males should work at trades with masters, till the land, or, failing this, they should be exiled. Girls should learn *buenas costumbres*. See also VII.4.1 of 1568 and 1628; cf. VI.3.21–22: "hagan asiento con personas a quien sirvan, o aprendan oficios," if this will not work, "los destierren de la Provincia"; VII.4.2.1 of 1595, repeated under

Charles II, expelling Spaniards, mestizos, mulatos, and zambaigos from Indian villages; VII.4.3 of 1609, *Españoles ociosos* should work in fields, mines, and in *exercicios publicos*.

49. E.g., *Gobernantes*, vol. 1 (Madrid, 1921), 53–75, "Carta de Cristobal Vaca de Castro al Emperador . . . Cuzco," 27 Nov. 1542, at p. 69: "In the Collao, handan muchos espanoles hechos bagamundos y rancheando los yndios y tomandolos lo que tienen." See also ibid., letter by the Viceroy Conde de Nieva, 16 June 1561, with a list of individuals being sent back; see further p. 390, letter by Conde de Nieva of 30 April 1562, referring to the earlier one, where the viceroy explains his decision: he fears that footloose persons will cause yet another rebellion: "De aquella provincia [sc. La Plata] y del Cuzco se suelen levantar los nublados y por mucho recado que se ponga siempre ay coasas que desasosieguen que esta tierra es de manera que diez honbres que se junten en alguna parte ponen en cuidado y una de las principales cosas con que aqui se a de tener quenta es con sacar de la tierra a los vagabundos y desasosegados y ansi yo enbio agora algunos a españa presos y desterrados y escrivo a su Magestad suplicandole que en ninguna manera se de licencia para que buelvan a estas partes ninguno de los que yo enbio." See further p. 391, mentioning the example Pedro de Ursua, who was killed by his men, among them the notorious Lope de Aguirre, who went on to commit further outrages until they were killed. The viceroy comments: "si de esta manera pasasen todos, buena dicha seria."

50. Instrucciones a Don Martín Enríquez, 3 June 1580, in *Los virreyes españoles en Amarica durante el gobierno de la casa de Austria. Peru*, vol. 1, ed. Lewis Hanke, *BAE* 280 (Madrid, 1978), 166–167.

51. Ibid., *Estado en que el conde de Villardompardo encontró el gobierno del Perú*, 25 May 1586, p. 189.

52. Mateo Alemán, *Guzmán de Alfarache* (first edition, Madrid, 1599; ed. Benito Brancaforte, with introduction and notes, Madrid, 1996); for a recent discussion of the picaresque genre, citing the earlier literature, see Angel Estévez Molinero, "La poética picaresca, Cervantes y 'un postre agridulce como Granada,'" *Bulletin Hispanique* 98 (1996): 305–326. On picaresque, see also Maravall, *La literatura picaresca*.

53. Garci Diez de San Miguel, *Visita hecha a la provincia de Chucuito por Garci Diez de San Miguel en el año 1567*, ed. W. Espinoza Soriano and J. V. Murra (Lima, 1964), 25–26, about the tambo of Chucuito: "en el tambo que hay en este pueblo para los pasajeros que van de camino les dan yerba y leña y agua como se tiene de costumbre y paja para las camas en lo cual se ocupan ordinariamente veinte incios y que desto no se les paga nada." The testimony goes on to state that about thirty Spaniards reside in Chuchcuito who were occupied in "granjerías" selling goods for more than their proper price.

54. For a description of Indian housing in the *reino de Quito*, see Lope de Atienza, *Compendio Historial del Estado de los Indios del Perú*, published by J. Jijón y Caamaño, *La Religión del Imperio de los Incas*, Appendices vol. I (Quito, 1931), chapters 5–9. In chapter 16, Atienza comments on the Indians' *poca caridad*, cf. below. The houses Atienza describes correspond closely to those depicted in Gaspar Miguel de Berrio's painting of 1758, "Descripcion del zerro rico e ymperial villa de Potosi," in the Charcas Museum, Sucre.

55. *Doctrina christiana y catecismo para instrucción de los indios* (Lima, 1584; Madrid, 1985), *Sermon XXII, del IIII mandamiento*, 618–619 (of the modern pagination): "Que por este peccado y otros que teneys ha permitido Dios que andeys perseguidos y hechos esclavos como si fuessedes bestias, porque no quereys vivir como hombres sino como caballos y carneros del prado, sin orden ni limpieça en vuestras almoas ni en vuestros cuerpos."

56. Ibid., *Sermon XXVII, De la Charidad y limosna*, 689.

57. Ibid., 688 and 685, respectively.

58. Ibid., 685, 688.

59. Vives, *De subventione pauperum*, Book 1, chapter 6, p. 437.

60. Ibid., p. 436; chapter 7, p. 440: "pecunia . . . transit in instrumentum honoris, dignitatis, superbiae, iracundiae, fastus, ultionis, vitae, necis, imperii."

61. In the 1550s, Domingo de Santo Tomás had realized that the exercise of Christian charity by private individuals, who were in any case loath to be generous, could come nowhere near relieving Andean poverty. This was why, unlike Vives, and unlike social reformers in Spain, who all advocated solutions on a local and regional basis, Domingo de Santo Tomás thought the problem had to be tackled from the center and globally. He therfore urged Philip II, in vain as it turned out, to allow no further immigration into Peru from Spain, because most of these impecunious newcomers who were hoping to make their fortunes and roamed the land as "vagabonds and idlers," were a threat to public safety, and made existing problems worse (AGI, Justicia 313, letter of 1 July 1550, fol. 5r.). See also AGI, Charcas 135, letter from Domingo de Santo Tomás, now bishop of Charcas, to Philip II, dated 25 October 1564, listing Greeks, Italians, Corsicans, Frenchmen, Germans, and Portuguese, all of them "gente sin rey." In addition, Fray Domingo, like some other members of the ruling elite, felt that Spaniards who were already in Peru should be made to stay, rather than taking their wealth back to the Peninsula. Finally, Fray Domingo urged the king that the grants of *encomienda*, of land and Indian labor, that had been made to individuals by the conquerors and the Crown should revert to the Crown.

62. Vives, *De subventione pauperum*, Book 1, chapter 2.

63. J. V. Murra, "Aymara Lords and Their European Agents at Potosí," *Nova Americana* 1 (Torino 1978): 231–243.

64. AGI, Charcas 45, Probanza of Joan Ayavire Cusara.

65. AGI, Charcas 56, Probanza of Don Fernando Ayra de Ariutu.

66. Capoche, *Relación*, 150–158, gives an account of the course of the controversy. For "Cada uno mire lo que compra," a rendering of the old maxim, *caveat emptor*, see the opinion of Fr. Luis Lopez, O.S.A., in Capoche, *Relación*, 153a. Capoche also has transcripts of opinions that Toledo gathered in Lima. For a discussion, and documents bearing on this controversy that are not in Capoche, see Josep M. Barnadas, "Una polémica colonial: Potosí 1579–1584," *Jahrbuch für Geschichte von Staat, Wirtschaft und Gesellschaft Lateinamerikas* 10 (1973): 16–70.

67. Capoche, *Relación*, 155b: "son personas libres y vasallos de S.M. y en lo que se pudiese han de ser favorecidos, viviendo nosotros en su tierra y enriquecdernos de ella y de sus trabajos." Some years earlier, in 1576, Acosta had passed through

Hunacavelica, where he composed a similar opinion, insisting on the rights of Andean miners, see Lohmann Villena, *Las minas de Huancavelica*, 102–103 with n. 17.

68. The right of self-help to remedy great need is an ancient one. An authority Acosta might have read is Cicero, *De officiis*, ed. and tr. Walter Miller (Cambridge, Mass., 1975), II.25, entertaining the question whether in great need it is permissible to steal a cloak from a tyrant. The answer is yes, provided that it is in the interest of "human society." Acosta's reason for letting Indians steal is precisely that it is in the interest of society at large.

69. Capoche, *Relación*, 164–165: "cunato mas justicia tendran estos indios que trabajando no se pueden sustentar, por ser poco el jornal. Este tal, conforme ley natural, se podra satisfacer del que le tuviese en aquella opresión, porque no solo se ha de mantener y vestir, que a un esclavo debemos esto, sino enriquecerse y aprovecharse, como hacemos nosotros en su tierra." See Cicero, *De officiis (On Duties)*, tr. Miller, III.29 ff.

70. On this transformation of mining work from compulsory to partially voluntary work, see Cole, *The Potosí Mita*, chapter 2, and now the important analysis by Enrique Tandeter, *Coercition et marché. L'argent du Potosí dans l'Amérique coloniale* (Paris, 1997), chapters 2–3. This is the definitively revised version of Tandeter's *thèse;* earlier versions were published in Spanish and English. On qualms of conscience in high places about forced labor at Potosí, see also K. V. Fox, "Pedro Muñiz, Dean of Lima, and the Indian Labor Question (1603)," *The Hispanic American Historical Review* 42 (1962): 63–88.

71. Noble David Cook, *Born to Die: Disease and New World Conquest 1492–1650* (Cambridge, 1998).

72. R. Levillier, *Gobernantes del Perú. Cartas y papeles, siglo XVI*, vol. 14 (Madrid, 1926), letter of 10 April 1597, pp. 37–38: "Es asimismo yntolerable travajo y bejacion la que padecen los yndios en la lavor de las minas, labranzas, crianzas y tragines de este reino que crecen cada dia y ellos se van acavando porque carga todo sobre los miserables que los españoles no vienen aca a travajar sino a servirse dellos y de sus hazendillas, y van treinta cinquenta ciento y ducientas leguas mas y menos de sus pueblos a las minas de Potosi y de otras minas donode los tienen dos quatro seis meses y un año en que con la ausencia de su tierra travajo ynzufrible y malos tratamientos muchos se mueren, o se huyen y no buelven a sus reducciones dejando perdidas casas, tierras, muger y hijuelos."

73. Levillier, *Gobernantes*, vol. 14 (Madrid, 1926), letter of 2 May 1599, p. 171. "Por evadirse los yndios deste Reino de los travajos y vexaciones que padecen en sus pueblos se ausentan y huyen dellos y se esconden y ocultan en chacaras montes y quebradas de do ha rresultado la desolacion de sus rreduciones en tal manera que del cuzco para arriba . . . estan todas solas y desanparadas de que se ha seguido no haver den quien cobrar las tasas pertenecientes a su magestad . . . ni gente que acuda a las mitas de potosi."

74. See Ann M. Wightman, *Indigenous Migration and Social Change. The Forasteros of Cuzco, 1520–1720* (Durham, N.C., 1990); Karen Vieira Powers, *Andean Journeys. Migration, Ethnogenesis, and the State in Colonial Quito* (Albuquerque, 1995).

75. An early example of this argument comes from the long memorial written to the Crown by the Conde de Nieva about the perpetuity of *encomiendas*, dated

Lima, 4 May 1562, in Levillier, *Gobernantes*, vol. I, 395–471, at p. 408. The argument here is that the price that the *encomenderos* offered to pay to the Crown for granting perpetuity was more than the land could afford without sinking into poverty.

76. For the state bankruptcies of 1575 and 1596, see Geoffrey Parker, *The Grand Strategy of Philip II* (New Haven, Conn., 1998), 87–88, 279; see also C. J. de Carlos Morales, *El consejo de Hazienda de Castilla 1523–1602. Patronazgo y clientismo en el gobierno de las finanzas reales durante el siglo XVI* (Valladolid, 1996).

77. *Consulta* of 1 February 1619, reproduced in Pedro Fernández de Navarrete, *Conservación de monarquías y discursos políticos*, ed. Michael Gordon (Madrid, 1982), 10. Fernández de Navarrete's classic was first published in Madrid in 1624. See J. H. Elliott, *Imperial Spain 1469–1716* (New York, 1964), 278–291 on high taxation, under-development, and peasant flight in Castile; pp. 317 ff., for the *consulta*. Cf. below n. 89 for Sancho de Moncada.

78. *Consulta* of 1619, in Fernández de Navarrete, *Conservación*, 9: Philip II should act "en ejecución de lo que dejó escrito el Señor don Alfonso el Sabio un una ley de la Partida donde dice: Acucioso debe ser el Rey en guardar su tierra, de manera que se non yermen las villas, nin los otros lugares, nin se derriben los mujros, non las torres, nin las casas, por mala guarda: é el Rey que desta guisa amara é toviere honrada é guardada su tierra, será él e los que hi vivieren, honrados y ricos, é abondados, é tenidos por ella: é si de otra guisa lo ficiese, venirle hia lo contrario desto." The argument that the king should reduce favors to the nobility was reiterated more vigorously by Rodrigo Fuenmayor during the 1630s, see Pedro Luis Lorenzo Cadarso, *Un arbitrista del Barroco. Estudio histórico y diplomático del memorial de Rodrigo Fuenmayor* (Universidad de La Rioja, 1999).

79. See the Relacion del Perú (Palacio de Santa Cruz, Universidad de Valladolid), addressed to the duke of Lerma: "este socorro y la conservaçion de aquel Reyno depende de la conservaçion de los Yndios dél, (q.) estava en tan grande diminuçion q. si con brevedad no se remedia, sin duda se acavara todo, y quando se quiera poner el remedio, no se podra poner porq. los Yndios cada dia son menos y las cargas q. tienen mas."

80. *Le relationi universali di Giovanni Botero Benese, divise in quattro parti* (Venice, 1605), Part I, Book I, pp. 17–18, on Portugal (at the time subject to Spain), observing that the power of Spain and Portugal has diminished because of their loss of population in overseas enterprises and wars: "la Provintia rimane priva, non solamente di essi; ma de' figliolo, che ne sarebbono nati. In tal maniera, ch'ella è quasi simila a un banco, che sborsa denari assia, senza ricercar cosa alguna. Hanno i Portoghesi, & i Castigliani seguito una ragione di stato affatto contraria a quella onde procede la grandezza, & potenza Romana. Conciosia che i Romani veggono, che nissuna cosa è più necessaria all'imprese grandi, e d'importanza, che la moltitudine della gente, mettevavo ogni studio non solamente in propagare se setssi, & multiplicare il numero loro co'matrimonii, con le colonie, & con altri aiuti tali."

81. See, for example, the Real Cedula of 1601, sent to Viceroy Velasco, where, reviewing reports and opinions sent from Peru, the Crown states: "deseando yo acudir al rremedio dello para que los yndios bivan con entera libertad . . . segun y dela forma de los demas que tengo en essos y estos reynos y otros sin nota de

exclavitud ni de otra subjecion y serbidunbre mas de la que como naturales vasal-los deven, y que mirando por su conserbacion propagacion y auemnto de tal man-era se acuda a esto que mediante el travajo yndustria lavor y grangeria de los mesmos yndios se atienda a la perpetuydad y conserbacion desas probincias" pub-lished in Levillier, *Gobernantes*, vol. 14, p. 303.

82. On the sin of desire (*codicia*), see *Catechismus ad parochos ex decreto Concilii Tridentini editus* (Lyon, 1677, and many other editions), Part III, an explanation of the Ten Commandments; at pp. 401 ff., the ninth and tenth commandments, not desiring one's neighbor's wife and property, are discussed. The catechism stresses that desire, *concupiscentia*, can be positive. *Concupiscentia* is accordingly divided into desire of the spirit, such as love of God's word, and desire of the body, resulting in drunkenness, adultery, and the like. Another kind of desire of the body takes the form of wanting the possessions of others. Little if any room is left for any posi-tive and laudable desire for worldly comfort and success. The *Doctrina christiana* comprising the catechism of the Third Council of Lima (above n. 55), in discussing the tenth commandment (p. 225, modern pagination), makes the same distinction, but much more concisely, the issue being that the possibility of positive desire for things of this world is not contemplated. The departure from this kind of teach-ing that is implicit in the statements of Acosta, and also in those of numerous secular writers and officials of the Crown, is all the more notable, and marks a fun-damental shift in Spanish political thought.

83. Guaman Poma, *Nueva Crónica*, 629–634; 637–638.

84. Ibid., 211: "es muy justo que se rreserve su madre para la cria . . . con ser barbaro y gintil, los señores Yngas mandaron guardar esta ley de los antiguos yndios."

85. Ibid., 201: "Estos servian de pasatiempo, hablar y chocarrear, como son enanos, tinre, vayaca, cumo, corcobado. . . . Cada uno de los que podian travajar y ayudar, los que tenian ojos servian de mirar, los que tenian pies andavan, los que tenian manos texian y servian de despenseros y quip camayos mayordomos. . . . En estos yndios y yndias tenia una horden muy buena del servicio de Dios y multiplico de jente para hinchir la tierra de gente, para la grandesa, aumento y servicio de la magestad del Ynga y principes, duques, condes, marqueses deste rreyno." In the translation, I have omitted "vayaca" because in the context I do not see how to translate the term.

86. Garci Diez de San Miguel, *Visita*, 220: "Los dichos indios son tan enemi-gos de hospitales que todos decian que no lo querian." In the outcome, the visita (inspection) decreed that they were to pay for a hospital nonetheless. By law, a physician's salary was to be taken out of royal revenues. But even in urban districts, this often did not happen, hence much litigation, e.g., by the physician Marcos de Mesa of the hospital for the poor and Indians in Chuquisaca against the overseer of the royal revenue (*fiscal*) in 1601. See Archivo Historico Nacional, Sucre, Votos ACh(1)s/c, for 22 February and 22 March 1601. The disinclination of paying for hospitals manifested by Andean people is rendered all the more intelligible.

87. Guaman Poma, *Primer Crónica*, 201: "Y estos tenia sus sementeras, casas, eredades y ayuda de su servicio y anci no avia menester hospital ni limosna con

esta horden santa y pulicia deste rreyno como ningun rreyno de la cristiandad ni ynfieles no lo ha tenido."

88. Olivia Harris, "Ethnic Identity and Market Relations," in *Ethnicity, Markets, and Migration in the Andes: At the Crossroads of History and Anthropology,* ed. Brooke Larson and Olivia Harris with Enrique Tandeter (Durham, N.C., 1995), 351–390 at p. 369: "Seen from the outside, the persistence of Indian identity among peasants facilitates their exploitation by non-Indians. However, from their own perspective, there are other, far more positive, reasons for their continuing classification as Indians, which have to do with their relationship with the land. While non-Indians may despise peasant culture, Indian peasants in their turn despise outsiders, who 'do not know how to work,' and who live by begging from them—for this is often how they perceive the exactions of mestizos. They even feel sorry for these people who have little or no land, who are afraid of real work, and who depend on others to produce food for them."

89. Regarding population decline in Castile between 1591 and 1631, see James Casey, *Early Modern Spain. A Social History* (London, 1999), 21, 49, 51; Michael R. Weisser, *The Peasants of the Montes: The Roots of Rural Rebellion in Spain* (Chicago, 1976), documents the phenomenon for the Montes region of Toledo, see pp. 64 ff. and 106 ff. For a contemporary assessment of the causes, see Sancho de Moncada, *Restauración política de España* (Madrid, 1619; ed. Jean Vilar, Madrid, 1974), Discurso Segundo, titled "Población y aumento numeroso de la nación española."

90. Christoval Pérez de Herrera, *Discursos del amparo de los legitimos pobres, y reduccion De los fingidos: y de la fundacion y principio de los Albergues destos Reynos, y amparo de la milicia dellos* (Madrid: Luis Sanchez, 1598), see pp. 41–43, the letter of the author to Philip III: for the "aumento y conservacion de muchos bienes espirituales y temporales en estos reynos," everyone should be occupied in a trade, and should avoid idleness, the "madre y origen de muchos vicios y pecados."

91. Cf. *Noticia general para la estimacion de las artes, y de la manera en que Se conocen las liberales de las que son Mecanicas y serviles, con una exortacion a la honra de la virtud y del trabajo contra los ociosos, y otras particulares para las personas de todos estados. Por el L. Gaspar Gutierrez de los Rios, professor de ambos Derechos y Letras humanas, natural de la ciudad de Salamanca. Dirigido al don Francisco Gomez de Sandoval y Rojas, Duque de Lerma, &c.* (Madrid: Pedro Madrigal, 1600), comprising an exhortation against idleness and urging respect for every kind of useful occupation, however humble.

92. *Bienes de el honesto trabajo y daños dela ociosidad, en ocho discursos. Por el P. Pedro de Guzman, natural del Avila, Religioso de la Compañia de Iesus* (Madrid, en la emprenta real, 1614), Biblioteca Nacional, Madrid, R18723, Discurso II.3.

93. Guzman, *Bienes,* Discurso VIII. Compare the population figures offered by James Casey, *Early Modern Spain. A Social History* (London, 1999), 21.

94. To what extent the projects of change and reform here mentioned, although they were not implemented at the time, did in due course hasten actual change, both in Spain and the Americas, is another subject, see David Ringrose, *Spain, Europe and the "Spanish Miracle" 1700–1900* (Cambridge, 1996).

william ian miller

Home and Homelessness in the Middle of Nowhere

In Iceland one must have a home; it is an offense not to—in some circumstances, a capital offense. A sturdy beggar was liable for full outlawry, which meant he could be killed with impunity.[1] The laws are hard on vagrants. Fornication with a beggar woman was unactionable;[2] it was lawful to castrate a vagabond, and he had no claim if he were injured or killed during the operation.[3] One could take in beggars solely for the purpose of whipping them, nor was one to feed or shelter them at the Thing on pain of lesser outlawry.[4] Their booths at the Thing could be knocked down, and if they happened to have any property with them, it could be taken from them without liability.[5]

How much of a homelessness problem there was we don't know. But there is a kind of panicky desperation that suffuses the laws that could indicate a fairly large population of unattached people, or merely that unattached masterless people were uncanny sources of contagion, disgust, loathing, and fear, divorced from their numbers. Beggars figure in the sagas too. Beggar women serve as transmitters of gossip, beggars are shown to be untrustworthy and are abused now and then,[6] but no saga shows anyone outlawed for vagrancy, although of those outlawed for theft, a significant number were no doubt unattached to any household.[7]

The Icelandic legal regime, one might say, was obsessed with pinning every person down to an identifiable household. Everyone was obliged to attach him- or herself to a household for a year term during a two-week period in spring known as Travel Days or Moving Days and one was also responsible for finding a domicile for one's dependants during that period if one could not maintain them on one's own.[8] For most people home meant being in service in someone else's household. The law's requirement of having everyone formally fixed to a domicile was the first step needed to fix people into a grid of accountability. When most legal process required summoning the person against whom you had a claim, it meant you had to know where to find him, or where such summons could be uttered so that it was a legally valid summons. The head of household could find himself liable for the wrongs and misadventures of his household members; he was liable as well for their support for a period if they were too ill to work.[9]

In a society in which the main unit of economic activity coincided with the household, a domiciliary law was a labor law as well as a regulation underpinning a viable system of legal process and legal responsibility. The laws were greatly concerned with getting the maximum productivity out of the miserable volcanic soils in a short growing season. People who did not mow the grass and make hay, tenants who underproduced, were subject to prosecution for underexploiting their lands.[10]

The idea of home, of domicile at least, was lodged dead center in the Icelandic legal structure. Home was where lawsuits began—at the defendant's home, that is. Home of either plaintiff or defendant determined venue, in which court at what Thing the case was to be pleaded. And the end of a lawsuit for any serious claim that resulted in a conviction was deprivation of home, not just because you were to be killed as an outlaw, but also because your rights in your home were subject to confiscation by the man who got you outlawed. Outlawry also affected the rights of others, not outlawed, with regard to their own homes. If anyone took in an outlaw he too was punishable with lesser outlawry, which meant he had to leave home and Iceland for three years. Law-abiding citizens had the affirmative obligation to share with others in the district the responsibility of providing housing and maintenance to the outlaw's dependants.[11]

But home in the sense of legal domicile could hardly have been a place where the heart was, surely not for those in service, though for the wealthier families the law embodies some special protection for the chief residence, the *aðalból*, which may have had some special emotional cachet for those possessed of one.[12] We would have to know just what a servant's legitimate expectations were of being retained for the next year before we could undertake to attribute to him much of a *feeling* of attachment to his legal domicile.[13] The very name of Moving Days suggests relocation each year for a significant portion of the population. One of the more insistent impressions one gets from the sagas is that people moved around a lot, via service and, among the wealthier segments, via fosterage. If there were fond memories of childhood, those memories would likely include several places, each populated by different people, with only some of the places also housing one's parents and siblings.

Then, too, one must wonder whether people's attitudes towards home vary, strange as it may sound, with the durability of the house, the actual building that qualifies as home. In Iceland, much to the chagrin of the archaeologist, houses were built of sod; they took a lot of maintenance not to melt away. A house made of stone, or brick, as that wise pig of the nursery tale knew, allowed one to bond to the house simply because it endured. Does this mean the Icelanders focused their attachment less to an actual building than to a particular view from a place, or to particular more enduring artifacts within the sod house? Does a sense of home intensify with fixity of place? We might construct a continuum of a sense of home with one extreme requiring a permanent attachment to an enduring building, with certain fixed visual sight lines looking out on what we call views, moving by degrees all the way down to the hunter-gatherer, or slash and burn agriculturist, or the nomad's tents and hollows in the ground. The servant might have had expectations of home more in approximation with a hunter-gatherer than he did with the head of his household for the year.

Then again the Icelanders never let themselves forget that they were new to the land; Norway never ceased to be part of the story of what home meant. Indeed they even figured some of their direction terms with reference to Norway. Thus their terms for southwest/southeast and northwest/northeast assumed one was positioned on the coast of Norway with land to the east and sea to the west. When they left Norway for Iceland they said they were going out or away; when they went from Iceland to Norway they said they were going "from out" or going back. They never ceased to see themselves as at the periphery with the center located a long way east across the North Atlantic.

But nonetheless, roots started to penetrate the lava on which they dwelt as they came to understand themselves as special for their remoteness, a people living in the middle of nowhere, without a king, and who were better poets and storytellers than anyone else in the Germanic north (or for that matter in the romance south). Home included Norway in a vague way, much as first-generation immigrants to America might speak of the old country, but in a complex way, for Norway was what they had to define themselves against to come to think of themselves as Icelanders. (This is not unlike the experience of English and Spanish settlers in the New World who, however, had a local hostile population to contend with that aided them in their sense of separateness from the ancestral homeland by giving them a present danger against which to redefine themselves.) Norway was the home of their ancestors, a place that the most enterprising of them sought to visit, and a place where there was a king to grant favors and prestige, a symbolic capital that was transportable to Iceland. There is more than a suggestion in the sagas that there was a reverse migration to Norway. In any event, back to the ancestral lands to the east was where they expected people sent packing by virtue of lesser outlawry or some arbitrated imposition of exile would sail off to.

But I want to get at sentiments if I can and this is tricky for it will force us to deal with outlaws and exiles, those people, in other words, most likely to know what home is because they are conscious that they miss it and even worse, miss it because it was taken away from them. Home for those who can take it for granted needn't inspire all that much thought, talk, or self-consciousness. Take it away or threaten to take it away and people might of a sudden construct a theory of home out of their misery. Privileging outcasts has its own problems. They exaggerate and invent remembered joys, joys which they only came to understand were joys once they were missed. Did the Anglo-Saxon narrators known as the Wanderer and the Seafarer really have all that much fun in the ring-giving ceremonies as in their present lamentable state they believe they did? Very likely, it was the pitfalls hidden in those joys which probably earned them their exiles, for receiving rings from your lord is only pleasurable if you are getting more or better rings than the man on the bench next to you. Otherwise envy and vengefulness are your lot in the hall and that can lead to ale-assisted brawls and manslaughter of one's bench mates or angry thoughts directed toward one's lord.

That leads me to the dead and ghosts, for a brief detour. The dead are exiles too, outcasts of a sort and even outlaws. The Norse dead cared about the homes they once owned, and if they were just household members and not homeowners they still showed a great attachment to the personal property they left behind in the place they resided, or even to the place itself.[14] They want to remain where they lived with what they owned. No one cares more about place and property than the dead; that is why they, along with dragons, guard hoards and cairns. Given the very proprietary interests of Norse ghosts it should not be surprising to learn that Norse ghosts were not really ghosts at all. They were the living dead, characterized not by airy spirit but by the grossest matter and tons of it. Icelandic ghosts get heavy in death; they gain weight. Oxen flounder trying to drag them away. They seem to become the very earth itself merging with their sod home—their heaviness becoming paradoxically the way they make their spiritual claim to domicile—and claim a powerful deadhand control over the property they enjoyed in life.

These afterwalkers let us glimpse the dark side of the love of home and place. Take the case of Killer-Hrapp. He was very hard to deal with alive, aggressive towards his neighbors, acquisitive, bullying. On his deathbed he instructed his wife to bury him upright at the threshold of the living-room door, "so I can watch over my house even more carefully."[15] Not even his heirs thrive in the place after his death. His son goes mad and dies and when his widow's kin try to claim the property it seems Hrapp is responsible for capsizing their boat and drowning them all. And he was not laid to rest until he was dug up, still undecayed, and cremated. Now dispersed to the winds, Hrapp couldn't pull himself together to trouble anyone anymore, although his lands still seemed cursed by an uncanniness that Hrapp imparted to them.[16]

Hrapp's love of his home, his property, is exclusive, a jealous love. To love his home means to let no one else share it or claim an interest in it. It means begrudging one's heirs their fortune in his death, and it surely means excluding his enemies. Hrapp is an emblem of what property lawyers have come to call the right to exclude. We have come to think of home in dewy-eyed ways of a warm hearth with a stringed musical accompaniment, with images of friendly inclusiveness, but as is the case with most all our syrupy visions, they are bought at the price of those cast out or not invited in. For it to be *our* home means it absolutely cannot be everyone's home. The number of people included in these touching scenes is always limited and even then the scene often includes one or two we wished weren't part of the package. Hrapp's conception of home is an aggressive sense of his own right to exclude; he thus wishes to be ever present when those he includes come onto or into the property, as well as to be there should anyone come onto it uninvited. Hrapp's love of home reveals itself as a spitefulness and hostility to the pleasures he fears others might be having at his expense, much in the manner that some of us may be suspicious of the incentives that buying life insurance has for generating ambivalence in our loved ones at our final parting.

Living Icelanders worried about the attachment of the dead to their domiciles. When the vaguely werewolfian Skallagrim dies sitting upright, his son Egil is urgently called by very anxious household members to deal with the corpse. Egil takes no chances. He approaches the corpse indirectly, closes its eyes and nostrils, and then cuts a hole in the south wall, no great matter in a house made of sod, and takes his father some distance away to bury him on a headland.[17] No one was taking chances with Skallagrim by carrying him out across the threshold.

Elsewhere ghosts reluctant to leave their abode are summoned to a door court, the door, like the threshold, representing a magical boundary between inside and outside. The afterwalkers abide by the judgment of the court and leave.[18] Folklorists have detailed the many ways of laying ghosts, which mostly involve confusing the corpse's sense of direction or bodily organization. Thus heads are severed and placed at the anus, catching the dead in the bondage of eternal recurrence in a Moebius strip.[19] Others are cremated and tossed to the winds, some are buried at places of inherent ambiguity because unowned or unownable: crossroads, the shore between the high- and low-tide marks, divides between valleys. Do not, manifestly, do not bury an integral corpse at the threshold or carry it out that way if you think that might teach it the way back or be construed by it as an invitation to return, even if you bury it at a crossroads.

So I have with grim intent made home sweet home, the attachment to domicile, first a matter of law and second a matter of sentiment, the sentiments being love of place, property, and one's own, and grudgingness, spite, and malice with regard to anyone else who might enjoy the same at your expense, which, by definition, means begrudging your heirs more than your enemies. The love of place seems nearly incapable of existing without engendering as necessary by-products the darker passions of acquisition, possession, and desires to retain and control.

Let us return to the living. A man named Gunnar has been ordered to leave Iceland for three years pursuant to an arbitrated settlement. Gunnar had killed many people, none without cause; in fact he had an untraversable plea of self-defense for each of the men he killed, but it was judged that peace stood a better chance if he were forced to leave for a while. When it comes time to ride down to the ship, Gunnar says his farewells and announces that he does not expect to return ever again. But on his way to the ship his horse stumbles. Gunnar manages to jump off and land on his feet, but while floating in the air, described by the sagawriter cinematographically before that was technologically possible, as if in slow-motion, Gunnar looks back up towards the slopes of his farm: "the slopes are beautiful; never have they seemed to me as beautiful before, golden fields, new mown hay—I am riding back home; I am never leaving."[20] Plop, then he hits the ground.

Put aside the rare mention of natural beauty—it is not man's relation to nature that interests me here, but his relation to his property, his home, and how that comes to appear to him when ordered to leave it. Remember Gunnar has announced he is leaving home for good, not just three years. There is an aura of doom about him. It has been prophesied that if he kills twice within the same nuclear family and then breaks any settlement made consequent on that killing, he will himself be killed. Gunnar defies augury, but not without giving reasons for doing so. His reasons do not sound in legality: that the settlement was unjust, that he had an unanswerable defense, and that why should it be he that has to leave rather than the people who attacked him. When the settlement was announced the saga notes in a typically understated way that "Gunnar said he had no intention of breaking the settlement."[21] His reasons are that his reason is overborne by the attraction of his home and the beauty of his own.

Some would see that he also thinks of his beautiful and difficult wife now that he is leaving her; that her beauty helps color the beauty of the slopes. Indeed the word for slope figures frequently in poetic kennings for woman. But the passage says nothing about her and though she is happy when Gunnar returns, there is no indication that we are to read that happiness as anything more than another instance of her delight in violating norms of proper behavior.[22] To the extent that Hallgerd is part of the attraction it is because the new mown hay and the beauty of the property confer luster on her, not the other way around. It is the farm that is feminized, drawing Gunnar to it in a manner more wistful, more loving, more erotically styled, than the overly belligerent manner of Hrapp's attraction to his own property. But Gunnar, though substantially more lethal than Hrapp, is distinctly less uncanny in spite of being given to singing verses from his grave.

There is another connection between Hrapp's love of home and Gunnar's and it is intimately tied up with the pain of thinking others may delight at your expense. When Gunnar announces his intention to stay, his brother, who has been ordered abroad too, tries to convince him to honor the settlement. Settlement breaking is shameful, he says, something he could never bring himself to do and something he cannot believe that his honorable brother would ever consider: "Don't give your enemies the joy of breaking the settlement; no one would expect it of you." Old Icelandic has a single compound for the pleasure enemies feel at your expense—*óvinafagnaðr*—literally, "enemies' joy," which is nothing more than Schadenfreude seen through the eyes of its unfortunate object, rather than the perspective of the delighted subject. How did English ever manage without these words?

Like Hrapp, Gunnar's love of home cannot divorce itself from an emotional and moral economy in which giving pleasure to others or, more precisely, denying them pleasure, figures prominently in attachment to place. And though Gunnar's brother thinks that the Schadenfreude will all be the enemies', it is not quite clear that he hasn't stumbled upon an important component of Gunnar's motivation for staying. Hallgerd, his wife, senses it; hence her joy. Gunnar is back to rain mayhem on his enemies rather than letting them experience the satisfaction of his departure. His attachment to home means sticking it to his enemies. There is some textual support for this once the dead Gunnar speaks verses from his grave. The verse makes it clear (to the extent Norse verse makes anything clear) that he means to bring pain to his enemies. The allure of his fields and new mown hay was as martial a vision as it was bucolic; it was also a vision of mowing down men.

Avenging himself on his enemies makes home look like home sweet home to Gunnar. Thoughts of vengeance, however, do nothing to improve the allure of home for Gunnar's brother Kolskegg, who seems to have an equal share in the property. "No, I won't stay," says Kolskegg, "I shall not shamefully break faith with this settlement nor any other trust I have undertaken. This will be the only thing that will separate us. Tell my kinsmen and my mother that I don't intend to see Iceland again, because I will hear of your death, brother, and then nothing will ever draw me back." So strong is the norm against settlement breaking that even the pull of avenging a much beloved brother will not bring him back. It is more: by staying Gunnar pollutes home for Kolskegg, making it a place of shame. Home will be the place where he will either feel the desire to avenge his brother but be legally disabled from taking it because of his brother's shameful act (not that that need prevent him from taking revenge) or not feel the desire and feel shame for that.[23]

But Kolskegg, in this passage, is still arguing, trying to convince Gunnar to relent. He knows no other way to make his point stronger about the seriousness of Gunnar's violation than to announce he will give up home, Iceland, and kin, give up on avenging his brother because his brother will have forfeited the right to be avenged. The passage is really quite moving because of what claims Kolskegg feels he must abandon, but then a sidekick's claims are limited precisely by being a sidekick's claims. A sidekick is less complex, and even if complex he understands himself to be secondary so that his complexities must remain unexplored or deferred; he is to be a foil for Gunnar. He is there to show, by giving up his own home, how egregiously tragic Gunnar's choice not to leave home for three years is. Home then has a different hold on heroes and sidekicks, even honorable brotherly sidekicks. For sidekicks the fields are not as golden, the slopes not as lovely, even though Kolskegg's legal share in the property is no less than Gunnar's.

Gunnar stays to be declared an outlaw. That deprives him of his right to his home and to the benefit of hospitality in other people's homes. Home in any form is just what is not allowed him. Outlawry is in fact a death sentence, but death is at the end of the causal chain the punishment contemplates. First it is about banishment from *heim(r)* in all its senses. The Norse word for world and euphemisms for death partake of the symbolism of home, abode, place, and space. Home is the place of the living in general (*heim*, adverb, is home *heimr*, noun, the world). To be born is *koma í heiminn*. To die is to leave this home. To lie unconscious is to be between *Hel* and *heim*. Outlawry means to deprive one of *heim* in all its senses, literal and pregnant. Its main style is to deny home and hospitality, to deny culture, the warmth of human habitation. The outlaw is thus the lone-wolf, the woods-stalker, the person who, along with the uncanny creatures of the dead and monster world, belong *utangarðs*, outside the pale.

The division of space into the social and the wild, *innangarðs* and *utangarðs*, is marked conceptually by the fence, *garðr*, that surrounds the home field. (Others have treated this in detail so I will be very cursory.)[24] The dividing line between within and without, though fairly sharp, still allows for gray zones, a transition zone. There are ambiguous spaces at the marches between in and out, hither and yon. The court of confiscation for an outlaw, for instance, must be held, *utangarðs* within "arrow-shot's helgi" of the fence where there is "neither field nor meadow."[25] The space of an arrow shot is a kind of consecrated zone between here and there, in and out, to which the society's legal process still runs. More haunting is the notion of the dog's bark, specifically, of being beyond it.[26] Man piggybacks on animal sensory acumen in matters of hearing and smelling to bring some kind of light to the dark beyond. Not so that that beyond gets made safer, but so that one has more time to defend against assaults originating from the world beyond. If the arrowshot is the space from which outlaws are launched into the wild, the dog's bark is the space that defends against the wild's launches into socially colonized space.

Gunnar goes back to his home and is killed there within months. His life as an outlaw is short. But two of the best-known sagas tell the stories of two men who lived desperate lives as outlaws for years. One of these men, Grettir, has something of the uncanny about him. His strength is so prodigious that it pits him against afterwalkers, mound-dwellers, she-trolls, with all of whom he shares a certain kinship. (His literary and folk-loric kinship to another uncanny soul, Beowulf, has long been noted.) Grettir was never much at home in the social world; he is barely socialized, refuses to work, insults people without cause, itches for fights and con-frontation. His one socially valuable function is his ability to neutralize other uncanny sorts: he is very good at killing or putting to rest berserks, monsters, and the unquiet dead. He never was much attached to home, at least while his father was alive, though his mother coddled him, nor was he given to much reflection. But he is afraid of the dark and it is to the dark that he is expelled. The fear of the dark, more than the dark itself, is the emblem of all that which lies beyond the circle humans have managed to carve out from threatening chaos.

Gisli fits better among men. Except for a few homicides he is mostly a good citizen; he worked hard and was very good at building things, pri-marily homes. He built what was to become his sister's, his own, and his wife's once he was on the lam, in addition to several hiding places. Grettir, however, seems to break up houses or burn them up, often through no fault of his own, but either by accident or by the necessary consequence of fighting ghosts within them. If Grettir was meant to live amidst uncanny creatures, Gisli is very much of this world, though ill-fated, and bizarrely obsessed with his sister's sexuality. But once outlawed, Gisli comes to have a strange relation with the dark too. He suffers in his sleep. He is tor-mented by dream women who prophesy his ending. So what do outlaws' dreams and fears of the dark have to do with home? This will take me on what appears to be a frolic and a detour but which will strive to connect the idea of deprivation of home with self-awareness, psychological sophis-tication, and the rise of self-consciousness, not as in Lacan or Freud, but as seen through thirteenth-century Icelandic eyes.

It is via outlawry, the perfected condition of homelessness, of being allowed neither quarter nor sustenance, with all convivial company denied, that produces one's awareness as a purely individuated person. Psychologi-cal depth seems to come with enforced sociological shallowness. It is psy-chological inner spaces that now fill the void occasioned by the deprivation of the social *innangarðs*. Exile to *utangarðs* creates psychological *innangarðs*. And those inner spaces are terrifying, not like the warm insides of the farmhouse, which in *Gísla saga*, however, reveal them to be roiling with illicit erotic and murderous desires. The dark that Grettir fears is the dark-ness of his own consciousness of himself as utterly unattached and forcibly excluded. And though Gisli was quite a dreamer of ill dreams before he was outlawed, those dreams prophesied doom for others; once outlawed, his dreams become self-referential. The outlaw is condemned to a kind of complete freedom by being denied the freedom of making any bonds at all. He is his own man banished into an awareness of himself as a pure and perfectly detached individual. No wonder the outlaws of the sagas become heroes; they are even lonelier than the most elevated hero who still plays his role within the bounds of society. The bums and tramps begging from farm to farm are just bums and tramps, but outlaws are, if not the Marcel Prousts and Underground Men of the glacial outback, at least the Hamlets and Miltonic Satans.

People always suspected that the risk of too much home was a kind of childish idiocy. In Old Norse the word for foolish is *heimskr*. There are proverbs to that effect: *heimskt er heimalit barn:* the home-bred child is an idiot. The proverb backs wholeheartedly the institution of fosterage, as well as travel, especially in the form of Viking raiding. In getting away from home lies the prospect of the wisdom that comes from seeing the world, the word for wisdom being, uncannily, *heimr* (world, home), so that a philosopher is *heimspekingr*, wise in the ways of the world or if we give *heim* its sense of foolish maybe the philosopher is just a foolish wise guy, as he is still contemptibly seen to this day: an educated fool. The wisdom that outlawry thrusts on Grettir and Gisli is not of the world as home—that world is lost to them; they know nothing of it except that they miss it. In its place they come to understand the notion of *missing*; they delve their inner spaces; fight with inner demons, desires and longing. I suppose some will be inclined to make this a matter of loss and lack in its Lacanian sense. But I find that a tediously dull way to gloss over the differences between then and now, even though Gisli, if not Grettir, can tempt one to go that way, what with Gisli's barely unconscious desire to kill anyone who sleeps with his sister, including her husband.

Gisli and Grettir experience their outlawry differently in a way that parallels their relations with others during their civil life. Gisli is very attached to his wife and she to him. Gisli builds her a house on a bleak unpopulated fjord, the kind of place, had it been further inland, that Grettir haunted. They do not have children, but they have a foster daughter both are attached to. In his last years Gisli spends much time in caves near his loved ones, but the little sociality he is granted by the loyalty and dedication of the two women who sustain him is funded proportionally by their own loss of social contact. None of them have a proper home so that Gisli might have some kind of home on the lam.

Grettir passes much time with otherworldy beings, occasionally helping people on the civil side by ridding them of ghosts and also getting
helped on occasion by powerful men sympathetic to his plight. He has
sexual liaisons with women and begets, it is thought, at least one child, but
he never marries. He too dwells in caves, but spends his last year on an
island, a plateau with sheer cliffs that plunge into the sea. A more poignant
image of a home that is not one could not be found. But he is not alone
there. His younger brother joins him, as well as a tramp, the very image of
homelessness within the pale, contrasting with the outlaw's homelessness
beyond it. Grettir is kin to both, one by blood, the other by convergence
of their legal and economic conditions. But the bum is not given an inner
life because he had nothing to miss in the first place. He had no belong-
ings to no longer belong to, and so he merely whines and complains. He
feels creature discomforts but attributes no meaning to them. So repre-
hensible is he that he ends up sharing most of the blame for Grettir's capture, murder, and mutilation. There is no honor in merely being homeless.

It is always a feature of papers and talks devoted to a specific conference
or colloquium topic that one makes a little too much of the topic that provides the occasion for the occasion, seeing everything through the eyes of
home and homelessness and twisting things into its orbit that have no
business there. I may be engaged in a kind of conventional overreaching
when I seek to make too much of the domain occupied by the Norse word
heimr. Though I should be suspicious of linking home and homelessness
with conceptions of world, worldly wisdom, foolishness, outlawry, self-
consciousness, legal domiciles, lack, loss, and even sexuality, I will nonetheless continue in that vein. But I suspect I might have been able to find just
as many connections had the topic been cisterns or elbows. So with that
caveat admitted and ignored we have yet another concept to add to the mix
which will bring together again Gunnar's violation of a settlement, ideas
of outlawry, and the strictly legal notion of domicile as it is formally determined during Moving Days. The concept is *grið*. It means home, with the
particular sense of being the place in which one is lodged or in service in
accordance with the law. It has, in other words, a formalistic and legal ring
to it. Thus a servant is a *griðmaðr* (serving man) or *griðkona* (serving woman).
To leave service is to *fara ór griði*; to be homeless is to be *griðlauss*.[27] But
to my delight, because it affirms certain connections I have been making
up to now, *grið* also means, in the plural, truce or formal peace. It is thus
the word for quarter, asylum, sanctuary. It even comes to mean life itself,
as that which you gain when granted quarter. *Grið*, in all its senses, is

exactly what is denied to the outlaw. To be an outlaw is to be without peace or sanctuary; the outlaw is thus *griðalauss* (plural), literally without peace, and *griðlauss* (singular), without home. To be a truce-breaker is to be a *griðníðingr*, one of the worst things anyone can be called and it is what Kolskegg hints that Gunnar will be known as. Thus when Kolskegg says to Gunnar that he will not violate this settlement or any other trust he has undertaken, the word he uses that I have rendered as "shamefully break faith" is *níðask* sharing a root with *níðingr*, that is to be the lowest of the low, a betrayer of trust.

To be legally domiciled is to be accepted within the peace and hospitality of the household, not to be legally domiciled is to subject oneself to being outside the peace of all households for it is an actionable offense not to be in the peace of some household. Nothing seemed to horrify the Icelandic sensibility more than the idea of unattached people. People traveling alone were everywhere objects of suspicion. They were outlaws or people who were up to no good precisely because they were people who could kill or steal anonymously and thus evade the responsibility of making themselves available for reprisal. Solitary people were wolves, without regard to the slander implied against those most social of animals. If the predominant feeling for the homeless among us is disgust and occasional pity, the predominant one among them was fear and suspicion.

The stranger, however, probably had more grounds for being frightened by all those domiciled locals than they did of him. He could ask for a limited *grið*, a peace or sanctuary of specific ambit and duration. He, by this gesture, was asking to be treated as a guest rather than as an enemy, both concepts—guest and enemy—inhering in the notion of stranger and captured etymologically in the common Indo-European root of the words *guest* and *hostile* (compare Latin *hostis, hospes*). Such truces were on occasion formally pronounced and in their anathemas there is a theory of *heimr*, encompassing both its narrow sense as a domicile and its broader sense of habitable world, the human world. The person who violates the *grið* granted to the stranger is to be called a *griðníðingr* and he is himself to be estranged,

> exiled and banished from God and good men, from the heavenly kingdom and from all saints and never to be fit for the company of men and driven from everywhere as a wolf where Christians go to church, heathens sacrifice, where fire burns, the earth grows, the baby cries for its mother, the mother bears a son, where fires are kindled, ships sail, shields flash, the sun shines, the snow drifts, the Lapp skis, the fir tree

grows, where the falcon flies the springlong day and the good wind holds both wings aloft, where the heavens turn, the land is settled, and where the wind carries the water to the sea, where men sow seed . . .[28]

It goes on but the point is fairly clear. The truce-breaker is to be denied human home; he has passed over to the other side. Home in its widest sense is where sociable humans venture as part of their normal activities; it includes the domain of animals that do not inspire midnight horrors or that do not play leading roles in bad dreams. If home cannot accommodate the wolf or the bat, it welcomes the falcon gliding languorously in its lethal beauty. Thus too the lethal beauty of armament as in flashing shields. Snow is domesticated too as it must be in the northlands; though it is not quite clear whether it is snow that is made tame by the skis of those uncanny Lapps, or whether it is rather Lapps who are tamed and brought in from the other side by the fact that they ski, just as a normal human would.[29] The non-judgmental inclusion of heathens in the same homely world with Christians bespeaks a pre-Christian origin for the text. Christians were not as willing to be as inclusive in their definitions of what belonged on the human side of the line; Christians had a nasty habit of morphing non-Christians into wolves and vipers.

Home, as is implicit in the anathema, is a relative term and an oppositional one. To the Icelander in Norway, home is Iceland. To the Icelander in Byzantium home is the domain of the *dansk tunga*, the Scandinavian language. In Iceland home narrows its focus to various specific places, not necessarily, given the moral claims of fosterage and service, to a specific place. But then these places will be opposed to other farms that manifestly are not home, but are home to others whom abroad you would recognize as Icelanders from back home. When I am abroad home is the United States. But when asked to particularize which state I come from, I am faced with certain ambiguities in the notion of home. I have lived for almost twenty years in Michigan, but though tenured and happy I feel vaguely transient. I am not rooted there. I grew up in Wisconsin and my parents still live in the house I grew up in. That still feels as much like my home as the home in Michigan. Home seems ineffably, for us, tied to the richness of childhood. And so my sense of homeness of the Michigan residence is really the vicarious experience of my children's experience of feeling at home there. For them Ann Arbor is home and to their minds it must be mine also because it is their home, and indeed their view is controlling. Home is an emotional thing. Being held to have a home at place X because the government says that is your home, or, as in Iceland, because you are in formal *grið* there, does not mean that that is where the heart is, or all of the heart in any event, for in Iceland especially, what with all that moving around, you were also attached affectively to other homes where you spent time or were cast in other roles. The idea and sentiment of home is temporal as well as spatial.[30]

In immigrant communities or in newly settled frontier regions the idea of home, as noted earlier, is further confused. When the first settlers came out they no doubt felt themselves Norwegians; their new dwellings would be home as against other settlers, but still would not quite be home in other conceptual settings. A deep sense of home might require the time necessary for these Icelanders to think of themselves as Icelanders and not just as dislocated Norwegians. When does the sense of ethnicity emerge? It is clearly there in spades by the time the sagas are written, which can be seen en masse as the most glorious claim of a proud and separate identity as there can be. In the sagas we also have one of the clearest markers of ethnicity: the ethnic joke. To the Icelanders, Norwegians are drunkards; Swedes are pagans, berserks, and rapists. And in turn the Norwegians think of Icelanders as a bunch of suet eaters and country bumpkins. There is nothing better for marking off ethnicity within the bounds of a common linguistic community than differences in diet, so that one finds the other disgusting for eating and drinking disgusting things. Different foods, more than different landscapes, make difference felt, because the idea of eating the inedible fixes difference saliently in a suffusion of nausea. Different landscapes have no such effect.

But clearly, as Kirsten Hastrup[31] has argued about Icelandic identity, the Icelanders' sense of themselves as Icelanders, and the concomitant sense of Iceland as home, was already in place at least a hundred years earlier than the time of the writing of the sagas. We have a self-conscious manifesto of Icelandic identity describing the society's birth, baptism, and confirmation: Ari Thorgilsson's *Íslendingabók* appearing nearly contemporaneously with the penning of the Icelandic laws in 1117. I would claim one could find earlier signs. The Icelanders knew that they didn't quite fit. Who else had no king? And within Christendom who else had their tithes computed not as an income tax but as a net-worth tax? They paid a property tax of 1 percent rather than an income tax of 10 percent, proof, by the way, that the expected yield on an asset was 10 percent. They were a people apart, way out in the middle of nowhere, as if outlawed themselves.[32] (We can drop the "as if" in the Australian and Pitcairn Island story of identity formation.) In fact, the story the Icelanders liked to tell about the settlement was that many of the people who settled the land had been outlawed for resisting the claims of overlordship of Harald Finehair. The Icelanders, like Australians later, built a new society far beyond the sea, beyond the known extent of middle-earth, and came there to build homes and eventually to see the place as home, but first they may have seen it as an exile to the wastes.

The sense of home works in two directions: from the bottom up. First build your house so that it is your home as against other homes. These other homes are characterized by relations that establish their otherness; these are thus the homes against which you feud, but from which you take your spouses and with whom you exchange feasts. And then groups of households get together and form a legal community which defines itself as against those it extrudes—the outlaws, the homeless, those who are *óalanda, óferjanda, óráðanda*, that is, not to be given food, a lift, or counsel— and finally as against those on the outside who want to take you over, like the Norwegian king.[33] Extrusion is the dark side of the process of active group formation. And from the top down: as when you are told to get out and go elsewhere, and if that "you" comprises a big enough group your elsewhere will make of the fens and wastes to which you have been exiled, an Iceland, an Australia, or an America, my new found land.

Home is uncanny in German, the *heimlich* and the *unheimlich* con-verge.[34] There is something uncanny both about home and about those who have none. Let me close with this: When raiding abroad Vikings would kill the infants of those people they plundered, tossing them up and catching them on their spears. When at home one did not treat one's ene-mies so. Their children, at least until they reached the age of being an acceptable vengeance target, were spared, or if not it was considered an egregious violation of the norms of feud. Yet right at home one could kill one's own infants, just as if they were Slavs, because in fact they were treated as creatures from beyond until brought into the pale, into the law, into the house, by sprinkling with water. Home thus to the new infant in a world of infanticide can be for those first hours of life the most precari-ous of places to be, born into outlawry until actively let in.

Notes

1. The laws of early Iceland, dating from the twelfth and thirteenth centuries, are collectively known as *Grágás* and are conventionally cited to the edition of Vilhjalmur Finsen, *Grágás* Ia and Ib, *Konungsbók* (1852), and *Grágás* II, *Staðarshóls-*

bók (1879). *Konungsbók* has been excellently translated into English with relevant variant matter from *Staðarhólsbók* and other mss. by Andrew Dennis, Peter Foote, and Richard Perkins, *Laws of Early Iceland*, 2 vols. (Winnipeg: University of Manitoba Press, 1980, 2000). For the relevant provision on killing sturdy beggars see *Grágás* Ia 139–40. There seems to have been an intermediate class of person, who was not attached to a single household nor yet quite a vagrant, but allowed to travel among households as part of the poor relief system for handling the dependents of outlaws (Ia 113, 115). I cite sagas to their chapters, which are maintained across editions and translations.

    2. *Gr* Ib 48, II 178. He was excused from paying for the assault only if he acknowledged it; should he deny it and it be proved against him he had to pay compensation. In any event he was obliged to maintain the woman during confinement should she conceive and was obligated to support the child.

    3. *Gr* Ib 203, II 151.

    4. *Gr* Ib 179, II 258.

    5. *Gr* Ib 14, II 123.

    6. *Gísla saga* chs. 28–29 shows beggars very anxious as to how ill they might be treated if suspected of wrongdoing.

    7. We do see, however, poor people lodged in and transferred between district households; see, e.g., Olaf Hildisson in *Þorgils saga ok Hafliða* ch. 4.

    8. *Gr* Ia 129. Any male of sixteen years could arrange his own residence; likewise a single woman of twenty.

    9. *Gr* Ia 134. According to the laws the primary liability for servants belong to their kin, but as a general matter those people in service in a household often qualified as poor relations of the household head. I have discussed this all in detail elsewhere and mention it only to paint in a background for what is to follow; see my *Bloodtaking and Peacemaking* (Chicago: University of Chicago Press, 1990), chs. 4–5.

    10. A landowner was constrained to rent his farm if he would not farm it himself (*Gr* Ib 92, II 461–462, 466) and a tenant was liable for a three-mark fine if he left any meadow unmowed and lesser outlawry if he failed to take up the tenancy by the seventh week of summer (Ib 136, II 499).

    11. *Bloodtaking and Peacemaking* 238, *Gr* Ia 94; Ia 86–87, 114–115.

    12. *Aðalból* receives distinctly less special treatment than odal land received in Norway. In Iceland the *aðalból* receives some insulation from levying for debts, but not all that much; *Gr* Ib 78.

    13. See, however, the case of Atli in *Njáls saga* (chs. 36–38) who asks to stay on for another year even though he is fairly certain that if he does it will cost him his life; he is devoted to the household and most of its members to him.

    14. E.g., Thorgunna, *Eyrbyggja saga* chs. 51–52; Glám, *Grettis saga* chs. 32–35.

    15. *Laxdœla saga* ch. 17.

    16. Cremating doesn't always work. The ashes get ingested by grazing animals which then start to act like afterwalkers themselves; *Eyrbyggja saga* ch. 63.

    17. *Egils saga* ch. 58.

    18. *Eyrbyggja saga* ch. 55.

    19. *Grettis saga* chs. 18, 35.

    20. *Njáls saga* ch. 75.

21. Ibid., ch. 74.

22. Contrast Gunnar's mother who was not happy to see him return, knowing that he was breaking a settlement to do so and no doubt figuring that his enemies would now unite with the law behind them to kill him.

23. Njál, Gunnar's friend, orchestrates a revenge for Gunnar, knowing that it is illegal but that public opinion will still support some kind of violent reaction on behalf of a man as great as Gunnar as long as it doesn't step on important toes (ibid., ch. 78).

24. See among others Kirsten Hastrup, *Culture and History in Medieval Iceland* (Oxford: Clarendon Press, 1985), 140–151; John Lindow, *Murder and Vengeance among the Gods: Baldr in Scandinavian Mythology*, FF Communications, vol. 116, no. 262 (Helsinki: Suomalainen Tiedeakatemia, 1997), 16–18.

25. *Gr* Ia 84.

26. *Gísla saga* ch. 3.

27. See Lindow, *Murder and Vengence*, 131–132.

28. *Grettis saga* ch. 72.

29. Lapps figure everywhere in the sagas as sorcerers, magicians, shapechangers, a people not quite of this world.

30. The same problem of temporal identification causes trouble with pinning athletes to teams. Was Wayne Gretzky properly an Oiler, a King, a Blue, or a Ranger?

31. Kirsten Hastrup, "Establishing an Ethnicity: The Emergence of the 'Icelanders' in the Early Middle Ages," in *Semantic Anthropology*, ed. David Parkin, ASA Monographs 22 (London: Academic Press, 1982), 145–160.

32. I suspect the process of separation and ethnicization was aided by the practice of naming groups of people after the valley or peninsula or farm on which they dwelt. So there are thus the people of Myrar, the Thornessings, the Haukadalers, Vestfirðingar, and then within these areas new names arose based on smaller geographic units.

33. *Njáls saga* ch. 141. *Gr* II 359.

34. On the *heimlich* meaning itself and its opposite, see Freud's classic discussion "The 'Uncanny,'" *Standard Edition* 17:217–256.

nicholas howe

Looking for Home in Anglo-Saxon England

Nowhere in Old English poetry is home evoked more memorably than when it is most threatened, as here in Riddle 15 of the Exeter Book:

> Sorrow is certain for me
> if any fierce opponent discovers me
> hidden where I live in my house,
> a dwelling place with my children; if I wait there
> with my young offspring, when the stranger comes
> to my door, then death is certain from him.
> Therefore I must fly in terror out of my home
> with my issue, must flee the danger.
>
> (ll. 6b–13)[1]

This passage offers a clue so the audience can solve the riddle by identifying its mysterious speaker. The disturbing image of home not as a source of safety but as a place of danger is achieved deftly through the description of the fleeing parent and children. The Old English word translated as 'home' in the penultimate line of the quotation is *eþel*, a commonly used term that can denote a domestic abode (as here) as well as a communal sense of cultural or national homeland. A modern reader familiar with the history of Anglo-Saxon England might conjure up an ingenious solution to the riddle as describing the flight of the English before the onslaughts of Danish Vikings in the ninth century when they abandoned their homesteads. Nothing in the language of these lines precludes this kind of solution.

The remainder of Riddle 15 makes clear, however, that its solution must be a matter of natural rather than political history because it describes a burrowing animal, most likely a badger but perhaps a porcupine or hedgehog.[2] That this wonderfully evocative description of a threatened home should be spoken by an animal rather than a human being is not entirely surprising, for Old English poetry rarely registers the presence of the domestic in a direct manner. The surviving texts of Anglo-Saxon England pay little explicit attention to home as a physical structure, a building with walls and a roof, a setting of family life. The structure that appears repeatedly and centrally in the heroic poetry of the period is the royal hall, the site of public ceremony where lord and retainers—and even some women—gather to celebrate life and thereby hold off the darkness that lies around them.[3] But a hall in Old English poetry is not exactly a home, at least it is not so in the typical sense of being a place where men and women live day in and day out with their children and members of their extended family. As Anita R. Riedinger has argued in a valuable study, *Beowulf* and its halls have distracted modern readers: "Yet everywhere in the background of most Old English poetry—even in works that vividly depict war and warriors, whose cultural center *is* the hall—there lies, in often the most profound kinds of ways, the concept of 'home'."[4] More specifically, one may note that the retainers in *Beowulf* spend the night sleeping on mead-benches in the hall known as Heorot, but they do so because they belong to a select group of warriors. King Hrothgar, we are told, withdraws from his hall at night so that he can sleep with his queen, Wealhtheow, in quarters elsewhere. Nor does Beowulf spend a night in Heorot after he has killed the hall-intruder, Grendel.[5] The hall may have functioned as a sort of surrogate home for young, unmarried warriors who shared a homosocial bond, that is, it was the setting for a kind of Anglo-Saxon barracks life. Only when we understand the hall of Anglo-Saxon poetry in these terms can we see how little resemblance it bears to the other forms of home found in medieval and renaissance societies as surveyed in this volume.

When we compare Old English literary works with those from the closely related culture of medieval Iceland, the difference in matters of home is immediately evident. As William Ian Miller demonstrates elsewhere in this volume, Icelandic legal and literary texts are all about home and homelessness. They give us some idea of what Icelandic homes looked like, what they were made of, how a dead body should be removed from one, how they formed a farmstead with barns and fields, and why being without a fixed domicile was to be avoided. From the sagas, especially, we gain a sense of daily, domestic life in all of its aspects, even including the most noble way to die within one's own home when besiegers have broken all honorable rules of combat by setting fire to it. To distinguish the Anglo-Saxons further, one notes that the Icelanders did their most important ceremonial business not in horn-gabled halls like *Beowulf*'s Heorot but in the tented turf-booths and open air of the annual assembly or Thing.

That the Anglo-Saxon English built their domestic buildings in wood and other perishable materials means that nothing like an extant house survives from the period. The archaeological record for domestic structures, as will be considered later, is largely limited to postholes, foundation trenches, cellar pits, and other subsurface evidence. From these traces, various reconstructions of Anglo-Saxon dwellings are possible to the extent that archaeologists can use the evidence of a single site to imagine very different structures. The Anglo-Saxons were so accustomed to building in wood, rather than stone, that the usual verb in their language for 'to construct' or 'erect' is *getimbran/getimbrian*, literally, 'to timber'. This verb was used for all types of buildings, even those rare ones made from stone.[6] The impermanence of wood construction means that we cannot enter into the three-dimensional reality of an Anglo-Saxon house, as we still can with some in Venice or other cities of early modern Europe. Unless, that is, we visit a reconstructed dwelling at a site such as "Bede's World" at Jarrow in the north of England.[7] But such visits, while piquing one's curiosity, do not allow one to view buildings with at least some of their original fabric intact, as do examples one can still see in places like Venice or Toledo.

Of the cultures studied in this volume, England from 700 to 1100 C.E. is perhaps the least forthcoming in its evidence for home and homelessness. If the Anglo-Saxons did not build houses for the ages, they also did not put home (in the sense of literal dwellings) at the center of their legal culture as did the Icelanders. Numerous Anglo-Saxon law-codes survive from throughout the period but they do not often refer to home and homelessness in explicit ways, though some of their clauses cast oblique, if fascinating light on the subject. Thus, one can ask what it means for shaping a culture's definition of home that some of its law-codes specified penalties for strangers that wander off the beaten path: "If a man from a distance or a foreigner goes off the track, and he neither shouts nor blows a horn, he is assumed to be a thief, to be either killed or redeemed."[8] This clause, from a late seventh-century code of Wihtred, king of Kent, is not anomalous and, indeed, appears in virtually the same form in the contemporary laws of Ine, king of Wessex.[9] In a society without an organized police force to protect neighborhoods and houses against the designs of outsiders, it made a certain sense to have strangers announce their presence especially, one presumes, when they neared residents' houses. If this clause is not directly about home, it certainly is evidence that the Anglo-Saxons distinguished between their familiar neighbors and strangers from elsewhere. Home, for an Anglo-Saxon, was partially defined as the place where one knew everyone else or, conversely, where one was known and recognized by those who also lived there. It was where you were not an outsider.

That the extant architectural and legal sources offer little directly accessible evidence does not mean that home played no role in the imagination of the Anglo-Saxons. Some of their literary texts do tell us how the English envisioned their experience—both literally and figuratively—through images and terms for home. The degree to which sources of evidence about home and homelessness vary across cultures is a crucial aspect of the topic when viewed comparatively.[10] It teaches us that looking for home, especially in the absence of extant structures, requires flexibility in the use of sources, a willingness to work with the available materials rather than an insistence that only certain kinds of evidence are relevant. To put it simply, if there are no extant houses, then one must find other ways to ask how a culture spoke of its sense of home, its place in the world. For societies with strong traditions of didactic poetry, such as Anglo-Saxon England, texts provide a means to ascertain the ways in which home affected the cultural imagination. Sometimes, the most useful point of entry for such an inquiry is not a great imaginative work from the period, such as *Beowulf*, but a more utilitarian compilation of customary lore.

Consider, for example, a few lines from the so-called *Rune Poem*, a work of twenty-nine sections that follows the sequence of the traditional Scandinavian alphabet but that is written in Old English. In each section, the poet glosses the meaning of the runic character's name by articulating cultural commonplaces. Under the runic character ◊ written out in Old English as *eþel*, the poet offers a statement that is meant to articulate the desired order of things in the Anglo-Saxon world:

> *Eþel* is much beloved by every man,
> that he might enjoy there in his house
> all that is right and proper in continual prosperity.
> (ll. 71–73)[11]

If the Anglo-Saxons displayed embroidery samplers on their walls, this passage could have served as their version of "Home, Sweet Home." For our purposes, it is particularly suggestive because it seems so banal in its statement of how one is to live prosperously in a house (*on bolde*). And yet the passage has more to offer because the word that goes untranslated above—*eþel*—has a range of meanings that is relevant to the larger sense of home. It can designate not simply an animal's abode (as in the riddle about the badger) but also can denote such larger and more amorphous categories as 'native land', 'country', 'ancestral region'. The authoritative *Dictionary of Old English* offers these various senses for *eþel*: 'one's own country', 'one's true home', 'home', 'homeland', 'land of one's birth', '(hereditary) land', '(ancestral) domain'.[12] The most recent editor of *The Rune Poem* translates *eþel* in this passage as "the family land" to suggest home as a place of loyalty defined more by kinship relations than by political alliances.[13] *Eþel* is home, then, in ways that also speak to larger allegiances, however they might be determined. And, if one might hazard a guess in the instance of *The Rune Poem*, *eþel* draws on a variety of emotive connections: as the land that has been held by a family for generations, as the site that links one to the memory of ancestors, as the territory of an incipient nation known as *Englalond*. *The Rune Poem* uses *eþel* to designate home in the sense of "our home and native land," to quote the anthem, *O Canada!*

Yet the force of this passage, and it has force because it does register a necessary cultural conviction, derives from the way *eþel* is given a local habitation in the phrase *on bolde*, 'in a house'. The place of allegiance does not depend entirely on some abstraction, but draws as well here on the word *bold* that customarily designates an actual structure, such as a dwelling, home, or building of importance such as a palace, hall, or mansion.[14] *The Rune Poem* suggests that home and homelessness in Anglo-Saxon England are best understood both as conditions of experience and also as terms for interpreting that experience: they are to be taken in both the most literal and the most figurative senses. Home is the place that shelters one against the elements and vicissitudes of life; it is also the place that gives one a sense of larger identity.

The Anglo-Saxons had a remarkably wide lexicon for designating home in its various senses. As Riedinger observes, "There are at least fourteen synonyms for 'home' in Old English poetry: *eðel, eard, geard, ærn, bold, reced, cnosl, cyþþ, worðig, wic, eodor, hof, hus*, and *ham*." While these words had various connotations—some suggesting homeland, others a physical building or enclosure, and yet others associations with family—"all could and usually did, mean 'home'.".[15] Among these synonyms, the most immediately relevant for our purposes are *ham* and its numerous compounds. The Old English word *ham* is, self-evidently, the origin for Modern English 'home' and carries a similarly wide range of senses: home, house, abode, dwelling, residence, habitation, house with land, estate, property, district, region, neighborhood, place where rest, refuge, or satisfaction is found, and, finally, native country.[16] Given the propensity of the Anglo-Saxons to coin words by combining elements, there are also many compounds in which *ham* appears, most immediately numerous place names in which it is joined to a personal name, as in *Buccingaham* 'Buckingham'. A complete discussion of Old English compounds using *ham* would threaten to fill the remainder of this chapter but some selected examples will serve to demonstrate its possible range in the Anglo-Saxon lexicon, though it should be noted that some are quite rare: *hambringan* 'to bring a wife home, marry'; *hamcuþ*, lit. 'known at home' or 'familiar'; *hamcyme* 'coming home or return'; *hamfæst*, lit. 'fast at home' or 'dwelling at home'; *hamhæn* 'domestic fowl'; *hamland* 'enclosed pasture land'; *hamleas* 'homeless'; *hamsiþian* 'to return home'; *hamstede* 'homestead'; *hamweard* 'homeward'; *hamweorud* 'the group of people associated with a home'. That *ham* can be combined to form each of the semantically significant parts of speech (noun, verb, adjective, and adverb) may also be noted in passing as a measure of its lexical usefulness.

These compounds suggest that *ham* could be used to ground life in place, as in the adjectives *hamfæst*, evoking that sense of fixity or security that comes with being at home, or in *hamcuþ*, identifying the familiar with that which is known at home. Similarly, when used in compounds describing direction, *ham* provides a sense of home as being where one is rooted in place, as in the verb *hamsiþian* and the adverb *hamweard*. The latter example is especially resonant when it appears in a passage such as the following from the Anglo-Saxon *Chronicle* as it relates the journey in 855 of King Æthelwulf:

> And in that same year he journeyed to Rome with much pomp and lived there for twelve months. He took in marriage the daughter of King Charles of the Franks as he was traveling homeward [*hamweard*] and arrived home [*ham*] in good health.[17]

As even this brief, relatively formulaic passage from the *Chronicle* illustrates, home is the place by which one defines much of what can happen in life. Is it familiar like home? Is it safe like home? What is the relation of a given place to home in terms of direction? Am I heading away from it or toward it? In a culture of roadmaps and numbered streets, of global positioning systems in automobiles, finding home seems simply a matter of following instructions because there are defined coordinates that mark every site on the planet. But *hamweard* need not always be reduced to a mechanical trip plotted out on the roadmap.

Whether Old English poets designated home by *ham* or *eþel* or any of the other synonyms available to them, they saw it most evocatively as the final destination, the place to which life's journey would lead the true Christian after death. In many of the Old English lyric poems, the afterlife is represented as the heavenly home, the place of eternal domain that does not perish and decay as do the buildings made by humankind on earth. Perhaps the most explicit statement of the heavenly home comes toward the end of *The Dream of the Rood*, where the dreamer-narrator of the poem explains the meaning of Christ's earthly life:

> May the Lord be a friend to me,
> he who earlier suffered here on earth
> on the gallows-tree for the sins of men;
> he redeemed us, and gave us life,
> a heavenly home.
> (ll. 144b–48a)[18]

The redemption of human sin through the crucifixion of Christ on earth yields entry into heaven, the eternal home. The poem thus turns after this passage, appropriately, to Christ's harrowing of hell and ends with his triumphant return to the kingdom of God, *þær his eðel wæs* 'for that is his home' (l. 156b). In this phrase, *eþel* moves toward denoting some larger idea of a homeland or territory of the saved. If its meaning refers less to politics than to salvation, this *eþel* is also presented in the poem as being semantically parallel to, and theologically identical with, the kingdom of God, *on godes rice* (l. 152b), that is mentioned several lines earlier. Old English poets loved polysemous terms that could be used to describe both the earthly and the heavenly life—such as *ham, ric, eþel*—so that they could better align the two realms.[19] Yet more, this verbal technique carries with it a central belief of Christianity: that the conditions of life in the earthly home are but a shadowy version of the life that the saved will know in the heavenly home. To use the same set of words to designate both forms is to suggest the mysterious ways in which the earthly home is the necessary precondition to the heavenly and, as such, is incomplete by itself.

This summoning up of the heavenly home is, at its best in Old English poetry, preceded by passages of haunting beauty in which the transience of the earthly home is unflinchingly described and yet also eulogized. The Old English poets are far more drawn to these poignant catalogues of all that has gone from the earth than they are to descriptions of the heavenly home. They are far better at lamenting all that has gone than they are at describing the celestial paradise in images drawn from, say, the Book of Revelations. The heavenly home, in their poems, is all the more mysteriously alluring for never being described in precise terms; indeed, therein lies its beauty. The implicit contrast with all that was beautiful but now has been lost from earthly life is enough to manifest the glory of the heavenly home in poems like *The Seafarer*.

The concluding statement of *The Seafarer* may well seem formulaic, even banal in its exhortation that the audience should think of the final blessed home in the heavens:

> Let us think where we may have a home
> and then consider how we might arrive there,
> and also struggle so that we may be allowed
> to enter into that eternal blessedness
> where life is dependent on love of the Lord
> and joyful bliss in the heavens.
>
> (ll. 117–22a)[20]

In the original Old English, the poet uses alliteration to link the significant terms of *ham* 'home', *hyht* 'joyful bliss', and *heofon* 'heaven' so that together they form an envelope pattern to contain the passage as a whole. His technique here is essentially homiletic: he has reached the end of his poem and he means to emphasize its central, Christian truth. In his translation of *The Seafarer*, Ezra Pound cut this passage because he believed it was the interpolation of a later, Christian poet.[21] Pound was right to see this passage as clearly distinct from all that precedes it, though before rejecting it as spurious he might have considered why it was that the poet made no attempt to speak of the heavenly home in anything other than the most abstract and seemingly unpoetic terms.

Precise description of the heavenly home would have required a kind of invention on the poet's part and thus might have seemed to verge on blasphemy. Moreover, such invention would certainly have distracted readers from the final exhortation that they think of how they are to make their journey to heaven. The poet's genius for description is not at issue here, simply his decision to reserve it for telling of life on this earth. His lines earlier in the poem about the return of spring are among the most memorable in Old English:

> The groves take on blossoms, the cities grow fair,
> the meadows turn beautiful, the world comes alive;
> all then urges the restless one,
> the spirit on its journey, the one who thinks
> to depart far across the sea streams.
>
> (ll. 48–52)[22]

Put another way, within the figurative logic of the poem the journey to the heavenly home begins with the departure from the earthly home—precisely when it is at its most flourishing. Therein lies the measure of renunciation, whether one chooses to read the poem literally as the account of a wandering spirit eager to explore new places or allegorically as the path of the soul to its final home. Either way, home is what must be left behind, and the poet signals as much through his description of its vernal beauty

For the poet of *The Wanderer*, the earthly home figures as the place of ruin and desolation, the site of loss and regret. In these ways, it also serves as the impetus for the exile to seek his true home with God. The speaker of the poem, separated from his home—*eðle bidæled* (l. 20b)[23]—laments the transience of earthly life through a series of questions: "Where is the setting of banquets? Where are the joys of the hall?" (l. 93).[24] All that remains, he tells us, is a fragment of a building, a tragic synecdoche of the earthly home: "A wondrously high wall decorated with serpentine patterns / Stands now as a trace of the beloved company" (ll. 97–98).[25] All that exists on earth is transient, loaned by God, as the poet says in a series of exclamations using the Old English adjective *læne* 'loaned, temporary, transient' as a kind of mournful refrain. By contrast, the poem ends by asserting that all in Heaven stands fast and immutable, outside the workings of time (l. 115).

The linked tropes of the earthly home as temporary and the heavenly home as eternal run throughout much of the religious poetry in Old English for the simple reason that they express a basic tenet of the Christianity shared by poets and audience. For them, the true home is not where one makes it in some contingent or improvised fashion but rather where it is found in the life beyond. That this should be so may explain a certain measure of *contemptus mundi* among Old English poets, or at least it would seem to do so were they not so devoted to evoking the poignant beauty of all that fades from the earthly home. Modern readers of *The Seafarer* and *The Wanderer* are likely to feel sometimes that their poets were drawn more to that which must be renounced on earth than to that which will be enjoyed in heaven. This reading, one I have shared at times, seems in the end to be misplaced, for it denies the imaginative conclusion that the poets expected from their readers: that the evoked pleasures of a lost world are but a pale shadow of the inexpressible grandeur of the eternal home.

And yet as a twenty-first–century reader facing the matter of home in Anglo-Saxon England, one wants something more than the inexpressible. While that may have been sufficient for the devout soul, it does not easily satisfy the historical imagination. Looking through Old English poetry not for the master tropes of earthly home and heavenly home but rather for moments of the domestic can yield scattered but valuable insights. If they do not in any obvious way cohere to form a unified vision of home as it was lived day in and day out, that may well be all to the good, for these passages can thus retain a certain immediacy over the centuries. More to the point, one can read them by going around, as it were, the interpretive model of the earthly and heavenly home.

Perhaps the most widely quoted passage from Old English poetry on the subject of married or domestic love appears in another of those poems of traditional lore, the so-called *Maxims I.* The poet's technique for evoking the desired order of the world is to issue a series of normative statements mixed with an occasional vignette that seems almost to open into high drama:

> The ship must be fastened with nails, the shield bound,
> the light linden board; and the beloved Frisian must be
> welcomed by his woman when his boat stands in;
> his ship has come and her husband as well to home,
> her own provider, and she invites him in,
> washes his dirty garments and gives him fresh clothes,
> lies with him on land as his love urges.
>
> (ll. 93–99)[26]

For all that this passage speaks movingly of homecoming and the domestic life shared by a man and woman, it is not without interpretive difficulties. Most immediately, why does an English poet speak of a Frisian woman? Is she somehow to be imagined as the ideal of the welcoming wife just as Frisians were reputed to be venturesome sailors? Are they meant to balance each other as homebody and seafarer? Most intriguingly, why does *this* poet represent the marital home as part of the desired order of the world when so few others of his peers do so? How are we to understand the surprising nature of this passage within the larger context of Old English poetry? Why should a scene of tender homecoming—of care given and desire gratified—seem so unusual in this poetry?

Readers of the *Odyssey* might for a moment read this passage from *Maxims I* as if it were a brief version of Penelope welcoming Odysseus on his return to Ithaca. The comparison is valuable chiefly for indicating the differences between this Greek epic and all of Old English poetry, for the *Odyssey* is filled with scenes of home and homelessness, of returning and departing, of being welcomed as a castaway by a young maiden and her friends or of fleeing the unwelcome hospitality of a one-eyed giant. Just as the theme of *philoxenia*, the welcome owed to the stranger, makes us understand what home meant to the Greeks of the *Odyssey*, so the relative absence of sentiments about homelife and domesticity in Old English poetry make us want to read the episode of the Frisian woman as deeply revealing of its culture. It may be, however, that one places great interpretive weight on this passage simply because it is so rare. That is, these lines about the Frisian wife and her husband in the home seem so natural or expected that we are likely to feel we *should* find their like throughout the cultural record of Anglo-Saxon England. The sobering fact, however, is that the poetry of the Anglo-Saxons is far more likely to urge thoughts of journeying to the heavenly home than it is to celebrate the return to the earthly home.

Yet we know that the Anglo-Saxons had homes and could build them with great skill. In the catalogue poem conventionally known as *The Gifts of Men* we find a wide survey of the abilities and talents that God is said to have given to human beings. These range across intellectual, athletic, martial, political, and artistic endeavors. Together they form a kind of compilation or index of all those skills that were valued in Anglo-Saxon England. Among them, and it is unusual in being inventoried twice in this relatively short poem, is housebuilding: "One is an excellent builder at erecting a home" (ll. 75b–76a).[27] What it might mean to excel at raising a *ham* is glossed earlier in this same poem:

> One can artistically plan the construction
> of each lofty building; his hand is skillful,
> wise and controlled, as is right for a worker,
> in order to erect the dwelling; he knows how
> to join fast the wide building against sudden collapse.
>
> (ll. 44–48)[28]

The attention here to craft, to the planning of the dwelling, is noteworthy because it suggests the degree to which such work was valued in the culture. The last line reflects the practice of using wood for construction because making tight joints is essential to ensure the stability of buildings and protect them against collapse. The statements of the *Gifts* poet are intriguing in this regard because they dovetail neatly with the archaeological evidence.

The casual reader of the definitive three-volume *Anglo-Saxon Architecture* by H. M. Taylor and Joan Taylor could well be forgiven for concluding that the people of this period lived in the open air or, if lucky, in tents and caves, because this work offers no discussion of domestic architecture.[29] To the extent that they limit themselves to stone churches, the Taylors reflect a long practice in Anglo-Saxon architectural studies of concentrating on the buildings that still stand above ground—in whole, in pieces, or incorporated into later structures—for all to see. More recently, archaeologists of the period have begun to ask more questions relating to domestic structures such as houses, halls, and barns. Yet there remains a quietly apologetic air to some of the discussion about wood construction, as here in C. J. Arnold's 1997 *An Archaeology of the Early Anglo-Saxon Kingdoms*:

> Carpentry was also extensively used to build the houses, barns and byres which were more common and fundamental to everyday life. The skills required were no less than for the intricate metalworking and jewelling skills of the period, but the effort and raw materials were on an altogether different scale.[30]

Indeed, *The Gifts of Men* cites not only housebuilding, as noted earlier, but also setting gems in jewelry as being among the praiseworthy human talents. In that spirit of honoring expertise, we can briefly summarize some of the more relevant archaeological surveys as they relate to questions of home in Anglo-Saxon England.

The most immediate point to make about Anglo-Saxon domestic architecture is that it was not a purely native or insular tradition but rather was influenced by styles and practices brought from the continental homelands by the Angles, Saxons, and Jutes when they migrated to Britain in the fourth and fifth centuries C.E. Adaptations were certainly made to reflect local conditions but the line of continuity remained strong and offers us compelling evidence for the ongoing presence of Germanic culture in post-migration England. Introductions to Anglo-Saxon archaeology suggest that while there were differences across England there were also, generally speaking, two common forms of domestic buildings: halls and *Grubenhaüser*. The halls in question were certainly not all of royal scale and magnificence such as *Beowulf*'s Heorot, though the excavations at Yeavering in the north of England suggest that some at least were of considerable size and were set in quite elaborate royal compounds that could include numerous outbuildings as well as a grandstand-like structure.[31] Most halls in Anglo-Saxon England were more modest in scale and functioned within a working agricultural landscape that included barns and other outbuildings. *Grubenhaüser* have, as a term and as a structure, generated a good deal of controversy among archaeologists who are not at all agreed on whether they should be translated and reconstructed as 'pit houses', 'grub huts',[32] or 'sunken featured buildings'.[33] There is, moreover, considerable debate about whether they were used as dwellings at all or simply as workshops and storerooms.

For an example of an early Anglo-Saxon village, we may turn to the well-excavated site of West Stow in Suffolk, which dates from the fifth and sixth centuries and which contains both wooden halls and sunken featured buildings. The seven halls on the site vary in size from 16 feet by 32 feet to 23 feet by 46 feet, that is, from 512 square feet to 1,058 square feet, and all lack evidence of internal subdivisions or walls. The thirty-four sunken buildings at West Stow are much smaller, 8 feet by 10 feet.[34] Each hall stood separate from the others, though each was surrounded "by a small cluster of sunken featured buildings."[35] According to Martin Welch's interpretation of the site, "it seems likely that families lived, cooked, ate and slept in the seven halls" while "the sunken featured buildings provided for a similar range of ancillary functions such as stores and workshops."[36] Among the likely purposes for sunken featured buildings was weaving, a craft that would benefit from the dampness of a partially sunken structure.[37] Later halls in Anglo-Saxon England were more likely to have internal subdivisions, presumably to wall off sleeping quarters from the main area of the building. Thus, in King Edwin's hall at Yeavering perhaps one quarter of the area is thought to have been used for sleeping.[38]

From a settlement in Cowdery's Down near Basingstoke (Hampshire) archaeologists have been able to gather considerable evidence about the techniques of wood construction used for building halls in Anglo-Saxon England. The site preserves evidence for various types of timber buildings, including those using "earthfast uprights both in individual 'post-holes' and in wall trench foundations." In each case, oak planks were pegged together to frame the walls and then were "infilled with wattle panels made from interwoven thin branches and windproofed by being daubed by clay."[39]

These daubed panels may have been painted and some of the timbers may have been ornamented with carvings. This form of construction allowed the Anglo-Saxons to minimize the amount of dressed lumber necessary for a given structure and thus would have made it less costly in terms of labor and materials. Roofing was of either thatch or thin wooden shingles. The specific ways in which the halls at Cowdery's Down were built have been reconstructed in various plans but the basic principles are clear: they were built solidly of immediately procurable materials using the available carpentering skills. That they have been reconstructed in quite different ways, as the sketches available in Leslie Webster's study indicate, provides a useful caution on the limits of our current knowledge about Anglo-Saxon domestic architecture.[40] While noting this caution, one can see that such buildings were vulnerable not only to fire, being constructed of highly inflammable materials, but also to damp and rot, being built directly on or below the ground without water-resistant foundations of stone or masonry. The average life of such a hall could hardly have extended far beyond two or three generations and probably would have required regular maintenance to last that long.

The reconstructed floor plans of Anglo-Saxon halls suggest that even at their largest they were considerably smaller than continental versions. Lest this difference be taken as evidence that the Anglo-Saxons were somehow less prosperous or sophisticated than their continental relatives, one may note that local conditions were a factor in this regard. More specifically, halls in the continental Germanic homelands were built to accommodate not only people but also animals in byres: "In these at least half of the building was subdivided into stalls, designed to keep cattle and other livestock in good condition through the relatively severe winters of these regions."[41] The milder English weather made such byre-houses unnecessary. The halls that were built in England for people seem not to have been especially cramped or confining; they were smaller because they had one less function to perform. Houses without attached stalls for animals were probably more salubrious if not more pleasant to the nose, though that response may be a modern prejudice born of too much soap and disinfectant.

To the extent that they were built to an older model that was modified to suit the climatic conditions of England, Anglo-Saxon domestic halls represent a form of cultural adaptation to a new locale. They suggest the ways in which a migratory people can hold to its old-country traditions while also accommodating the different conditions of the new homeland. This process of cultural adaptation to a new land, as it was written in the timber halls of the period, points to a further issue that relates directly to matters of home and homelessness in Anglo-Saxon England: that the island was the post-migratory home of continental tribes that did not forget their origins in Germania and indeed used those memories to form cultural myths of identity.[42]

What then can home signify in the most literal as well as most abstract sense to a people with long memories of migration? The enduring fact of migration is that it be remembered as a transit between two places, between a home that has been left behind and the one that has been found or, more likely, seized on arrival. As I have argued elsewhere, the interpretive model used by the Anglo-Saxons to remember their migration from northwest Europe to the island of Britain was drawn from the Old Testament story of the Israelite Exodus.[43] Like the Jews, the Anglo-Saxons were a people (according to their own myth of migration) that had been chosen by God to possess a promised land. Home was thus not simply a site of long settlement, a matter of territory or geography, it was also—for both Israelites and Anglo-Saxons—a place blessed by a divine covenant. More specifically, the Anglo-Saxons had left regions in Germania where they knew spiritual captivity, because there they were pagans, to cross the North Sea and arrive at a homeland that over time became the setting for their conversion to Christianity. The Anglo-Saxons' myth of migration endured for centuries because it helped to explain within providential history how it was that they were able as pagans to seize the island from its Christian inhabitants. It told them how it was that God favored them as possessors of the island rather than the Celts who had occupied it when the original Christian conversions occurred. The migration myth served, in short, as a warrant for the Anglo-Saxons to possess the island and make it home.

More precisely, it was the land that fell within the covenant that the Anglo-Saxons believed they had with God. Home for the Anglo-Saxons was the land itself, the work of God's Creation, far more than it was anything built on the land. Human beings sentenced to live within time built such structures, and thus all of them—not excluding their stone churches and rare stone halls—were subject to decay and destruction. The Anglo-Saxons historicized their sense that everything built on the earth was ephemeral, that is, they interpreted this knowledge that nothing human-made endured by setting it within the temporal sequence of human history.[44] In poems such as *The Ruin* and *Maxims II*, the Anglo-Saxons described the remains of stonework construction they saw on their landscape as the "old work of giants" who had distantly preceded them on the island.[45]

That such structures were most likely the work of Romans rather than giants is our knowledge, our form of periodization, and does not negate my argument that the Anglo-Saxons understood this stonework as the remnants left behind by a race that had occupied the land in an earlier time.

That home was for the Anglo-Saxons the land itself rather than anything built on it can be seen vividly in the documents they wrote to record certain legal acts, such as the grant of property from one owner to another or a bequest made by a living person that was to be distributed after his or her death. These texts were memorial in intent, that is, they were meant to preserve oral ceremonies against the passing of time as well as the forgetfulness and deceit of human beings. Documents of both types are filled with references to bequests of land but they very rarely specify houses or other buildings on the land. Anglo-Saxon wills refer to all sorts of portable property, including weapons, books, ecclesiastical vestments, and the like, but define real estate as land, most usually using the Old English word *land*.[46] The number of surviving Anglo-Saxon wills is relatively small, but they are consistently alike in having clauses such as the following in which every use of "estate" in the translation renders *land* in the original:

> This is the agreement which Ulf and his wife Madselin made with [God] and with St Peter when they went to Jerusalem. That is, the estate at Carlton to Peterborough after their death for the redemption of their souls; and the estate at Bytham to St Guthlac's; and the estate at Sempringham to St Benedict's at Ramsey.[47]

The absence of references to houses and other buildings in most wills and land charters reflects, of course, the fact that wealth in Anglo-Saxon England was based on agriculture, on the working of the land for planting crops or grazing animals.[48] That land was the source for producing wealth made it the object of enduring value and thus worthy of being bequeathed. By comparison, in an industrial or post-industrial economy, much land is valuable not for its productive capacity but for the buildings that sit on it, that in fact render it non-productive in an agrarian economy.

Anglo-Saxon wills do on occasion designate the size of the estate in question, as when Thurketel of Palgrave gives fifteen acres and a *toft* or homestead to Leofcwen.[49] For the most part, however, they designate the land in question simply by a name, as when the same Thurketel gives "Simplingham" to his wife and "Wingefeld" to his nephews. Such names, as they designated the *land* or estate in question, must have had common currency in the immediate area and thus needed no further demarcation because their boundaries would have been known. Even the one will that does delineate the *land* in question by specifying its boundaries does so without reference to houses or other buildings:

> These are the boundaries of Balsdon: from the steam at *Humelcyrre;* from *Humelcyrre* to *Heregeresheafod* from *Heregeresheafod* along the old hedge to the green oak; then on until one comes to the paved road; from the paved road along the shrubbery until one comes to Acton; from Acton until one comes to Roydon; from Roydon back to the stream. And there are five hides of land.[50]

Boundary clauses of this sort are very common in Anglo-Saxon land charters, and they also infrequently refer to built structures in the course of designating the circumference of the land parcel in question. To some extent, one can argue, this practice suggests that the Anglo-Saxons conceived of the land itself and all that grew on it as more enduring than anything human beings could build on it and thus as more useful for legal purposes. There is much evidence, which I have surveyed elsewhere, to support this interpretation, though some boundary clauses contain natural features that can hardly be thought of as enduring for more than a human generation or so.[51]

Nonetheless, these legal documents speak vividly to the notion that the Anglo-Saxons thought of home through the concept of land rather than the fact of houses. A house was not a home for them, though the land on which it sat could be honored in that way. These same land charters and wills also provide a very compelling reason for why the Anglo-Saxons thought of land itself as home. Many of these documents record gifts of land from secular owners to ecclesiastical foundations, usually monasteries. A gift of land given to such a body must by its very nature be for perpetuity within human history if it is to have the desired effect of aiding the donor's quest for eternal salvation. The will made by Ulf and his wife Madselin before going on pilgrimage to Jerusalem specifies that their gift of an estate to the abbey at Peterborough was meant "for the redemption of their souls." Offering land for the redemption of one's mortal soul may seem opportunistic, even mercenary to us, but it was very much within the normal practices of Anglo-Saxon Christianity. H. D. Hazeltine puts the matter succinctly: "Rights in terrestrial possessions are exchanged for rights in the heavenly mansions; and these rights are exchanged by grants which at the same time are contracts."[52]

There is another way, perhaps less legalistic though certainly as binding, to conceive of this exchange. The land given by human beings to religious bodies so that their members will pray for the good of the donor's soul after death was never the absolute possession of human beings nor their true home. As the poet of *The Wanderer* reminds his audience, all things on earth are *læne*, transitory because given by God. Thus, to give land to a monastery, for instance, is to return it to God's keeping and also to acknowledge that one's true home is not here on earth in a house made of wattle and daub or even stone.[53] Rather it is in the heavenly home that cannot be described by those on earth. On this, at least, those who composed poems and legal documents in Anglo-Saxon England seem to have agreed. Home is, finally, the place that lies beyond direct human experience or apprehension. It can be entered only by those who knew how to live well on earth in a transitory house of wattle and daub.[54]

Notes

1. "Me bið gyrn witod, / gif mec onhæle an onfindeð / wælgrim wiga, þær ic wic buge, / bold mid bearnum, ond ic bide þær / mid geoguðcnosle, hwonne gæst cume / to durum minum, him biþ deað witod. / Forþon ic sceal of eðle eaforan mine / forhtmod fergan, fleame nergan" (*The Anglo-Saxon Poetic Records*, Vol. 3, *The Exeter Book*, ed. G. P. Krapp and E. V. K. Dobbie [New York: Columbia University Press, 1936], 188). Unless noted otherwise, all translations are by the author.

2. For these solutions, see Craig Williamson, *A Feast of Creatures: Anglo-Saxon Riddle-Songs* (Philadelphia: University of Pennsylvania Press, 1982), 171–172, where the riddle appears as Number 13 because of Williamson's editing of the collection.

3. For discussions of the hall in Old English literature, see Edward B. Irving, Jr., *Rereading Beowulf* (Philadelphia: University of Pennsylvania Press, 1989), chapter 4, "The Hall as Image and Character"; and Alvin A. Lee, *Gold-Hall and Earth Dragon: Beowulf as Metaphor* (Toronto: University of Toronto Press, 1998).

4. Anita R. Riedinger, "'Home' in Old English Poetry," *Neuphilologische Mitteilungen* 96 (1995): 51–59, at 51.

5. For these passages in *Beowulf*, see respectively, ll. 728–30a (warriors sleeping in the hall); ll. 662–65a (Hrothgar); and ll. 1299b–1301 (Beowulf).

6. A classic example of *getimbran/getimbrian* being used in this way occurs in the Old English translation of Matthew 7:24: "Eornustlice ælc þæra þe ðas mine word gehyrð and þa wyrcð byð gelic þam wisan were se hys hus ofer stan getimbrode." "Therefore anyone who hears my word, and does it, is like the wise man who builds his house on stone." For the Old English text, see *The Old English Version of the Gospels*, ed. R. M. Liuzza (Oxford: Oxford University Press, 1994), E.E.T.S., O.S. 304; vol. I, p. 15.

7. For a virtual tour of "Bede's World," see www.bedesworld.co.uk.

8. Dorothy Whitelock, ed., *English Historical Documents*, Vol. 1, *c. 500–1042*, 2d ed. (London: Eyre Methuen, 1979), 398.

9. Ibid., 401.

10. For a wide-ranging survey of the various ways in which home can be considered, see the special issue "Home: A Place in the World," *Social Research* 58.1 (1991), especially John Hollander, "It All Depends," 31–49.

11. "(eþel) byþ oferleof æghwylcum men, / gif he mot ðær rihtes and gerysena on / brucan on bolde bleadum oftast" (*The Old English Rune Poem: A Critical Edition*, ed. Maureen Halsall [Toronto: University of Toronto Press, 1981], 90); see also her discussion of this passage, pp. 148–150.

12. See *The Dictionary of Old English*, "Fascicle E" (Toronto: 1996), *s.v.*, *eþel*.

13. *The Old English Rune Poem*, 91.

14. See *The Dictionary of Old English*, "Fascicle B" (Toronto: 1991), *s.v.*, *botl*.

15. Riedinger, "'Home' in Old English Poetry," 51.

16. This list contains all of the possible definitions offered in the Bosworth-Toller, *Anglo-Saxon Dictionary* and *Supplement*. When the *Dictionary of Old English* publishes its entry for *ham* in the near future, there will no doubt be changes and corrections to this list. For a discussion of the development of Modern English *home* in its various senses, see Hollander, "It All Depends," 44–46.

17. "And þy ilcan geare ferde to Rome mid mycclum wurðscipe. ⁊ þær wunade .xii. monað. ⁊ he feng to Karles dohtor Francna cining þa he hamweard wæs. ⁊ ge sund ham com" (*Two of the Saxon Chronicles Parallel*, ed. Charles Plummer [Oxford: Clarendon Press, 1892], 67; Version E of the *Chronicle*, *s.a.* 855).

18. "Si me dryhten freond, / se ðe her on eorþan ær þrowode / on þam gealg-treowe for guman synnum. / He us onlysde ond us lif forgeaf, / heofonlicne ham" (*The Anglo-Saxon Poetic Records*, Vol. 2, *The Vercelli Book*, ed. G. P. Krapp [New York: Columbia University Press, 1932], 65).

19. For more on the use of polysemy in Old English poetry, especially *Beowulf*, see Fred C. Robinson, *Beowulf and the Appositive Style* (Knoxville: University of Tennessee Press, 1985), especially chapter 2, "Apposed Word Meanings and Religious Perspectives."

20. "Uton we hycgan hwær we ham agen, / ond þonne geþencan hu we þider cumen, / ond we þonne eac tilien, þæt we to moten / in þa ecan eadignesse, / þær is lif gelong in lufan dryhtnes, / hyht in heofonum" (*The Anglo-Saxon Poetic Records*, Vol. 3, *The Exeter Book*, 146–147).

21. Ezra Pound, *Translations*, introduction by High Kenner (Norfolk, Conn.: New Directions, 1963), 207–209.

22. "Bearwas blostmum nimað, byrig fægriað, / wongas wlitigiað, woruld onetteð; / ealle þa gemoniað modes fusne / sefan to siþe, þam þe swa þenceð / on flodwegas feor gewitan" (*The Anglo-Saxon Poetic Records*, Vol. 3, *The Exeter Book*, 144).

23. As the main entry for *eðel* in the *Dictionary of Old English* notes, the word is often "contrasted with 'exile' variously expressed."

24. "Hwær cwom symbla gesetu? Hwær sindon seledreamas?" (*The Anglo-Saxon Poetic Records*, Vol. 3, *The Exeter Book*, 136).

25. "Stondeð nu on laste leofre duguþe / weal wundrum heah, wyrmlicum fah" (*The Anglo-Saxon Poetic Records*, Vol. 3, *The Exeter Book*, 136).

26. "Scip sceal genægled, scyld gebunden, / leoht linden bord, leof wilcuma / Frysan wife, þonne flota stondeð; biþ his ceol cumen ond hyre ceorl to ham, / agen ætgeofa, ond heo hine in laðaþ, / wæsceð his warig hrægl ond him syleþ wæde niwe, / liþ him on londe þæs his lufu bædeð" (*The Anglo-Saxon Poetic Records*, Vol. 3, *The Exeter Book*, 160).

27. "Sum bið bylda til / ham to hebbanne" (*The Anglo-Saxon Poetic Records*, Vol. 3, *The Exeter Book*, 139).

28. "Sum mæg wrætlice weorc ahycgan / heahtimbra gehwæs; hond bið gelæred, / wis ond gewealden, swa bið wyrhtan ryht, / sele asettan, con he sidne ræced / fæste gefegan wiþ færdryrum" (*The Anglo-Saxon Poetic Records*, Vol. 3, *The Exeter Book*, 138).

29. H. M. Taylor and Joan Taylor, *Anglo-Saxon Architecture*, 3 vols. (Cambridge: Cambridge University Press, 1965–1978).

30. C. J. Arnold, *An Archaeology of the Early Anglo-Saxon Kingdoms* (London and New York: Routledge, 1997), 73.

31. For ground plans of Yeavering and other royal sites in Anglo-Saxon England, see Alastair Service, *The Buildings of Britain: Anglo-Saxon and Norman* (London: Barrie and Jenkins, 1982), 29.

32. Eric Ferne, *The Architecture of the Anglo-Saxons* (London: Batsford, 1983), 15.

33. Martin Welch, *Discovering Anglo-Saxon England* (University Park, Penn.: Pennsylvania State University Press, 1992), 21.

34. Ferne, *The Architecture of the Anglo-Saxons*, 15–16.

35. Welch, *Discovering Anglo-Saxon England*, 25.

36. Ibid., 26–27.

37. Ibid., 28: "A damp atmosphere makes weaving easier, particularly when producing linen from flax and a covered man-made hollow would certainly fulfil this requirement."

38. Service, *The Buildings of Britain: Anglo-Saxon and Norman*, 29. For an illustration of a reconstructed noble household in tenth-century Lincolnshire, with hall, weaving shed, kitchen, and sleeping quarters, see Christopher Dyer, *Making a Living in the Middle Ages: The People of Britain, 850–1520* (New Haven, Conn.: Yale University Press, 2002), figure 3.

39. Welch, *Discovering Anglo-Saxon England*, 18.

40. Leslie Webster, "Anglo-Saxon England, A.D. 400–1100" in *Archaeology in Britain since 1945*, ed. Ian Longworth and John Cherry (London: British Museum, 1986), 136–138; see also, Welch, *Discovering Anglo-Saxon England*, 19.

41. Welch, *Discovering Anglo-Saxon England*, 36.

42. Riedinger, "'Home' in Old English Poetry," 58.

43. See Nicholas Howe, *Migration and Mythmaking in Anglo-Saxon England* (Notre Dame, Ind.: University of Notre Dame Press, 2001), esp. chapter 3, "*Exodus* and the Ancestral History of the Anglo-Saxons."

44. On ideas of history in Anglo-Saxon England, see Roberta Frank, "The *Beowulf* Poet's Sense of History" in *The Wisdom of Poetry: Essays in Early English*

Literature in Honor of Morton W. Bloomfield (Kalamazoo: Medieval Institute Publications, 1982), 53–65.

45. For *The Ruin*, ll. 1–2, see *The Anglo-Saxon Poetic Records*, Vol. 3, *The Exeter Book*, 227; and for *Maxims II*, ll. 1–3, see *The Anglo-Saxon Poetic Records*, Vol. 6, *The Anglo-Saxon Minor Poems*, ed. E. V. K. Dobbie (New York: Columbia University Press, 1942), 55.

46. Ferne, *The Architecture of the Anglo-Saxons*, 21, who remarks, "Even the wills which start to appear [late in the Anglo-Saxon period] are singularly unforthcoming about standing property."

47. "Þis is seo foreowearde þe Vlf Ᵹ Madselin his gebedda worhtan wið Ᵹ wið sce PETER. þa hig to Ierusalem ferdon. þat is þat land æt Carlatune into Burh. æfter heora dæge heora saule to alysendnesse. Ᵹ þæt land æt Bytham into Sce Guthlace. Ᵹ þat land æt Sempingaham. into sce Benedicte to Ramesege" (text and translation from *Anglo-Saxon Wills*, ed. Dorothy Whitelock [Cambridge: Cambridge University Press, 1930], 94–95).

48. See further Dyer, *Making a Living in the Middle Ages*, 13–42, esp. pp. 19–21 for a discussion of village formation in Anglo-Saxon England.

49. *Anglo-Saxon Wills*, 68.

50. "þis sind þa landmearca to Byligesdyne of ða burnan. æt Humelcyrre. fram Humelcyrre . . . Heregeresheafode. fram Heregeresheafode æfter ðam ealdan hege to ðare grene æc. þonne forð þæt hit cymð to þare stanstræte. of þare stanstræte Ᵹ lang scrybbe þæt hit cymð to Acantune fram Acyntune þæt hit cymð to Rigendune. fram Rigindune æft to þara burnan. Ᵹ þær. Is. landes fif hida" (*Anglo-Saxon Wills*, 40–41). It should be noted that some translators of Anglo-Saxon boundary clauses, including Whitelock, will sometimes use a modern place-name for the Old English place designated in a charter or will, thus misleadingly suggesting that some of these texts do refer to houses or other standing properties (e.g., in the charter just quoted, Whitelock translates "Giddincgforda" as "Giffords Hall" rather than the literal "Gidding's Ford").

51. See Nicholas Howe, "An Angle on This Earth: Sense of Place in Anglo-Saxon England," *Bulletin of the John Rylands Library* 82 (2000): 3–27; and "The Landscape of Anglo-Saxon England: Inherited, Invented, Imagined" in *Inventing Medieval Landscapes: Senses of Place in Western Europe*, ed. John Howe and Michael Wolfe (Gainesville: University Press of Florida, 2002), 91–112.

52. *Anglo-Saxon Wills*, xx.

53. In this regard, I am reminded of William James's claim in *Pragmatism* that "All 'homes' are in finite experience; finite experience as such is homeless," as quoted by Hollander, "It All Depends," 46, n. 16. See James's *Pragmatism* (Cambridge, Mass.: Harvard University Press, 1978), 125.

54. For their suggestions and assistance with this study, I thank Roberta Frank, Christopher A. Jones, and Carol Neuman de Vegvar.

index

Acosta, José de, 103, 106
Æthelwulf, 148
Albacete, Spain, 73
Alemán, Mateo, 118n.52
Alfonso X, king of Castile and Léon, 105
Aljamiado literature, 64–65
almsgiving, 91–92, 101, 106–7
Ambrose of Milan, 111n.12
Al-Andalus/Andalucia, 58–59, 77
Anglo-Saxon Chronicle, 148
Anglo-Saxons. *See* England
Arabic language and literature, 62, 64, 70–72, 74
Aragon, 77
Arnold, C. J., 154
Atahuallpa (Incan emperor), 94–95
Ayala, Martín de, 64
Ayavire Cusara, Joan, 102

Balbi, Alessandro, 22
Balbi, Giulio, 23
bandits. *See* thieves
Barbarigo, Zuan, 23
baths, community, 63
"Bede's World" (Jarrow, England), 145
beggars, 40–41, 43, 91–93, 101, 125
Bembo family, 17–23, 27–28
Beowulf, 134, 144–46, 155
blind persons, 92, 107–8
Botero, Giovanni, 106

Brown, Patricia Fortini, 4, 13–55
Bruges, 91–92
building materials, 2, 6, 8, 45, 97–98, 127, 145, 154, 155–56

Ca' Bembo Santa Maria Nova, 17–18, 20–22, 27
Ca' Corner della Ca' Grande, 16–17
Capoche, Luis, 97
Caqui, Diego, 102
casa da statio, 17–24
caste systems. *See* social order
Castile, 105–6, 108
Catullus, 110
Cavazza, Tomaso, 28–29
charity and charitable institutions, 10, 27–39, 92, 95, 98, 101, 106–9. *See also* hospitals and hospices
children, 72, 78–81, 127. *See also* orphans
cholards, 2–3
Chronicle (Anglo-Saxon), 148
Cicero, 120n.68
cittadini, 15, 27, 40
colonized peoples, 5–6, 66–67, 93–110
community baths, 63
Commynes, Philippe de, 14
Comunero Revolt (1520-21), 67
Condulmer, Angelo, 39
construction skills, 153–54
Contarini, Andriana, 27
Cornaro family, 16–17

Corte dei Preti, 29–32, 35
Corte San Marco, 33–35, 39
Council of Lima (Third), 100–102
counter-identities, 77
courtyards, 2, 22, 27, 29, 32–33, 35, 59, 76
Cowdery's Down, Hampshire, 155–56
Cruz, Lucía de la, 70
cultural adaptation, 7, 154, 156–57
Cuzco, Peru, 94–95

da Brolo, Costantino and Bartolomeo, 44
darkness, fear of, 134, 144
dead, the, 128–30
"Death of the Hired Man" (Frost), 9
decorative features, 5, 29, 32, 45, 81
deportations. See diaspora
Derelitti, 41
Dey, Utman, 80
diaspora, 5, 57–59, 63–64, 72–81, 108, 113n.23. See also exile and exiles
dietary difference, 139
diseases, 104
displacement/dispossession, 5–6, 96, 99, 108–9
Domingo de Santo Tomás, 94–98, 106, 119n.61
doors, 130
Dream of the Rood, The, 149

economic status, 4, 15, 35, 39–40
Egil (Egils saga), 129–30
England, 2–3, 8, 128, 143–60
Enríquez, Fernando Muley, 75
Enríquez, Martín, 99–101, 103
Enríquez de Guzman, Alonso, 99
epel ("domestic abode" or "homeland"), 143, 146–47, 149
ethnicity, 139
exclusion, right of, 129
Exeter Book, 143–44

exile and exiles, 2, 13, 104, 126, 128, 130–31, 133–37, 151. See also diaspora
expulsions. See diaspora

facades. See street frontages
fences, 133
Ferdinand V, king of Aragon and Castile, 60–61, 63
Fernando III, king of Castile and Léon, 59
floorplans, 2, 21, 30, 35, 37, 98, 100, 156
forced labor, 96–97, 108
France, 2–3, 79
Freud, Sigmund, 134
frontier regions, 127–28, 139
Frost, Robert, 9

Galera, battle of, 72–73
garðr ("fence"), 133
gente valdía ("superfluous people"), 6, 99–100, 107, 109, 119n.61
ghettos: Jewish, 4, 43–47, 60; Morisco, 58, 60–62
ghosts, 7, 128–30
Gifts of Men, The, 153–54
Gísli (Gísla saga), 134–35
Giustinian, Marco, 23–24
Granada, 59, 63, 66–67, 71, 73, 75–77
Greco, El, 101
Grettir (Grettis saga), 134–36
grið ("home"), 136–37, 139
Griego, Juan, 94
Grubenhaüser ("sunken feature buildings"), 155
Guaman Poma de Ayala, Felipe, 107–8, 110
Gunnar (Njáls saga), 130–33, 136–37
Gutiérrez, Alonso, 77
Guzman, Pedro de, 110
Guzmán de Alfarache (Alemán), 100

halls, 144–45, 155–56
ham ("home"), 8, 147–50, 153
Hardenberg, Friedrich von. *See*
    Novalis
Hastrup, Kirsten, 139
Hazeltine, H. D., 159
heavenly home, 7–8, 149–53, 160
heimlich/unheimlich
    ("homelike/unhomelike"), 9, 140
heim(r) ("home," "the world"), 133,
    135–37
Hieronimo, 36
home, words for, 8–9, 133,
    135–37, 139–40, 143,
    146–50, 153
Homer, 153
hooks, bell, 70
Hospital of Saints Peter and Paul,
    29–30
hospitals and hospices, 29, 36–39,
    41–43, 95, 108
household inventories, 25, 43, 45
houses: building materials for, 2, 6, 8,
    45, 97–98, 127, 145, 154, 155–56;
    construction skills and, 153–54;
    courtyards of, 2, 22, 27, 29, 32–33,
    35, 59, 76; decorative features of, 5,
    29, 32, 45, 81; fences and, 133;
    floorplans of, 2, 21, 30, 35, 37, 98,
    100, 156; hiding places in, 59–60,
    64; roofing materials for, 156;
    street frontages of, 2, 5, 17–18, 29,
    45, 59; thresholds/doors of,
    129–30; water/sewer systems for,
    44, 62–63
housing projects, 29–36, 38–39
Howe, Nicholas, 143–63
Hrapp (*Laxdœla saga*), 129, 131
Huancavelica, Peru, 97, 120n.67
huts, 97–98

Ibn 'Abdun, 10, 58–59
Iceland, 6–7, 10, 125–40, 144–45

identity, 1, 47, 147; "counter-", 77;
    cultural, 57–59, 64–65, 68, 74;
    family, 16, 24; memory and, 58,
    157; self-awareness and, 10,
    128, 134–35
immigrants, 40–41, 127–28, 139
Incans, 6, 10, 93–110
Incurabili, 41
Ine, king of Wessex, 146
innangarðs/utangarðs (the "social" and
    the "wild"), 133–34
Innocent XI, pope, 76
Inquisition, 59, 64, 68–71, 74–75
Isabel I, queen of Castile, 63
Islam. *See* Moriscos
Italy, 105–6

Jérez, María, 74
Jews, 4, 14, 43–47, 60, 66, 79,
    85n.39, 157
Jiménez de Cisneros, Francisco, 63

Lacan, Jacques, 134–35
land/landscape, as home, 13, 127,
    130–33, 147, 157–59
landlords and tenants, 22–27,
    35–36, 45
Landnámabók, 7
Lapps, 138
Las Casas, Bartolomé de, 114n.28,
    117n.47
laws and legal documents, 3, 6; on
    domiciles, 126, 130, 136–37;
    household inventories, 25, 43, 45;
    on Jewish resettlement, 44; land
    charters, 158–59; on poverty and
    vagrancy, 40–42, 92, 99, 104, 125;
    on property, 128, 158–59; purity
    of blood statutes, 66, 89n.91;
    requiring conversion to
    Christianity, 58, 63; on strangers,
    145–46; tax records and, 22–23, 25,
    27; wills, 3, 20–22, 32, 158–59

Lazarillo de Tormes, La vida de
(anonymous), 93, 102
Lazzaretto Nuovo, 41
Lazzaretto Vecchio, 41
León, Luis de, 69
liberation theology, 114n.27
Libros Plúmbeos, 76
Lupaqa peoples, 95

MacCormack, Sabine, 5–6, 91–123
Maxims I, 152–53
Maxims II, 157
measles, 104
memory, 5, 7–8, 13, 58, 127–28,
147, 157
Mendicanti, 41
Meshullam family, 44
Michiel, Tomà, 25, 27
migration, 6, 8, 104–5, 108–9, 127–28,
139, 156–57
Miller, William Ian, 6–8, 13,
125–42, 144
miserables ("wretched ones"), 98, 101,
103–4
mita/mittayoc ("taking turns at work"),
95–98, 102–4, 108–9
Molina, Licenciado, 79
monfíes ("bandit gangs"), 72
Morales, Leonor de, 70, 74, 86n.45
morerías, 58, 60–62
Moriscos, 4–5, 57–81; cultural
resistance by, 59–60, 64, 68–71,
74–75; forced conversion to
Christianity and, 58, 63–64, 67–68,
71; Inquisition and, 59, 64, 68–71,
74–75; occupations of, 89n.91;
rebellions and, 63, 67, 72–73, 75
Moryson, Fynes, 39
Moving Days (Iceland), 126–27, 136
Muley Enríquez, Fernando, 75

Ninancuro, Francisco, 94
Njál (*Njáls saga*), 6

Norway, 127–28, 139
nostalgia ("homesickness"), 9
Novalis, 10

Odyssey (Homer), 153
Olivieri, Pietro, 33, 35
Ondegardo, Polo de, 96–97, 108
orientalism, 84n.24
orphans, 29, 36, 41
Ospedale dei Crociferi, 36–38
Ospedale di Gesu Cristo di
Sant'Antonio, 41
Ospizio di Sant'Agnesina, 39
Ospizio Priuli, 38–39
Ospizio Zen, 36
outlaws, 126, 128, 133–37. *See also*
thieves
óvinafagnaðr ("enemies' joy"), 131–32

Padilla, Ysabel de, 73
past, sense of the. *See* memory
patricians, 15, 23, 25, 27, 39–40
Perry, Mary Elizabeth, 4–5, 10, 57–90
Peru, 5–6, 93–110
Philip II, king of Spain, 73, 92
Philip III, king of Spain, 57, 77–78, 105
Pietà (hospital), 41
pilgrims, 29, 36
Pizarro, Francisco, 95
plague victims, 41
popolani, 15, 27
Potosí, Peru, 95–98, 102–4, 108
Pound, Ezra, 150
poverty, 29–43, 91–110
Priuli, Lodovico, 38–39
Procurators of San Marco, 24–25,
28, 32
Ptolemy, 117n.47

rebellions. *See* wars and rebellions
refuge, home as, 4–5, 10, 59, 64, 70,
74, 136–37
Riedinger, Anita R., 144, 147

Robusti, Jacopo. *See* Tintoretto
Rome, 79
roofing materials, 156
row houses, 29–32, 38–39
Ruin, The, 157
Rune Poem, The, 146–47

sanctuary. *See* refuge, home as
Sansovino, Francesco, 14–16, 18, 47
Sansovino, Jacopo, 16, 53n.72
Schadenfreude, 131–32
Schweitzer, Hans Heinrich, 42
Scott, James, 69
Scuole Grandi, 28–29, 32–33, 35–36, 39–40
Seafarer, The, 7–8, 128, 150–51
self-awareness, 10, 128, 134–35
self-help, 103, 106, 109
Seville, 59, 61, 63, 68, 74–76, 78
sick and infirm persons, 29, 41–42, 107–8
Skallagrim (*Egils saga*), 129–30
Slavs, 14
social order, 4, 32, 35, 47, 102, 105, 109; *cittadini,* 15, 27, 40; patricians, 15, 23, 25, 39–40; *popolani,* 15, 27
Soto, Domingo de, 92, 99
Spain, 3; conquest/settlement in New World by, 5–6, 93–110, 128; Moriscos in, 4–5, 57–81
stealing for survival, 103, 106, 109
strangers, 137, 145–46
street frontages, 2, 5, 17–18, 29, 45, 59

taqiyya ("external conformity"), 65, 71
tax records, 22–23, 25, 27
Taybili, Ybrahin, 80
Taylor, H. M., 154
Taylor, Joan, 154
temporal identification, 139, 157
tenants. *See* landlords and tenants
thieves, 72, 91, 125, 145. *See also* stealing for survival

Thorgilsson, Ari, 139
thresholds, 129–30
Thurketel of Palgrave, 158–59
Tintoretto, 18
Toledo, 60, 145
Toledo, Francisco de, 103
Torres y Portugal, Fernando de, 100
tramps, 135–36. *See also* vagabonds and vagrants
Tunisia, 80
Turkey, 79–80

Ulf and Madselin, will of, 158–59

vagabonds and vagrants, 6, 41, 91–93, 99–100, 104, 108, 125, 135–36
Valencia, 77, 80
Valencia, Pedro de, 77
Valverde, Vicente de, 112n.18
veils, wearing of, 65–66
Velasco, Luis de, II, 104
Venice, 2, 4, 13–47, 79, 145; Jewish ghetto in, 43–47; landlords/tenants in, 22–27; poverty in, 27–43; sick/infirm in, 41–42; social order in, 13–22
Vida de Lazarillo de Tormes, La (anonymous), 93, 102
views, 127. *See also* land/landscape, as home
Vivaldi, Antonio, 41
Vives, Juan Luis, 91–92, 98–99, 102

Wanderer, The, 7–8, 128, 151–52, 160
al-Wansharishi, 61–62
wars and rebellions, 63–64, 67, 72–73, 75, 108, 113n.23
water and sewer systems, 44, 62–63. *See also* courtyards
Webster, Leslie, 156
Weiditz, Christoph, 65
Welch, Martin, 155
West Stow, Suffolk, 155

Wihtred, king of Kent, 145
wills, 3, 20–22, 32, 158–59
women: charitable institutions and,
    36–38; as cultural preservationists,
    68–71; inheritance rights and,
    20–21; as resistance fighters, 72–75;
    veiling of, 65–66

Yeavering, England, 155
Ylaquita, Diego, 94, 106

Zarçamodonia, 72
Zen, Ranieri, 36
Zorzi, Gabriel, 23
Zurbaran, Francisco de, 101